What does the harrowing experience of w
living through it? What happens when the
views of others—from parents and family
Peace, Olivera Simić reveals dimensions of
alone understood. With her we engage in loss or homeland, language and identity.
The scars that are left are rarely, if ever, made as visible as they are in this book.
A deeply human narrative set within the growing body of feminist writings on war.

—KATHLEEN BARRY, author of *Unmaking War Remaking Men*

The lines of enmity and amity that course through the Balkan wars and their aftermath in diverse diasporic communities have found their biographer in Olivera Simić. Like Rebecca West, she has written a song of experience—an intimate but also reflective book of living through the devastating politics of the former Yugoslavia. Recalling a past that remains present, it grapples with the pressing questions of what it means to live with and, importantly, live on, with the predicaments of survival and hope. This is a book to be read here and now.

—PETER D. RUSH, Director of the International Criminal Justice programme, Institute of International Law and the Humanities, University of Melbourne

Olivera Simić has written a moving, highly personal account of her experiences during a turbulent decade. She brings home, better than any other account I have read, how people on the ground experienced the war in Yugoslavia. She shows how surviving a war changes one's psychology, including how one thinks about the present and the future, while turning memories of the pre-war era into nostalgia. I am so happy that Simić has written this book; I was unable to put it down and read it in one sitting.

—SABRINA P. RAMET, author of *The Three Yugoslavias: State-Building and Legitimation, 1918–2005*

Too often, when we read or hear news of wars in places we know only how to locate on a map, we forget that in each story there are people, people with histories and emotions and lives which are often irreparably damaged by the time the page is turned or the radio broadcast ends. Olivera Simić reminds us that war hurts people in so many, many ways and is never really over. It's an important and timely reminder of the truth.

—MADELEINE REES, Secretary General, Women's International League for Peace and Freedom (WILPF)

Olivera Simić offers us a unique voice of dissent, in the face of immense loss and continuing trauma, prepared to face complex truths about war and hopeful that we may yet learn to resolve conflicts without violence.

—DIANNE OTTO, Director, Institute for International Law and the Humanities, Melbourne Law School

Olivera Simić passionately opens herself to the vulnerability of expressing an intense loss of homeland and belonging. Her pain is deep, penetrating the depths of the soul. In telling a courageous story of experiences of war, the reader is carried on an incredible journey of what it means to survive peace. This is an engrossing story. I commend this book as an intimate narrative of hope for a non-violent future.

—ELISABETH PORTER, author of *Peacebuilding: Women in International Perspective*

Bursting with often difficult yet unforgettable stories, *Surviving Peace* describes Olivera Simić's dealings with war and violence, and with life during 'dirty' post-conflict peace. It speaks to all whose lives have been touched by massive tragedies, social transformations and dislocations due to war. And it will speak to all those wishing to help prevent wars and create true and sustainable peace. Simić remains constructive and positive, optimistic that 'another future is possible'. *Surviving Peace* is an important step in that direction.

—IVANA MILOJEVIĆ, author of *Breathing: Violence In, Peace Out*

In her inspirational and engaging memoir, Olivera Simić has ensured that no one will forget the former Yugoslavia. Her experiences of war and the paradoxes of survival are an individual story, but also universal, as she shares her struggle to find meaning, belonging and identity in post-conflict Bosnia-Herzegovina.

—CLAIRE MOORE, Australian Labor Senator

Surviving Peace uses insights from psychology, trauma studies, philosophy and sociology and interweaves them with intimate memories of life before, during and after the war. Olivera Simić shows us how experiences of war and postwar shape people's connections to themselves, to others, and to places and times that have marked their lives.

—DUBRAVKA ŽARKOV, Associate Professor in Gender, Conflict and Development, International Institute of Social Studies/EUR, The Hague, Netherlands

This is a powerful and compelling book that opens a dialogue about a traumatic and hurtful past. It brings to life personal and political tragedies with courage, strength and compassion. Olivera Simić is a brave woman, and this book shows that she knows better than most the painful consequences of speaking truth to power, and the courage that is needed to do so. For those who have followed events in the former Yugoslavia periodically and from a distance, glancing occasionally at headlines and news flashes, *Surviving Peace* explains what happened and what it means. Her hope, that despite the trauma and devastation a future that transcends ethnic, nationalist and religious lines may prevail, is an inspiration.

—JULIANNE SCHULTZ, editor of *Griffith REVIEW*

Photograph by Madonna Adcock

Olivera Simić is a feminist, human rights activist and academic at the Griffith Law School, Australia. Originally from the former Yugoslavia, Dr Simić has lived and studied in Eastern and Western Europe, the USA and South America. She has published one monograph and three co-edited collections, book chapters, journal articles and personal narratives. She completed a Doctorate of Law at the University of Melbourne in 2011. She now teaches international law and transitional justice at Griffith Law School and lives in Brisbane. In 2013, she was a nominee for the Penny Pether Prize for Scholarship in Law, Literature and the Humanities, and won the Peace Women Award from Women's International League for Peace and Freedom (WILPF, Australian branch).

Other books by Olivera Simić

Regulation of Sexual Conduct in UN Peacekeeping Operations (2012)

Peace Psychology in the Balkans: Dealing With a Violent Past While Building Peace (2012) with Zala Volčič and Catherine R. Philpot (eds)

Transitional Justice and Civil Society in the Balkans (2013) with Zala Volčič (eds)

The Arts of Transitional Justice: Culture, Activism, and Memory After Atrocity (2014) with Peter D. Rush (eds)

Surviving Peace

A Political Memoir

Olivera Simić

SPINIFEX

First published by Spinifex Press, 2014
Spinifex Press Pty Ltd
504 Queensberry St
North Melbourne, Victoria 3051
Australia
women@spinifexpress.com.au
www.spinifexpress.com.au

Copyright © Olivera Simić, 2014

All rights reserved. Without limiting the rights under copyright reserved above, no part of this publication may be reproduced, stored in or introduced into a retrieval system, or transmitted, in any form or by any means (electronic, mechanical, photocopying, recording or otherwise) without prior written permission of both the copyright owner and the above publisher of the book.

Copying for educational purposes
Information in this book may be reproduced in whole or part for study or training purposes, subject to acknowledgement of the source and providing no commercial usage or sale of material occurs. Where copies of part or whole of the book are made under part VB of the Copyright Act, the law requires that prescribed procedures be followed. For information contact the Copyright Agency Limited.

Editors: Pauline Hopkins, Susan Hawthorne and Renate Klein
Copy editor: Maree Hawken
Cover design: Deb Snibson
Typesetting: Palmer Higgs
Typeset in Bembo and Futura
Indexer: Karen Gillen
Printed by McPherson's Printing Group
Cover photograph of Travnik © Aleksandar Trifunović. Reproduced with permission.

Parts of this book originally appeared in papers published in the *International Journal of Women's Studies*, *International Feminist Journal of Politics*, and the *German Law Journal*. A version of Chapter Four was first published in the *Griffith Review*.

National Library of Australia Cataloguing-in-Publication data:

Simić, Olivera, 1973– author
Surviving Peace: A Political Memoir / Olivera Simić

9781742198941 (paperback)
9781742198910 (eBook: ePub)
9781742198903 (eBook: Kindle)
9781742198897 (eBook: pdf)
Includes bibliographical references and index.

Bosnian Australians—Biography
Refugees—Biography
Peacekeeping forces—Bosnia and Hercegovina
Yugoslav War, 1991–1995—Refugees
Sarajevo (Bosnia and Hercegovina)—History—Siege
1992–1996—Personal narratives
Yugoslav War, 1991–1995—Peace—Psychological aspects
949.7024082

This project has been assisted by the Australian Government through the Australia Council for the Arts, its arts funding and advisory body.

MIX
Paper from
responsible sources
FSC
www.fsc.org   FSC® C001695

All gulfs open up in war. The act of love turns into an act of hatred. It turns into the betrayal of the woman and into the betrayal of humanity ... In all wars, atrocities stifle the victims' scream for help. Therefore, those who are in a position to scream ought to do so as loudly as they can.

—Iren Meier in *Women's Side of War* (2008, p. 390)

Contents

ACKNOWLEDGEMENTS

Every book is a product of both a gift and a labour: it requires the gifts of listening and writing, and demands dedication and close engagement. Books emerge from conversations and commitment. They are born after long mind and spirit labouring which is supported and influenced by family, friends and colleagues. This book is no different.

I am indebted to Susan Hawthorne of Spinifex Press for structural editing, and to my other editors, Pauline Hopkins and Renate Klein. Their interest in this book, and their advice and encouragement as it progressed, resulted in a much more accessible manuscript than it was before. I also thank Maree Hawken for in-depth copy editing. The hand-drawn maps were provided by Petar Alar and I would like to thank him for drawing them especially for my book.

Many thanks also to Maria Tumarkin, a Melbourne-based writer and cultural historian. Maria was the true believer that there was indeed 'a book in me' and gently pushed me to write the book proposal with her wholehearted assistance and support. I thank Kathleen Barry for her careful reading of early drafts and for constructive comments. I would also like to thank Ivana Milojević for her generous feedback on early drafts of the manuscript and invaluable conversations.

I was fortunate to meet Joan Nestle, now my dear friend, with whom I spent many hours talking about the hardships and joys of living in exile, far away from friends and family but closer to new peaceful and sustainable futures. Joan was the force behind my first personal narrative, written on my arrival in Australia, which will no doubt continue to open the door to many more stories to come. Thanks so much Joan.

Associate Professor Peter Rush has kindly read, edited and commented on most of my previously published narratives. Thank you, Peter, for your ongoing support and close engagement with my work. I am grateful to Stojan for his unwavering support, love and trust in me. Last, but not least, thank you, Andrej, for teaching me what unconditional love is all about and for giving another meaning to the world around me.

This book is dedicated to the extraordinary women who have survived war while their lives were ripped apart by violence. I applaud their courage and strength to go on and seek out humanity despite the deep pain and loss they have experienced.

Socialist Federative Republic of Yugoslavia (SFRY until 1992)
Map by Petar Alar (2013) based on Mardešić, Petar and Zvonimir Dugački (1961).

Map B

Bosnia and Herzegovina (from 1992)

Map by Petar Alar (2013) based on University of Texas Libraries (n.d.) 'Bosnia maps'.

PREFACE

The Past Lives On

We should kill our pasts with each passing day. Blot them out, so that they will not hurt. Each present day could thus be endured more easily; it would not be measured against what no longer exists. As things are, spectres mix with our lives so that there is neither pure memory nor pure life. They clash and try to strangle each other, continually.

—Meša Selimović, *Death and the Dervish* (1996, p. 183)

I was born in a country that no longer exists. I grew up in the former Yugoslavia and witnessed my country falling apart. I have experienced the deep and enduring pain of losing my country, my friends and neighbours; of losing the safe and solid ground under my feet, for ever. The motivation for writing this book was the desire to put down in writing my personal experiences of war and of the ensuing 'peace'— the experiences which affect every part of my life and often leave me feeling that I am merely *surviving peace*. My experience of surviving both war and peace has marked my life for ever and allowed me to develop a better understanding of the reasons why people sometimes act in disastrous ways. It has affected the whole of my spiritual and intellectual being. And it has driven my academic work in the direction of exploring the causes and consequences of war in my homeland (and beyond), as well as the trauma, resilience and utmost courage of its people.

Having this personal background, and being a feminist scholar and a human rights lawyer, I find myself in the situation where, on the one

1

hand, I am a woman who has experienced the pain and tragedy of war (an 'insider'); and, on the other hand, I am expected to be an 'impartial, objective scholar' with distance from the events being researched (an 'outsider'). This is extremely difficult to achieve. The dissonance of these two roles creates an ongoing internal conflict. I occupy both insider and outsider positions in relation to the environment and subject matter being explored. In my personal and professional life, I continually face—and attempt to balance—the challenges and contradictions created by the convergence of these roles. The balance is often elusive.

In this book, the personal 'insider' perspective assumes the lead. As an insider, I have in common the language, experience, culture, distinctiveness and sex of the population I reflect on. I have a strong understanding of the dynamics and the interplay of social relationships that inform the situations in my home country. As an 'outsider', I have been critically and extensively engaged since 2004 with the scholarly literature written about the people of this region.

I have been living with my daunting memories of the Bosnian war since it officially came to an end in 1995.[1] Paradoxically, instead of bringing me peace, the end of the war has produced an inner war that I struggle with every day. For a long time it was difficult to willingly revisit the past that was haunting my dreams, but now I feel that my own story must be told. In feminist research women are considered to be experts regarding their own lives who communicate and reveal the narratives about the events that took place in their lives, their feelings about those events, and their interpretation of them (Foss and Foss, 1994, p. 39). This book has assisted my personal healing, but it also aims to broaden a general understanding of the issues faced by people with war trauma in their day-to-day lives.

Although mine is an individual story, I believe that on many levels it is also universal. My experiences of war and survival are similar

---

[1] On 15 October 1991, the parliament of the Socialist Republic of Bosnia and Herzegovina (BiH) in Sarajevo passed a 'Memorandum on the Sovereignty of Bosnia-Herzegovina' despite opposition from most of the Serb parliamentary representatives. On 12 August 1992, the name of the self-proclaimed Serb Republic of Bosnia and Herzegovina was changed to Republika Srpska (RS). War had already broken out on 6 April 1992 and lasted until 14 December 1995 when the final version of the Dayton Peace Agreement was signed in Paris. It was mainly between those Bosnians who wanted to uphold the independence of BiH and the forces of RS.

to those of other war survivors. As a teacher, I often use personal experiences to introduce topics dealing with conflict and the pursuit of peace. This helps students relate to the often abstract theoretical ideas and research in the field of peace and conflict studies and law. Students have commented that they have found this approach unusual, and that they are highly appreciative of an academic speaking openly about her own vulnerability. This is another reason why I have been motivated to embark on this emotional journey which sometimes links intimate experiences with existing scholarship.

This book is also about the painful processes of acquiring new and, for many of us former Yugoslavs, unwelcome and unwanted identities. It is about the paradoxes of surviving the war, and the challenges of finding meaning and belonging in its aftermath. While everyone understands how important it is to survive war and preserve human life, there is less understanding of what the life of a survivor looks like. It is not often publicly acknowledged that life after war can be as difficult and haunting as it was during wartime.

In an attempt to bring attention and value to our experiences, this book provides an intimate and critical examination of some common concerns facing all post-conflict survivors, including how to acknowledge past horrors, and make some sense of them. It looks at the paradoxes of survival, and the ongoing struggle to find meaning and belonging. It investigates the long-term impact of disturbing traumatic experiences, and of personal and collective experiences, in the aftermath of war and violence. Faced with traumatic experiences, how do people behave and what motivates them to act in a particular way?

A sense of loss and despair characterises the postwar period from which emerges hope. There are challenges such as postwar identity reconstruction, the feelings that arise and are left unspoken, as well as the unresolved issues. The countries in the former Yugoslavia, including Bosnia and Herzegovina (BiH), have been through multiple transitions: from war to peace; single party rule to pluralist democracy; communist planned economy to liberal market economy; international protectorate to independent country. According to some scholars BiH's simultaneous transitions have reached an impasse (Donais and Pickel, 2003). It is a country that was ravaged by almost four years of civil war (1992–1995) that claimed 100,000 lives, while

2 million people were driven from their homes, becoming refugees and 'internally displaced persons'.

BiH is a young, fragile state in which one of its constituent peoples, Serbs, do not believe. According to Milorad Dodik, president of the Bosnian Serb-dominated Republika Srpska (one of the two current political entities in BiH; the other is the Federation of Bosnia and Herzegovina) BiH is "a country on life support, a diseased country held together by the international community" (in Dzidic, 2013). Unfortunately, this statement is not far from the truth. Almost 20 years after the war, the country is still troubled politically, economically and socially. However, BiH was not always 'on life support', but was a strong and ethnically diverse community. In *The Fall of Yugoslavia* (1996) Misha Glenny describes BiH:

> Bosnia and Herzegovina casts a spell on all who live there and who were privileged in the past to acquaint themselves with the republic ... [I]t is through the middle of Bosnia that East meets West; Islam meets Christianity; the Catholic eyes the Orthodox across the Neretva ... Bosnia divided the great empires of Vienna and Constantinople; Bosnia was perhaps the only true reflection of Yugoslavia. It is both the paradigm of peaceful, communal life in the Balkans and its darkest antithesis (p. 161).

Similarly, one of the greatest Bosnian writers, Meša Selimović (who was born to a Bosniak family but later declared himself a Serb), described Bosnians as living "at a crossroads of the worlds, at a border between peoples, in everyone's way, always at a fault to someone and first to be struck ..." (1996, p. 330). He portrayed BiH and its people as "the saddest little district of the world, the most miserable people of the world ... torn away and not accepted, alien to all and everyone ..." (p. 330).

Situated in the Balkans, BiH is often seen as the "dark side" of Europe (Todorova, 1997, p. 482) and associated with violence, barbarism and incivility (Bakić-Hayden and Hayden, 1992). It is at the crossroads of many civilisations and cultures and lies in the heart of south-east Europe. BiH is a country of ancient towns and cities with a vast array of landscapes, cultures, traditions and people. However, its rich history has often been used as a tool of war, as Tim Clancy, a Bosnian travel-guide writer, notes: "[It's history] has been twisted and distorted to such an extent that making head or tail of who did what, when, where, why and how 600 years ago, or even just 100 years ago, has largely lost its historical integrity ..." (2007, p. vii). Clancy points out how foreigners he talks to about BiH know very little about the country, and how their knowledge is largely framed by the media. He questions the myth of BiH as a 'country of violence' (p. viii):

> If this was a barbaric society with only intervening periods of civilisation then how on earth could they [Bosnians] live, grow and prosper during the Cold War and remain allies with the major powers of East and West? How could they host the largest Winter Olympics of the era in 1984? How could one stand in Bascarsija in Sarajevo and hear the call to prayer from the many minarets with the resonating sound of church bells in the background?

BiH is a land where, despite the war ravages, one can still find a Jewish synagogue, an Ottoman mosque, and Catholic and Christian Orthodox churches on the same corner (especially in Sarajevo). In BiH, eastern and western civilisations met and often clashed, but certainly enriched and reinforced each other throughout its long and rich history. Most of its inhabitants are of Slavic origins with three main ethnic groups which are three constituent nations in postwar BiH: Serbs (Orthodox Christians), Croats (Roman Catholics) and Bosniaks (Muslims). Bosniaks are sometimes referred to as 'Bosnian Muslims', or 'Bosnians', although the latter is also used to denote all inhabitants of the country (regardless of ethnic origin) in terms of citizenship.

Today, many Bosnian Serbs and Croats reject calling themselves 'Bosnians' because of apparent 'appropriation' and equalisation of ethnicity and nationality by Bosniaks. One could say that in postwar BiH, only Bosniaks fully consider BiH as their country. Bosnian Serbs and Croats are more inclined to identify with Serbia and Croatia respectively. Many do not feel BiH is their home. As for myself, I will always say that I am a Yugoslavian, but Bosnian too. Still, I feel I have no homeland any more.[2]

---

[2] Throughout this book I use 'Bosnia and Herzegovina', 'BiH', and 'Bosnia' interchangeably. 'Herzegovina' is also spelt 'Hercegovina' in the literature.

BiH is a country in which the character of the recent war is still not defined: all ethnic groups claim that they 'defended' themselves from the 'others'. They each have their own truth about the war and might call it 'a civil war', 'a defensive war', or 'an offensive war', depending on the ethnic group they identify with: Serbs, Croats or Bosniaks. Because of these contested truths about the war, it is of significant importance, as Vesna Nikolić-Ristanović and Nataša Hanak argue, to insist on "discovering the truth on crimes committed by all sides and connecting them into 'one truth' in order to understand what happened and to overcome denial" (2006, p. 383). Likewise, Judith Herman notes that "[r]emembering and telling the truth about terrible events are prerequisites both for the restoration of the social order and for the healing of individual victims" (1992, p. 1). In my academic writing I feel a responsibility to talk about the crimes committed by 'my own' people. That is, I believe, the only legitimate way I can talk about the war and the past that haunts me.[3]

Many survivors of wars around the world will identify with the difficulties I've experienced while living with war trauma in a number of peaceful countries. This book is written for survivors of war, their families and friends, but also the general public in an effort to broaden their understanding of both friends and strangers who live with such memories and experiences.

The book is not written in chronological order. It is instead a journey of memories, flashbacks, particular narratives, history and conversations. It is about the transition from peace to war and back to 'peace' again and my own experiences during this process, in particular in relation to my ever-changing identity. Each chapter looks at various identity 'impositions' that have become part of my life.

Surviving Peace acknowledges the fact that trauma and the long-term consequences of war are ongoing. It is a matter of learning how to live with, and deal with, the consequences in a constructive

---

[3] I have written at great length about crimes committed in my homeland; see for example: Simić, Olivera (2013b) 'Memorial culture in the former Yugoslavia: Mothers of Srebrenica and the destruction of artefacts by the ICTY'; (2012a) 'After the war in Bosnia: Radmila's life under handbrake'; (2011) 'Bringing "justice" home: Bosnians, war criminals and the interaction between the cosmopolitan and the local'; (2009c) 'What remains of Srebrenica? Motherhood, transitional justice and yearning for the truth'. See Bibliography for further examples and full details.

way, so they do not make it impossible to move on. The strategy that works for me is to make sense of war by telling stories about it. It is widely known that, after telling their stories, survivors transform the meaning of their traumatic personal experiences and enter the stage of "wounded healer" (Bartsch and Bartsch, 1995, p. 145). As wounded healers, survivors carry their wounds with them but do not inflict them on others. Rather they use them as the basis for their social or political actions (p. 145). Surviving any war is tough, but surviving peace can sometimes be even tougher: torn between war and peace, between the wish to move on and the almost obsessive impulse to keep looking back. Surviving means finding the balance between these two states of mind, because neither of them will ever let go of us fully.

People from the former Yugoslavia were victims of bad political decisions, but they are also survivors, activists, peace builders and academics. It is my hope that this book will help to open a dialogue about the hurtful past. As a Bosnian woman who has left her homeland and now lives in Australia, I often feel like part of a living network crossing the borders of human division, together with those who wish to understand complex histories and reconcile all sides implicated in the Bosnian war saga. Because I have chosen to speak the unspeakable and remember what many wish to forget, I hope my words will encourage and urge others to do the same, to demand justice and strive for reconciliation. It is hard to create spaces in which we can speak without the fear of being judged, to speak in the languages we choose, and in countries we were not born in, and yet I am confident that I and others will continue to take the risk. Speaking and writing about loss opens the heart, connects souls, and reaches out to the world with a plea to all to for ever 'unmake war' (Barry 2010).

Olivera Simić
15 April 2014
Brisbane, Australia

CHAPTER ONE

Journeying Through War and Peace

When the leaders speak of peace
The common folk know
That war is coming.
When the leaders curse war
The mobilisation order is already written out.

—Bertolt Brecht, 'When leaders speak of peace' in *Selected Poems* (1975, p. 133)

A year ago I was invited to present a paper at a law and history conference in Melbourne. While I was setting up, the chairperson of my panel approached me and asked how he should introduce me to the audience. As soon as I began muttering a few words, he interrupted, asking: "Where are you from?"

"Yugoslavia," I replied.

The confusion was etched on his face. "But that country doesn't exist any more."

I replied with a grin, "Okay then, I was born in a country that exists no more, the Socialist Federative Republic of Yugoslavia. That country might no longer exist, but it existed at the time of my birth. I also speak a language that exists no more, for that matter."

My colleague was apparently so bewildered by my statement that he later felt the need to share our exchange with the audience. Several people approached me afterwards and told me that it was very unusual to hear someone still introducing herself as Yugoslav. Not many people would do so these days, they suggested.

But I do. I am a Yugoslav without Yugoslavia. I identify with the country I was born in; I am homesick for the place that exists only in my distant memory: the beautiful old towns, rivers and mountains, and the part of the Adriatic coast that was Yugoslavia. I speak a language that was declared dead when the war broke out in 1992. I was fortunate not to lose a close family member, but like many Yugoslav people, I lost so much. The beginning of the war meant the end of my physical belonging to the country I was born and grew up in, the country I loved, the country I left and soon abandoned. I tried to move on, to forget destruction and war, to run away from it all. But, as Meša Selimović writes: "Numerous times have I tried to run away, and I always stayed, although it does not matter where one physically lives. Bosnia is inside of me, like blood" (1975, p. 323). The further I was from home, the closer home was to me, to my heart, to my mind. The connection to my homeland was not severable by distance but, as many migrants will know, on the contrary, was made stronger by it. The smell, the sound, the sky and the sun of my home haunt me. They are always with me.

My home town, Banja Luka, is the second-largest city in Bosnia and Herzegovina (BiH) and the largest city in Republika Srpska (RS). It is RS's administrative capital and an important regional centre for education, business, arts and culture, although Sarajevo remains the capital. Banja Luka is well known for its parks and avenues and the Vrbas River which is why it is often called 'the city of greenery'. The oldest cultural heritage site is the Kastel built by ancient Romans and fortified by Ottomans who settled on the banks of the Vrbas. It is located in the centre of the city and often hosts theatre and music festivals, as well as art exhibitions. I spent my youth in and around the river which is a popular spot for swimming, diving, rafting, canoeing and kayaking. Some of the best taverns were built next to the river and my favourite, 'Scout', was right on the bank. We spent many nights drinking, singing and laughing next to the rough, greenish water of the Vrbas—not anticipating that many of us would never again enjoy its beauty.

My parents are both Orthodox Serbs and were members of the Communist Party before the 1990s. I was raised in a middle-class family and educated in my home town where I lived until the war started. I was proud to be a 'Yugoslavian girl' and belong to what

I regarded as a heterogeneous multicultural, multilingual and multi-religious community.

My family was a typical Yugoslav family. Like many of my friends, I grew up in a two-bedroom unit, sharing a room with my older brother. At the time I believed that this room was 'my room', although it was not only shared with my brother but would also be turned into a living room whenever we had guests. I considered these living arrangements to be perfectly normal back then. I never thought it should be any different or that, heaven forbid, I lacked privacy. The right to privacy—sacred in Western countries—was absent in socialist Yugoslavia, and I only learned of its existence once I found myself outside the borders of my country. We were all living happily in our small units not knowing that, in the West, 60 square metres of living space was considered to be totally inadequate for a family of four.

In *How We Survived Communism and Even Laughed* (1992), Croatian journalist and writer Slavenka Drakulić describes this day-to-day reality and the absurdity of our 'simple' lives in the former Yugoslavia. Trivial aspects of our lives in Eastern Europe, such as cramped apartments, shopping, cleaning houses and cooking, are brilliantly captured by Drakulić. Drawing her analysis primarily from her own autobiographical essays, she talks about how communism influenced the lives of people living in Eastern Europe by invisibilising—in an almost benign way—some of their fundamental individual rights, such as self-expression and privacy. After all, as she notes, communism is "more than a political ideology or a method of government, it is a state of mind" (1992, p. xvi). Indeed, it was a way of life, and with it came the philosophy that collective values always prevailed and were considered far more important than the individual. Communism discourages individualism and creativity. We co-existed only as part of a tribe and were raised to put the interests of our community and neighbours before our own. Any manifestation of individualism was considered selfish and offensive, and any person who put their own interests first would be bullied and ostracised by the community.

Still, our country ensured that we all had free education and medical care. We did not know about homelessness. Our borders were open and many Yugoslavs travelled to shop in Italy, Germany and other countries in Western Europe. We were the envy of other citizens of Eastern Europe, especially those 'under the Soviet boot', such as Poland, or what was once Czechoslovakia. We could do things they were forbidden to even think about. We watched Hollywood movies and listened to pop and rock music from all around the world. My parents had all the records by ABBA and Boney M, and my teenage hero was Billy Idol. We wore jeans, smoked cigarettes and considered ourselves 'hip'. We kids from the cities despised those living in villages and considered them uneducated and primitive peasants. We were divided along rural/urban lines—not along ethnic/religious ones. Many of us still consider these times as precious, so it comes as no surprise that some people from the former Yugoslavia are still nostalgic about the period when strongman Josip Broz Tito held the country and its people together.

The real trouble began with Tito's death on 4 May 1980, when I was only seven years old. I still remember vividly the day he died. I was with my friends in the communal space in front of the building where we lived. We were busy playing 'Izmedu dve vatre' ['Between Two Fires'], throwing the ball to one another, when I heard my mother calling me: "Olja, come home now." I never dared to argue with my mother. She was strict and I had learnt not to challenge her. So I picked up my yellow Disney ball and went home. My father was sitting on the kitchen bench listening to the news on the television. It was late Sunday afternoon, and I could smell roast chicken and potatoes, my favourite meal. I was hungry, but did not dare to ask for food. Somehow I knew I would not get it, and might even be scolded. I instinctively went into the kitchen to look for my mother who spent most of her days cooking. She was not there. I found her on our verandah, curled up on a small, red stool, smoking and crying. With a cigarette in one hand, she wiped the tears rolling down her cheeks with the other. She raised her dark-brown teary eyes and said, "Tito has died." I stared at her. There was sorrow but something more in her voice too. She was devastated by the news but not necessarily because she loved him. In retrospect, I think she was already worried about what was to come.

In the preceding years, all across the country there had been great concern about the prospect of a future without Tito, hanging over us like a black cloud. I sat on the white plastic chair next to her and did not know what to say. I could hear the distant voices now coming from our TV. My father turned up the volume. His face was filled with shock and grief and it sent a shiver down my spine. Echoes of the same TV channel were coming from the other units in our four-storey green and yellow building. Everyone was watching the latest devastating report on Tito's death. I knew I was supposed to be sad, and I remember I tried to cry but I could not. I felt ashamed, not really knowing why. Elvir Kulin, a Bosnian ex-combatant, described in his memoir the general reaction to Tito's death:

> The most traumatic event in the lives of all Yugoslavs was the death of Yugoslavian President Josip Broz Tito in May 1980. Tito was beloved by many people, and I saw my neighbours with tears in their eyes when they heard the news. I noticed that my parents and people in the neighbourhood were worried about what it would be like without Tito. They were concerned if Tito's successors would have his wisdom and experience to run the country with different ethnic groups and religions each wanting to assert their authority. I was only five then and didn't know or care much about politics ... According to a Bosnian Muslim death custom, when someone close to you died, you turned off the TV and put a clean piece of cloth over it. When Tito died, my parents did this to our TV for 40 days, and I was upset I couldn't watch it (2005, p. 13).

My parents, and in particular my mother, are to this day nostalgic about Tito's time. For years afterward my mother would say, "We had such a good life when Tito was alive. What we have now is not a life any more." With his death and the demise of communism, Yugoslavia was on the brink of disaster. It was as if, with his death, we all died too. And, in a sense, we did. The time of peace and relative happiness vanished for ever.

Growing up in a Yugoslavia that silenced any expression of religious identity under its mantra of 'brotherhood and unity', I was unaware of my own ethnicity, and that of my family, until the time of Tito's death. One afternoon, in the spring of 1986, I came home from school and asked my father who I was. He did not understand my question. I explained that I had not been able to give an answer to my teacher when asked about my ethnic origin. My father said, "We are Serbs." As a thirteen-year-old I did not give a second thought to what my father told me that day. The fact that I did not know my ethnic origins and religious background was not unusual then, since it was not generally discussed. Not long after that I became painfully aware of what 'ethnic' belonging meant.

Despite all the worries about our future after Tito's death, most people could not have imagined a full-blown war being even a remote possibility, either at that time or twelve years later at the beginning of 1992, when war was indeed at our doorstep. We had no idea that the war in BiH would be such a bloodbath because people were so ethnically mixed. But, as Bertolt Brecht once said, "war ... always finds a way" (1941/1972). In April 1992, war certainly did find its way and engulfed us all until December 1995. When it broke out I was nineteen years old, had just finished high school, and believed that the whole world was at my feet. I loved my city, enjoyed my friends. Together we discovered vodka, and gin and tonic; we smoked locally made Plavi Ronhil cigarettes and chased boys. It was 'cool' to smoke back then—behind the backs of our parents, of course. We did not know what 'war' meant, how to prepare for it, what to think about it.

The Second World War was still a vivid memory for our parents and grandparents, but although we had been taught about it at school, my generation had never actually experienced war. We did not know what to make of an official declaration of war in our country between those Bosnians (mostly Bosniaks) who wanted to uphold the independence of BiH, and those (mostly Serbs) who did not, the forces of RS. We pretended that nothing was happening, that it did not matter to us at all. Still, my parents and other older people could sense danger in the air. They knew that old grievances between Serbs, Bosniaks and Croats had not been settled after the Second World War. My parents and grandparents had never dealt with the past at a community level and had never gone through any reconciliation processes despite the horrific crimes that various ethnic groups had committed against one other. Strongman Tito had banned any discussion about inter-ethnic killings and enforced a collective 'amnesia' amongst Yugoslav people. In her memoirs, Tito's wife, Jovanka Broz, noted that Tito never denied the mass killings and extermination camps, such as Jasenovac in which hundreds of thousands of Serbs, Romas and Jews perished in the Second World War, but he and the leadership of Yugoslavia "put it aside after the war" (Jokanović, 2013, p. 59). Jovanka said that the leadership was

> busy with many issues that needed to be dealt with, some very urgent
> life issues ... [W]e moved that aside but we paid a price later on ... [L]ots
> of resistance ... and injustice accumulated over the years and then finally

erupted as a volcano ... [B]ecause of the 'brotherhood and unity' no one was allowed to talk about past atrocities (p. 59).

For us, the younger generation, war was an abstract idea, something we simply could not imagine. In any case, at that stage the war had not reached our homes, and draft calls had not yet been issued, at least, not in the city where I lived. War was raging in Croatia (the neighbouring republic) but it seemed far away from us. We would watch the TV news about the shooting and slaughtering in Vukovar and other Croatian cities but it did not really bother me or my friends. Our oblivion to the obvious chaos that was happening less than 500 kilometres away is hard to explain. I held the same indifferent views about it as I had once held for the Iraq–Iran war (1980–1988) which we had watched live on our TVs. Although this war was happening in *my* country to *my* people, it had not yet happened to *me* or to someone I knew. I was too busy going out, partying, and making plans to embark on my first trip down to the Adriatic coast without my parents.

In *Regarding the Pain of Others*, Susan Sontag writes about how it seems normal for people "to fend off thinking about the ordeals of others, even others with whom it would be easy to identify" (2004, p. 89). Sontag analyses the role, uses and meanings of images, in particular images of war and destruction, and whether such images can move people to "do something" or will leave them indifferent. She describes her meeting with a woman from Sarajevo in 1993 whose reaction to the TV scenes of war in neighbouring Croatia had been similar to mine:

> In October 1991 I was here in my nice apartment in peaceful Sarajevo when the Serbs invaded Croatia, and I remember when the evening news showed footage of the destruction of Vukovar, just a couple of hundred miles away, I thought to myself, 'Oh, how horrible', and switched the channel. So how can I be indignant if someone in France or Italy or Germany sees the killing taking place here day after day on their evening news and says, 'Oh, how horrible', and looks for another program. It's normal. It's human (p. 89).

So we turned our heads and kept on living as if nothing were happening. But very soon we were to experience the very same kinds of scenes we had watched from our comfortable armchairs in that short-lived pre-war peace. War found us unprepared in 1992, even though there had been plenty of warnings. The villages were the first to be subjected to its full-blown destruction and casualties when they were attacked by warring military forces. This was a war in which those in the 'ethnic minorities' were either killed or expelled by those in the 'majorities': Serb villages were attacked by the Croatian and Bosniak armed forces, and vice versa (Nizich, 1994, pp. 25–52). While men from rural areas were the first to be drafted into the war, poor women from these areas were disproportionately the victims of rape and sexual enslavement (Soh, 2008). Although women of all ages were affected, girls between 8 and 12 years old were among the 'favourite' prey of soldiers.[4] Those of us who lived in the cities and were lucky enough to belong to the presiding ethnic group could continue for a little longer to live under the illusion that war might not reach us. As Lara Fergus, in her novel *My Sister Chaos*, writes: "The problem was finding the end point, knowing at exactly what stage a war had become a direct danger to you, knowing when you should stop trying to live your life and start running for it. I was looking, but I couldn't see it" (2010, p. 51). Our problem too was to predict and determine a direct danger to us; to know when we should start leaving our residences and run for our lives.

I was focused on my daily life. My first trip to the coast with my childhood friends, Danijela and Gorjana, was now very close. We were also excited about the future and made plans to study together in Sarajevo. These dreams would all fall apart within weeks. The innocence of our youth was violently interrupted. We had to grow up overnight and make life-changing decisions. My best friends began to leave the city which was becoming a dangerous place for non-Serbs. Although there was no war in Banja Luka, war crimes

---

[4] I have recently come across the case of Mirjana Dragičević, an eight-year-old girl who was raped on 28 December 1992 in her home village of Donja Bioča by three foreign soldiers (Mujahideens, Islamic fighters from Arabic countries) who fought for the Bosniak army. The men gang-raped Mirjana in front of her mother Rada, and then shot both of them. Mirjana died instantly but Rada survived. Mirjana's four-year-old brother saved himself by hiding under a bed but heard the whole ordeal. Today, Rada works as a waitress in Han Pijesak and lives alone in very basic conditions. None of the three men were ever charged for the rape and killing (*Mirjana,* 2005). This is just one of many previously untold stories of murder and lack of accountability for crimes committed that we discover each day, almost 20 years after the war.

were already being committed in our midst; they were, according to Human Rights Watch, "virulent and pervasive" (Lupis, Mihelić and Nizich, 1994, p. 2). In a matter of weeks, the Serb-dominated city was 'ethnically cleansed' through systematic persecution of the Bosniak and Croat populations. People were being forced to migrate and leave their homes behind them; some were arrested and taken to detention centres in the city centre, while others were herded into a makeshift concentration camp near Banja Luka, called Manjača.[5] Those detained were accused of being 'spies' and having radio transmitters in their houses so they could report to 'their armies'; or they were accused of hiding weapons. In most cases the allegations were false. Such arrests were happening across BiH in those cities and towns that had disproportionately higher numbers of one ethnic group—which was the case in most parts of the country. The majority group would take over the position of power and establish its 'rule of law' which decreed that all people belonging to ethnic minorities should be killed, imprisoned or expelled. Women were tortured and raped, and so-called rape camps were established throughout the country.[6]

At that time, the well-known and highly respected Bosniak family, Čivljak, who for generations had made gold jewellery, were slaughtered overnight. The family were dear to many people in Banja Luka who could not comprehend such a heinous crime. They had been hard-working, decent people who had remained in the city, believing that no one would hurt them as they had done nothing wrong. Unfortunately, many people died due to such trust in their neighbours and fellow citizens. I recall that people talked about how the jewellers' bloodied bodies had been found in the morning in their bath-tub. The killing happened while I was still in Banja Luka, feeling

---

[5] The Manjača camp began operating in 1991 during the war between the then Yugoslav National Army and Croatian forces. At that time numerous Croatian prisoners of war were detained at the camp. With the commencement of war in BiH, the camp began to fill with detainees, predominantly Bosniak civilians from the Banja Luka region. The camp was shut down due to international pressure in late 1993 but was reopened in October 1995. It has been estimated that a total of between 4,500 and 6,000 non-Serbs passed through the camp (United Nations, 27 May 1994).

[6] It is a well-known fact that Serbs ran these camps containing non-Serb women. There are also lesser-known reports that Bosniak and Croat armies and paramilitary forces ran brothels and rape camps. A number of reports also alleged the operation of private prisons controlled by various Bosniak and Croat forces or individuals (United Nations, 27 May 1994).

relatively safe. Their unit was in my neighbourhood, and their murder sounded the alarm bell for Bosniaks and Croats that it was time to run for their lives.

In order to escape this real threat to their lives, Danijela and her family had to pack up and leave Banja Luka within a couple of days. Although I had grown up with her, only at the beginning of the war did I learn that her father was a Bosniak and her mother a Croatian. Our ethnicities had never come between us. We never discussed them. Suddenly, their ethnicity became the sole reason for their expulsion from the unit they had lived in for the previous 19 years. Danijela's parents had both been born and raised in Banja Luka. It was devastating to see them packing a few of their belongings and leaving in a rush. They could not take everything with them in their small family car, so Danijela left some of her favourite items with me. I remember seeing her father sitting and sobbing in the hallway of our building. He could not comprehend what was happening to them. Earlier that week, he and his wife had also been fired from their jobs because they were not of the 'right' ethnicity. I remember saying goodbye to Danijela and her family, but none of us were fully aware that they would never come back.

I lost touch with Danijela soon after the war began and I doubt that I will ever see her again. Her family spent a few years in Croatia and eventually resettled in the USA. She has never returned to Europe and I have been told that she has no intention of visiting her home city ever again. She is afraid of flying but also, I suppose, of facing the past. And I am part of that past. It is hard to believe that such a strong friendship could fall apart.

My friend Gorjana decided to migrate to Germany with her then boyfriend, Ranko. Gorjana was also from a 'mixed marriage': her mother was Serb and her father Croat. Again, I only discovered this fact at the beginning of war. At that time, Radislav Vukić, a Serb politician, gynaecologist and director of the Banja Luka Health Centre, infamously announced in the media that he would not allow women who were not Serb to give birth in Banja Luka hospitals. According to him, only Serb women could have access to hospitals and care, while women of other ethnicities had to leave the town and give birth to their babies elsewhere. We could not believe what we were hearing as it sounded too farcical to possibly be true.

Vukić also said that all ethnically 'mixed marriages' should be dissolved through divorce and abolished from then on, and that children from 'mixed marriages' were only good for making into soap (United Nations ICTY, 14 July 1997). In the spirit of the absurdity of this last announcement, Gorjana and her older sister cracked jokes. Gorjana said she would become 'Nivea soap' and her sister 'Palmolive'. They put these soaps next to their TV and we all laughed about it. We could not take such preposterous comments seriously. Little did we know that such a terrible threat was no joke at all.

At first I cherished staying in touch with Gorjana who, like many of us, felt the imperative to emigrate at the beginning of war. This friendship too, however, has become very fragile. Time is doing its work. My friends' faces blur together in my mind. They belong to the past, to some other time that often seems like a dream. We don't inhabit the same world any longer. Our lives continue in the same universe but on three different continents. Our paths probably won't cross again. And even if they do, where and how would we start making up for the lost time? From which point in time should we 'catch up' with our lives? Would our different 'ethnicities' come between us now? The past, the connector of our once-upon-a-time friendship, exists no more. Thinking about it or talking about it brings up those suppressed feelings of grief. But without thinking or talking about the past what is left between us? Could we talk about the present and the future, without discussing that which is our main connection?

In her memoir *Otherland: A Journey With My Daughter* (2010), Maria Tumarkin cites her mother's views on lost, but never forgotten, childhood friendships and what these meant to her. When emigrating from Ukraine to Australia, Tumarkin's mother had to say goodbye to many of her childhood friends whom she would never see again:

> We lived a shared life and we no longer do. I do not think we could possibly pick up where we left off. To remain real friends you have to be part of each other's lives. But when you don't have that and when you live completely different lives, your relationship is inevitably changed at its very core (p. 228).

In contrast to Tumarkin's mother, I was not aware back then that I was saying goodbye to my closest childhood friends, one of whom I would probably never see again. We were all certain that this farewell was temporary. But, our relationships were lost for ever and we stopped being part of each other's lives.

In 1992, not long after my two closest friends had emigrated, I was almost drafted into the army after the war started. I received a draft notice from the Serb army (Vojska Republike Srpske), which was already in control of my home town, to be part of a civilian protection unit. I still vividly remember the day when I went to pick up the blue uniform and black rubber boots with my father. We had no idea what it all meant but we were afraid they might take me away from my home. In a state of terrible fear, my parents made one of the most difficult decisions of their lives. They decided to send me away. I was 19 and had never been alone in a foreign country before. I did not want to leave. I was young and confused, terrified of staying but also of going somewhere alone. I would rather have joined my 21-year-old brother who had already been drafted. I wanted to be close to him although we did not even know where he was.

My father's family lived in Ukraine (the former Soviet Union) but going there was out of the question. My uncle and other relatives, who had left Yugoslavia after Tito had split with Stalin in 1948, had always struggled to survive, especially at that time in 1992 when the Soviet Union also abruptly fell apart. So my parents decided that it would be best for me to go to neighbouring Serbia, especially as my mother was originally from there and had lots of friends who offered to help out. I wanted to go to Western Europe, but my parents were too afraid to send me somewhere 'unknown' and distant. To them, Western Europe was like another continent, unfamiliar, unexplored and consequently dangerous. My youth and my sex exacerbated their fears; in their minds I faced a risk of being abducted by sex traffickers or other criminals. After a sleepless night, my parents put me on a bus with packed suitcases and sent me away to Serbia.

I spent the war as a refugee in Serbia, travelling back and forth to see my parents (and if possible, my brother) whenever I had a chance. These trips were always risky, but my parents could not stop me; the need to see my family was stronger than my fear of death from stray (or intentional) bullets, or grenades dropping from anywhere. I was travelling via the 'corridor', the lifeline road that connected RS and Serbia. There were often delays while we waited for shelling in front of us to stop. At times we had to stay in 'no man's land' for hours until we were told that it was safe to continue. The cities I was travelling through were Serb-dominated but many on the border with Croatia were occupied by the Bosniak army (Armija Bosne i Hercegovine).

The war had forced me to separate from my family for the first time in my life, but this was supposed to be only a 'temporary' solution. I thought, as many of us did, that "the war would soon be over, as if it were a rainstorm rather than a conflagration" (Ugrešić, 2008, p. 21). Little did I know that I would never return to live permanently in my home town.

I went to Niš, a city in the southern part of Serbia, was granted refugee status, and enrolled in law school. I lived in Serbia from 1992 through to the 1999 NATO bombing. Only in 2000, eight years after that first emotional bus trip out of my home town, did I return to live in BiH. By then I had graduated with a law degree from Niš University.

For a few years I worked in various international organisations in Sarajevo and Banja Luka in different capacities and involving a range of assignments, including 'ethnic minority return assistance' projects,[7] as well as projects related to combating human trafficking. 'Ethnic minorities' are considered to be people who live in urban or rural spaces occupied by so-called ethnic majorities. People are given such labels simply by interpreting and attaching their names to a particular ethnic group. The classification is applied irrespective of whether someone identifies with that ethnicity. Before the war, I never felt that I belonged to the Serb ethnic group. After the war, regardless of my personal lack of ethnic identity, I will always be 'classified' as a Serb. This is because my first and last names are Orthodox Christian and my parents are Orthodox Christians.

My identity has changed and shifted over the years since the official end of the war. In post-conflict BiH, and in the world generally, I am no longer simply a Bosnian woman: I am first and foremost a Serb woman. Because I've suddenly acquired this unwelcome label of a specific, but somehow alien, ethnic identity as a key feature of my

---

[7] These were projects run by the International Catholic Migration Commission (ICMC) which I worked for in Banja Luka. I was employed to help returnees, ethnic minorities (Bosniaks and Croats), to resettle in Banja Luka after the war. My team also reached out to other towns and villages with Serb resettlers to help them renovate their pre-war, often severely damaged, properties.

being, it has become difficult to cross ethnic and national borders, to work with people from various cultural and ethnic backgrounds and, in particular, to write about the crimes committed by 'my' people.

My activism and writings have often been seen as a betrayal of my own ethnic group, as 'anti-Serb'. No matter how much I would like to escape the new 'ethnicisation', ethnic identity has indeed become the most important attribute of a Bosnian, one that can open a door or close it for good. Unfortunately, as Bosnian-American writer Aleksandar Hemon argues, the ethnic identity training in BiH now begins very early, in both the family and the classroom. From an early age, children in today's BiH are 'trained' to become either Serbs, Croats or Bosniaks. According to Hemon, while the war was bad, its devastating and long-term consequences continue, as "peace has turned out to be ridiculous and demeaning" (Hemon, 2012). In this 'peace' we have all become what Herbert Marcuse (1964) named 'one-dimensional' humans, reduced to our ethnicity alone.

The dismantling of Yugoslavia tore apart its collective identity and a new one is still being created and constructed. Yugoslavianhood exists only as a memory of childhood. This is also true for the language that was spoken which was later split into 'different' languages (Forča and Puača, 2007, p. 64). 'Ethnohood' has become the main indicator of our identities, produced by local politics and governmental institutions (Vlaisavljević, 2010, p. 30). Ethnic identities are considered irreversible, unchangeable and inevitable. As Chaim Kaufmann argues, "ethnic identities are fixed by birth" (1996, p. 138). He maintains that ethnicity is the "hardest" of identity categories because it depends on "language, culture, and religion, which are hard to change, as well as parentage which no one can change" (1996, p. 140). This identity hardens during violent conflict, such as was experienced in BiH. 'Ethnohood' produces 'minorities' and 'majorities'—something that did not exist under Tito's socialist regime. Tito spoke of "socialism casting away minority and majority ... [T]here is neither minority nor majority, there is one people ..." (in Campbell, 1998, p. 93). Today's BiH has produced a society in which ethnic divisions can be clearly seen and are endlessly enforced.

I too lost my Yugoslav identity and was forced to gain a strange, unwelcome new one. My mother tongue, Serbo-Croatian, was the only language I knew and spoke growing up in my motherland,

Yugoslavia, but it ceased to exist with the dismantling of my country. This was the language in which I pronounced my first words; the language in which I learned to say *ljubav* [love] with six letters, and to say *rat* [war] with only three; the language I used to describe the world.

It is also a language that contains traces of a long history of war in the region. In *Ministry of Pain*, a novel about Yugoslav emigrants in Amsterdam, Dubravka Ugrešić (2008) writes about exile and the attempt to preserve the language that was declared dead. Tanja, a young professor from Zagreb, is given a one-year post teaching what is still called 'Serbo-Croatian' at the University of Amsterdam. She finds that the class is filled with fellow refugees. Her students attempt to explain the cause of the war by blaming the language: "There's something fundamentally fucking wrong with a language that, instead of saying, 'The child is sleeping soundly', or 'sleeping deeply', says 'sleeping the sleep of the butchered' " (p. 90). Our mother tongue was "our common trauma" and "a weapon, after all: it branded, it betrayed, it separated and united" (p. 44).

The war erased my country, my language, my youth—the life I had known until I was 19. The once universally used Serbo-Croatian was split into national languages as the break-up of Yugoslavia ushered in omnipresent politicised linguistic engineering (Greenberg, 2008). Although my language was sentenced to death and replaced by other languages, namely Serbian, Croatian and Bosnian, I continue to use its old, pre-destruction name, since nothing has changed in my pronunciation, spelling or vocabulary. But, so-called language experts were hired by the power elites to make changes to our mother tongue, to 'seal' our new postwar identity. Croatian radio, for example, began broadcasting programs on a daily basis to 'teach' Croatian people 'proper' Croatian language. New words were gradually invented to replace old ones. Language had become (and still is) a political statement and identity card. It was firmly attached to ethnic identity, and people who accepted new identities eventually adapted to new vocabulary and language. According to this new connection between ethnicity and language, it became logical and expected that Serbs speak Serbian, Croats Croatian, and Bosniaks Bosnian. The name given to the language we spoke had become a political and ethnic identity statement. All three languages are now official languages of the country and, accordingly, it is considered that citizens in BiH can speak and use any of them. But rarely, if ever, will you meet a Bosniak who will say that s/he speaks Serbian, a Croat who speaks Bosnian, or a Serb who speaks Croatian.

What we call the language we speak has become an important determiner of who 'ethnically' we are. Perhaps even more importantly, it indicates to others our political stance and ethnic identity. As Tone Bringa writes, just as with our first names, the language one speaks is used as an ethno-national marker directly related to family background and locality (1995). Language is perceived as the "innermost sanctum of ethnicity" and as the most evident sign of ethnicity (Schöpflin, 2000, p. 116). Yet, we all continue to understand one another, as these three 'new' postwar languages are actually one and the same language, but now with different accents, dialects and dozens of new words. In the beginning we made jokes about new words that appeared from nowhere and became part of Croatian/Bosnian vocabulary, but within a few years they had become the norm. Faced with the dilemma of where I belong and into which ethnic 'ghetto' I should place myself, I decided to belong to none of them, and therefore continue to call my language 'Serbo-Croatian', and my country of birth, my non-existent country, 'Yugoslavia'.

The whole language issue in my former homeland raises many complexities for me. What should be the easiest question to answer has become the most difficult: "Which language do you speak?" It has become a repeated reminder of war and loss. I often pause when I hear this question. I never know what the 'right' answer is because I feel there is always a deeper reason for asking it; like trying to find out my ethnic allegiance and place me in a specific 'ethnicity box' that my people created for themselves after the war. But I do not want to be judged by my ethnic origin and surrounded by prejudices and stereotypes. I want people to get to know me as I am, to learn about my work and how I define myself. Belonging to a group, as Jessie Hronešová points out, is strengthened by external ethnic markers, such as first and last names which, coupled with the label given to the language we speak, are used to intensify boundaries between the various groups (2012, p. 56). Internal and external ethnic markers and labels make our daily co-existence complex and difficult.

I find that some people think that we former Yugoslavs, by default, 'belong to' a certain ethnic group when they hear our name or hear the language we speak. They are not interested in how we define ourselves. As my colleague and friend, Professor Miodrag Živanović, once said to me: "[T]here are no more human beings in Bosnia, only Serbs, Croats and Bosniaks" (pers. comm., July 2012). We have all, willingly or unwillingly, consciously or unconsciously, become reduced to our ethnic identity. The language helps me to walk the fine lines between witnessing and participating, between being and being the one who self-reflectively judges the encounters I experienced.

Writing now in a language other than my own paradoxically provides a refuge for expressing the most difficult thoughts. I feel safe when writing in English, even though wrestling with its expressions and rhythms presents yet another challenge. I can hide behind this language, behind its multiple meanings, structures and cadences. I feel 'de-ethnicised' and can more easily attain objective distance when re-encountering my own history. This makes me feel both lost and found in the world of discourses and interpretations.

The question of identity has become a fundamental one for all Bosnians and other ex-Yugoslavs who now search for themselves through history, religion, spirituality, and exile. Our labels of ethnicity have overridden our very being and make it impossible for us to be recognised first as people, and only then as an 'ethnicity'. It has become a question of survival, of life and death, of dealing with the past and moving towards the future, of living between lost and new identities, of crossing the borders within oneself or staying behind, paralysed and invisible. In all this mayhem, I have found myself in a position that I do not want to occupy. Our bodies and minds were displaced, our country and language erased. Many of us were forced to change our spaces of physical and mental belonging. As Dijana Milošević, director of the Belgrade theatre company Dah, and someone with whom I spent lots of time in conversation about the aftermath of war in our country, said to me:

> Individual identity is shaped in part by national identity and the physical map of the country where one was born. When this map changes, the whole notion of identity is changed, and this process can be violent and painful, as the example of the former Yugoslavia continues to show us (pers. comm., 12 December 2011).

Reduced to my ethnic identity and perceived first as a Serb, and then as a Bosnian woman, I've found myself in a number of situations where people (not only Bosnians) have shown resentment after learning of my ethnic origin. More painfully, I have also felt resentment from my own family because, during the last 10 years, I have chosen to write about the crimes committed in my name. The ethnic identity that I have been reduced to in peacetime has become a chain around my neck that threatens to choke me. It determines everything I do, say or write. It takes away my breath and the strength necessary for my work and life. Every time someone starts to inquire about my 'ethnic identity' I find myself walking a minefield of people's judgments and closed-mindedness. How to introduce myself, my story, and not become 'the Serb'? How to say who I am without being judged, blamed or victimised? My anxiety, and fear of spontaneous responses, the need to be on guard, and the loss of ease in such conversations, is a legacy of war that I did not choose.

I am not the only one who feels lost in a vacuum, trapped between the collective identity I lost and the ethnic identity forcibly attached to me. A Bosnian refugee in Germany reflected on these dislocations:

> I can't live somewhere I can't identify with. I can't identify with the government in Bosnia and I can't identify with Germany either. I'm someone from the former Yugoslavia, but that no longer exists. First, I'm a human being, then a Bosnian, then someone from Bosnia of the Muslim religion. But I'm not religious. I don't feel Muslim (Campbell, 1998, p. 94).

The ethnic identity that has been imposed on me has determined my life and career. Because I am regarded first and foremost as a Serb, I am viewed as a traitor, as are others who write about crimes committed in their names. Our work has been branded as shameful by the respective communities we come from. It is not surprising then that my own family (in particular, my father), have been upset because of my scholarly engagement with literature which talks about Serb crimes, as I will discuss in the next chapter.

CHAPTER TWO

Traitor or Truth Seeker?

> you dream of flight with wings with claw some days
> you sob because all the elegies for the dead all the strings
> played with furious pathos will not stop the clot of war
>
> —Susan Hawthorne, *Valence: Considering War Through Poetry and Theory*
> (2011, p. 12)

"You have to stop writing," he tells me from 30,000 kilometres away. I am sitting in my study with the telephone receiver in my hand. His voice sounds unreal. Did he just say what I thought he said? In disbelief, I don't know what to tell him. Pause. Silence. His words are hanging in the heavy air between us.

"You should write about the crimes committed against Serbs. Serbs suffered too."

I stammer, unable to respond. I fix my gaze on the blue wall in front of me while I listen to him. My mind is buzzing: *I know that, Dad, but I choose not to. You can't tell me what I should write about. I don't write because you want me to write; I write from rage, bitterness, and deep feelings of injustice and shame. It's someone else's task to write about the crimes committed against Serbs, but not mine. I might occasionally do that, but I want to write about the crimes committed by 'my people' in 'my name'. I write about them because I dream these crimes. I dream Srebrenica; I dream about the dead, and the living left behind. The demons of this horror come back regularly and haunt me.* Still, none of these bubbling thoughts are said to him. I have no courage. Instead, I make some excuse and say I am in a hurry and need to go.

I am shaking when I finally hang up the phone. I feel physically ill. I stretch across my bed and lie there staring up at the ceiling. My limbs feel dense and vague, my mind is still buzzing. I feel angry and ashamed for not being brave enough to tell him what was on my mind; the thoughts and feelings that I have been suppressing for all these years. But I know that honesty would not help him understand. Like many of our compatriots, my father and I have lost a capacity to listen to things we are not eager to hear. It has become difficult, if not impossible, to engage with my father or his friends in any meaningful, non-confrontational conversation about war issues that are so important to us. The *full* war narratives (comprising both innocence and victimhood) have become so sacred that Bosnian people cannot allow themselves to think about anything that might disrupt these stories (Helms, pers. comm., November 2013).[8] But the real reason for not telling him straight out what I really think is that, deep inside, I am afraid he might say that he does not want me to be his daughter any more. I close my eyes and force myself to take a deep breath. I was not ready for this reaction, although I could see it coming. My father has never supported my writing and thinking regarding the causes and consequences of war in our homeland. This wasn't what he wanted for me. He did not want to stand for any of it.

Minutes pass, maybe an hour. The house is quiet. I feel more alone than ever before, trying to just disappear from it all.

My father and I are both obsessed with the war, Srebrenica and the dead, but for remarkably different reasons. He is in denial that genocide ever happened, while I desire to uncover all possible details about those four days in July 1995 when Bosnian Muslims in the town of Srebrenica (Bosnia) were killed by the Serbian army (see Simić, 2009, 2011, 2013).

Ever since I first started writing about the war crimes committed by the Serbs, my father has made it his life's mission to convince me to do otherwise. He thinks that I am writing about these crimes because I live in the West, and that this is not only expected of me but also

---

[8] Elissa Helms is the author of *Innocence and Victimhood: Gender, Nation, and Women's Activism in Postwar Bosnia-Herzegovina* (2013).

'convenient', and the only way I can pursue my academic career. He probably thinks that his daughter is not a 'traitor' by her own choice, but has to dance along to the dominant Western views of Serbs. She must sell her soul to the devil, not because she wants to, but because it is the narrative expected from her for the sake of her work. This is how he justifies my writing; this is what helps him to not hate me, to not feel heartbroken and disappointed in his only daughter.

Since 2006 I have lived in Australia, a country that has sheltered me and my writing, but I visit my parents in Bosnia and Herzegovina (BiH) at least once a year. Throughout the year my father goes to book launches for like-minded Serbs, buys locally written books, and piles them up in his bedroom in preparation for my arrival. It has become our ritual that the first thing he proudly shows me is a few kilograms of manuscripts on genocide and 'ethnic cleansing' which analyse the crimes committed against Serbs. Printed by dubious private BiH publishing houses, these so-called academic books (and novels) often do nothing but promote hate speech and a one-dimensional 'truth' about war.

Since the war, BiH has seen a mushrooming of such publishers who will accept and reproduce almost any manuscript if authors have the money to pay them for printing and distribution. Often people who are keen to get their views published will borrow (from their families and friends) just enough to have one edition of their book printed. In this atmosphere—and without any peer reviews or professional screening of the manuscript—anyone can publish anything with impunity and call themselves a 'writer'. I specifically avoid such books which are, as I see it, purely based on pursuing further ethnic hatred and division. But my father and his like-minded friends are avid readers. I believe that these books provide him with a perfect mirror: always confirming and never challenging his views.

My father has always loved to read, and when I lived at home I would often watch him from the hallway as he sat for hours at our old wooden dining table with one hand holding an open book and the other cradling his chin so that he would not fall asleep. Occasionally he would shout: "Yes!" while reading, and frequently, he would call out to my mother: "Listen to this" and then proceed to read aloud several passages from a book he felt passionate about. Mama would usually be in the middle of cooking, which she does (to this day) behind the colourful curtain that divides the kitchen from the rest of the dining room. This has been her sanctuary for as long as I can remember; the space where she is left alone in her own world. The curtain prevents the odour of the cooking oil from swirling throughout the unit. But it does much more than that: within this two-square-metre space she has been able to enjoy her ritual of smoking in peace, despite strong and ongoing disapproval from my father over the past 45 years. Still, even in that 'safe' space she could not escape having to listen to my father's occasional loud declamations. She would rather not hear them, but does not protest. Her only response has always been silence.

My father is convinced that Serbs are simply victims of the recent war, and to him the whole world seems unjust for denying the victimisation of his people. He is not alone in this view. Many Serbs distrust outsiders and resent world opinion. From the beginning of the civil war in 1992, the United States provided the smallest proportion of assistance to Serb refugees and did not hide its sympathy for Bosniaks and Croats. Although Serbs boycotted the referendum for the independence of BiH in 1992, the international community recognised it as a sovereign country, a move which plunged the country into civil war when the newly constituted army of Republika Srpska (RS) attacked Sarajevo and started the brutal four-year siege in which thousands of predominantly non-Serb civilians lost their lives. It is claimed that in the BiH war almost 31,000 Serbs were also killed and that, according to Serbs, this was nothing short of genocide (Hunt, 2011, p. 113).

My father is an example of the old communist-turned-nationalist generation who feed their minds by re-telling popular stories of Serbian victimhood and bravery. All his friends are Serbs and he prefers not to mix with members of the other ethnic groups living in BiH. He tells me that there is no point in associating with Bosniaks and Croats because there is nothing to discuss with them. All he wants to talk about is politics and it would be difficult to find a common language with people other than his 'own'. This is probably correct. All three ethnic groups have their own truths, blaming each other for gross violations committed during the war, and it is almost impossible to have respectful conversations about politics and war in today's BiH.

Although I never read my father's books, I don't have the heart to refuse to bring them back with me to Australia. I flick through them because I know that my father will seek my opinion. Many are written by local academics who 'know' the 'real truth' about the war in the former Yugoslavia. Without exception, they are only about crimes committed against Serbs. Over the years it has become more and more difficult to talk to my father about politics and war. I try to avoid having conversations with him because any attempt ends in a disagreement.

On a recent visit to my parents' home, I had no sooner unpacked my luggage and sat down for a coffee when my father locked his eyes on mine and asked: "So, are you still writing about Srebrenica? You know that Srebrenica is a lie ..." His arms were across his chest as he spoke. Each time I visit he looks more frail. His hair has become completely white and is thinning on top. His eyes seem much smaller than they used to be, but still have that spark and wit. He has grown shorter with age, and thinner; his clothes hang on him.

He did not ask me how my flight was, or how my life was going in that distant country that will always remain a mystery to him; a country that my family and fellow compatriots refer to as 'too far'. In my father's world, Australia is a place full of people who have fled from war, poverty, political persecution or terror with a dream of beginning a new life. And it is true that a great many of "the Australian population are either immigrants or descended from immigrants, with ancestral homes far beyond the ocean's horizon" (Scott, 2013, p. 147). Australia had become home to his daughter too, and since he regarded it as a rich, developed (and war-resistant) country, my father assumed that I must consequently feel safe, with a comfortable lifestyle that allowed me to fly home once a year. Not many other migrants had achieved this. I surely must be happy: I finally had a 'normal' job and security, far away from the daily social, political and economic crises back in BiH. From his point of view, with all my education, I was now living 'happily ever after' in the 'promised land'. How could I not be satisfied? What else could anyone from a war-torn country wish for apart from financial and social stability? His monologue continued in this vein for some time.

I listened to him on and off until he started to talk about the latest 'community news', the rumours that circulate in my home town: that the massacre at Srebrenica did not happen; that the people allegedly killed now live in Canada or the USA and vote in elections for ultra-nationalist Bosniak parties; that these people even attend their own memorial service each year in Srebrenica; that the famous documentary broadcast across the world showing the execution of six unarmed men from Srebrenica by the 'Scorpions' (the Serbian paramilitary unit) was a fake montage made by those who hate the Serbs;[9] that the people shown dead in that footage were acting, and after the cameras stopped rolling they got up and walked away; that the victims of the Srebrenica massacre killed one another; that the then President of BiH, Alija Izetbegović, 'needed' Srebrenica to provoke the international community and NATO into bombing the Serbian army in BiH in 1999 to end the war. My father knew all the tales and was eager to share them with me. I had heard them too. The difference between us was that I considered them to be lies, while he regarded them as truth. It was pointless to object as it would only lead to another argument. I sighed, shook my head, and said nothing. I was exhausted.

Still, he went on and on with his diatribe. I was jet-lagged, half asleep, after twenty-two hours in the air. I could not believe that this was the first thing my father was telling me after not having seen me for a year. This was our welcome hug and kiss. I listened to him for a while, trying to savour my first cup of Bosnian coffee (prepared by my mother) in a year. Having a coffee with your family and friends is such an important ritual and I was trying to relish the moment as much as possible. I thought to myself, *I will just let him get it all out, as he always does.* But this time I could not. I snapped. Anger rose in me, my arms dropped in frustration. The air was dry and I had trouble breathing. My voice was trembling, my hands shaking, as I shouted at him: "Leave me alone! I don't care about your denial and 'true stories'. No matter how hard you try, you won't change my mind; it is too late for that. I am not a little girl any more; I have my own brain, knowledge and principles. Just forget about it. Give up. This conversation has to come to an end."

---

[9] The killings occurred in the village of Trnovo after the fall of Srebrenica and were video-taped by the Scorpions. Six Muslim men and boys were forced to lie down with their hands tied before being shot in the back by their captors. The footage was aired on most television stations in the region, shocking people across the Balkan countries. The victims were identified as: Safet Fejzić (17), Azmir Alispahić (17), Sidik Salkić (36), Smail Ibrahimović (35), Dino Salihović (18) and Juso Delić (25) (Humanitarian Law Center, 11 January 2008).

I had only been back ten minutes and already regretted coming home. I wished I could fly back to Australia immediately. My family home had become something it had never been before: the source of insecurity and pain, something to run away from. This latest incident with my father reminded me of how war had destroyed us all. We continue to breathe, walk, talk and dream war. All we can talk about is war.

It has never been more obvious to me than during that afternoon, exactly what the overused terms 'war-torn social fabric' and 'intergenerational trauma', mean on the ground, in real life. The encounter with my father was a textbook example of how aftermath-of-war madness affects the relationships between the closest family members. My father is a very important and special person in my life. He played a key role in my upbringing and most of my memories of childhood involve him. We have always been very close to each other. Because of this, my decision to write about the things he denies with all his heart must be especially difficult for him. The disappointment in his only daughter hangs over us like a dense black cloud.

For my own part, I can hardly recognise my father any more. I struggle to understand him and his desperate and ongoing need to justify Serb crimes. He lives in a city where the vast majority of residents are Serbs and he only associates with them, and is deaf to other stories of pain and death. Still, what is bizarre and difficult to comprehend is that my father, like many of his generation, was not an ultra-right nationalist before or during the war. In fact, before the war he was a proud member of the Communist Party. But sadly, like many in the former Yugoslavia, he was swayed by the nationalist argument, and since the war ended, has emerged as a fierce nationalist. This is something that most people outside the borders of my former homeland find surprising: before war broke out, inter-ethnic relations were generally good. It is a contemporary myth that we hated one another and were fierce nationalists beforehand. While there were ultra-right nationalists before the 1990s, the truth is that war helped multiply those sentiments exponentially. As a consequence, very few people remained loyal to the idea of a multi-ethnic society with multiculturalism at its heart. Even fewer remained communists, loyal to the humanist ideal of equality between nations. Indeed, it would not be an exaggeration to say that the majority of people in my homeland have become right-wing nationalists.

Before the war, our best friends were a Bosniak family whom my parents had known for more than 20 years. I grew up with this family and considered them my family too. Yet when the war began in 1992, overnight they became 'enemies'. According to my mother, these friends had told her that she should pack her bags and move to Serbia. My mother, who was originally from Serbia and met my father while studying in BiH, was shocked, as was my father. That day marked the end of the relationship. My mother still misses them, and often cries when she talks to me about their friendship, and special moments they had shared over many years.

Despite the fact that my parents had been insulted and hurt by their closest friends, when food was scarce during the war my father still risked his life for the sake of this family by riding his bike to the next suburb, and bringing them some potatoes, milk or sugar from our own stores. He would pull his blue hood over his head and visit them knowing that he, or one of his family members, could be killed if he were caught. At that time, my father would have been regarded as a traitor for helping an 'enemy'. The Bosniak family's only crime was that they were of the 'wrong' ethnicity and religion (they were Muslims).

We all knew about and supported him in his 'treacherous' activity, and I admired my father for doing this. Yet he has never spoken about these times outside of our family home. Instead of being proud, he worries that someone might find out about his benevolence. Even today, almost 20 years after the war, his act of bravery would be seen as traitorous and he could be ostracised from his community. People in BiH are only encouraged to share stories of betrayal and killing, not of empathy and caring. Political elites in my homeland have no interest in drawing on any humanity that existed before or during the war between different ethnic groups.

In *Good People in an Evil Time* (2005), Svetlana Broz, the granddaughter of the former Yugoslav head of state, Marshal Tito, collected first-hand testimonies of ordinary people who resisted both the killings and an ideology of destruction under the most terrible circumstances. Her book refutes the stereotype of 'ancient hatred' and of inevitable natural animosity between the peoples of the Balkans. These are the stories of people such as Mile Plakalović who drove his taxi through the streets of Sarajevo (in 1993) when the bombing was at its worst, plucking the wounded from the sidewalk and delivering food and clothing to the old and young. My father's story could be one of the countless testimonies that Svetlana encountered in her writing, stories of people who put their humanity before their ethnicity; but he wants it to remain hidden.

However, regardless of his views, my father did not ask me to turn my back on my Bosniak and Croat friends in my home town. Whenever I returned home from my exile in Serbia (where I lived from 1992 to 1999) I would also visit my Bosniak family friends, although it was a time when, even in the middle of the day, a bomb could be thrown through the window of any Bosniak house without any reprisals. Life was worth nothing. Men with beards, and armed with guns and knives, walked around the city, and I was terrified whenever I saw them on the streets. I felt in a permanent state of danger, always alert and ready to run. In such an environment, my parents were terrified whenever I embarked on such outings. I would often leave my mother in tears and excruciating fear for my life, but they never protested or tried to prevent me from going out and visiting whomever I wanted. No words can ever express the admiration I have for my parents because of this.

I will be visiting my parents again this year and my father has already announced that he has another package of books for me. He is yet again prepared to greet his only daughter with books about alleged killing of Serbs, as her 'welcome home' present. Despite my protests, this ritual continues. He knows how much I love to read and he hopes that I will change my mind once I have read them all.

It is difficult to explain to him (and others) my urge to write about things from which most people would rather run away. Some people from the former Yugoslavia have asked me how I can continually read and write about the war crimes that Serbs committed. Some have openly resented my writing and have made mocking comments (similar to those of my father): "Yes, *what else* can you write there [in the West] where they *hate Serbs*? It is in your *own interest* to write about *Bosniaks* as victims." These comments have been sarcastic, patronising and, at times, hateful. I have been in situations where people from the former Yugoslavia would get up from my table or stop talking to me when they heard what I write about. I try to be calm and pretend I don't care; but I do. It is hurtful and it doesn't feel right. I am not glossing over the war crimes that my fellow Bosniaks committed. I am fully aware of them.

Moral Responsibility

There have been times, however, when I too have had doubts: Why look at the recent past? Why look at the past at all? Can I be objective if I am so close to the subject of my research? But after careful consideration I realised that I no longer believe in objectivity. There is no such thing as 'objective knowledge', and for me, as a feminist writer, there is no distance between myself as 'subject' and my country as my research 'object'. I have an urge to find out what happened to my country, my people, and myself and, using a feminist lens, to examine the facts I have discovered through my personal experiences and research.

I write because of feelings of moral responsibility and shame for injustices and terrible acts committed in 'my name'. Of course, I cannot be held accountable for atrocities perpetrated by the members of my ethnic group; that is their burden. However, I can and do feel a responsibility to demand justice and examine crimes committed by 'my clan'. I have to fight against wrongdoings, and against any attempts to justify those crimes, and also, against hate speech and ethnic hatred. In *Eichmann in Jerusalem* (1977) Hannah Arendt writes about the importance of individualised responsibility and about guilt as an individual matter. She argues against the notion of 'collective guilt' and speaks about Germany where, despite pleas against counterproductive collective guilt in the 1960s, there were many "very guilty individuals" who "*feel* nothing of the sort" (p. 251). These individuals were untouched by the judicial process, and more importantly, were allowed to go free because there were no strong demands from the community for their prosecution. According to Arendt, the "normal reaction to such a state of affairs should be indignation, but indignation would be quite risky" (p. 251). To her, talk without consequent action is no more than rhetoric, a cheap moral evasion, employed to release certain feelings without challenging communal apathy in any substantial way. It helps individuals to evade their present responsibility to deal with present injustice. She notes:

Those young German men and women who every once in a while—on the occasion of all the *Diary of Anne Frank* hubbub and of the Eichmann trial—treat us to hysterical outbreaks of guilt feelings are not staggering under the burden of the past, their fathers' guilt; rather, they are trying to escape from the pressure of very present and actual problems into a cheap sentimentality (p. 251).

Arendt notes that there is no such thing as collective guilt or collective innocence, but that every government should assume "political responsibility for the deeds and misdeeds of its predecessors, and every nation, for the deeds and misdeeds of the past" (p. 298). Each generation, by virtue of being born into a historical continuum, is burdened by the sins of their fathers. However, this does not equate with personal responsibility, and only in a metaphorical sense can one say that a people *feel* guilty for what their compatriots have done (p. 298).

In *Guilt About the Past* (2010) Bernhard Schlink also notes that

when we speak of guilt about the past, we are not thinking about individuals, or even organisations, but rather a guilt that infects the entire generation that lives through an era—and in a sense the era itself. Even after the era is past, it casts a long shadow over the present, infecting later generations with a sense of guilt, responsibility and self-questioning (p. 1).

I believe that my writing demonstrates my responsibility to tell and preserve the stories of war. Schlink predicts that "for [the] foreseeable future Germans will be shackled to their past" (in Connolly, 2012). Similarly, I might also relive my past through my present, and a war that put 'shackles' on my wrists, for the rest of my life. Delving into the past gives me purpose. Writing about it provides me with a sanctuary in which I feel free to shrink inside the deepest darkness of myself and give birth to words and texture. Anna Funder, in her novel *All That I Am* (2011), writes about the life of a famous German playwright, poet and revolutionary Ernst Toller, and other anti-Hitler activists in pre-war Berlin and London. One of the characters says of Toller: "[H]is insights come from that dark part of him. If he denies that, he'll be cut off from what feeds his writing" (p. 245). I too feel that, paradoxically, without this dark experience in my life, without surviving the BiH war, I would not have become the writer that I am. The war gave me a reason for writing and living as I do today.

I feel compelled to write, and I treasure the refuge that writing brings to me. It is a cathartic process which involves dealing with difficult things and putting words to them. As Philippine-Australian author, Merlinda Bobis, puts it:

> Writing visits like grace. Its greatest gift is the comfort if not the joy of transformation. In an inspired moment, we almost believe that anguish can be made bearable and injustice can be overturned, because they can be named (2011, p. i).

Indeed, the belief that I can right some of the wrong by telling the difficult stories is what keeps me pushing to write more. I write in English, my second language, so that my immediate family cannot read most of my papers, although they know enough about my writings from other people to be concerned about it. I do not think I will ever find peace with my father or ex-combatant brother in this regard. I once complained to a friend that the relationship I now have with my brother is appalling and almost non-existent. I had hoped for some words of comfort from her but instead she snapped: "What do you expect from him? He was in the war. You are writing about the crimes committed by the army of which he was a member. Why should you expect support and respect from him?" I was so struck by her words that I didn't know what to say. It hurt me because it was true; she was right, I am a 'traitor' in his eyes too. My colleague and friend, writer, and feminist academic (originally from the former Yugoslavia), Ivana Milojević, writes about the destruction of the family fabric:

> Writing my stories and their stories made me suffer, made me cry, and made me struggle with how much I was allowed to reveal. It made me ask tough questions about authenticity and ethics, self-serving attributional biases and the politics of victimhood, as well as whether I was a traitor or a truth seeker (2013, p. 5).

Similarly to Ivana, I often find myself struggling with, doubting, and agonising over my writing. My level of confidence keeps going up and down, but the experiences I lived through, and those told to me by other women and men, are the driving force that keeps my work moving. I firmly believe that witnesses from the past need to speak up so that amnesia does not prevail. If we let silence speak "the past will be condemned to be forgotten as though it had never been" (Arendt, 2009, p. 270). The responsibility that I, and others, assume is not just a means of 'feeling good about ourselves' or, as Judith Butler argues, "for the purity of our souls," but for "the shape of the collectively inhabited world" (2005, p. 110). But speaking up comes at a cost. Until recently I did not think that my writing was the source of my brother's anger towards me. I thought that, because he is not proficient in English and has never been interested in reading, I would be shielded from his criticism and rage. But I was terribly wrong. He knows what my writing is about, although his opposition to it is not expressed directly. We have never discussed it—but then we have hardly any communication at all.

The Masculinity of War

My brother does not talk about the war. He was only 20 years old when he was drafted in 1992 by the Serb army, and being a soldier changed him for ever. He could have packed his bag and deserted, as many of his friends did, but he did not want to do that. He was worried that something might subsequently happen to our family; that our parents would be forced to leave their jobs. He also felt the responsibility to stay and join his childhood friends who had already been drafted. He knew nothing about war, he hated no one, but he did not see a way out. He was, after all, raised in a country where men were supposed to be heroes and protectors, and always respond to the call to arms. As some male participants in Milojević's and Markov's study on students' views on the introduction of the civilian service in Serbia (2008) said:

- A real man has to know how to use weapons, and if needed, to protect his family and country, and not to wait for somebody else to do so.
- To me, being a soldier means honour. That also means that you are a mature, capable person and not asocial.
- Men through the army become stronger, more disciplined and serious, but only if they served the army with 'the uniform, and the gun in their hands'.
- … if our fathers could [serve the army] today's young men can do the same also (p. 183).

My brother was expected to comply with the requirements of masculinity—to display endurance, bravery and self-control—and enlist in the army. And so he did. He spent the war on the front line and witnessed his friends being killed in an instant. I presume he also witnessed them killing others. Those were the days when his youthful innocence died.

My parents had been almost driven to madness with the fear that he might lose his life. My mother chain-smoked and cried most of the time. Early one evening in November 1992, when I was visiting my family from my exile in Serbia, I witnessed a scene that pierced my heart. My mother was standing in the hallway in our small unit in Banja Luka with the phone receiver pressed against her ear. She had called the military base in our home town to check if my brother was still alive as we had not heard from him since he was drafted in June. The military officer on the other end of the phone was reading out the list of names of soldiers who had died that day. We knew that many of my brother's peers in his own unit had been killed. I watched my mother as she sobbed while listening to these names. She was as pale as a ghost and seemed to have aged ten years. Her lips were swollen, and her eyes were fixed on the black telephone in front of her. She held her breath while waiting to hear the name of her only son, her first-born child. Is he alive or not? Her brown hair was a mess, tears rolled down her cheeks. I could see her red dress trembling from the nervous shaking of her body. She swayed slightly while trying to take a deep breath. And even though she did not hear the name of her son among the names of other mothers' sons that were dead, after the call she collapsed. I took her limp body in my arms and embraced her. I felt tears rolling down my flushed cheeks as well. Everything around us seemed to stand still. Everything was unreal. We stayed embraced for what seemed an eternity.

My brother and his peers were convinced that they needed to go to war to protect their country and their wives, mothers, daughters and sisters. Their manhood was to be tested and proved by protecting the females that belonged to their ethnic or religious group. But women were not consulted or asked whether they wanted such protection. No one asked me or my mother whether we wanted a war; whether we wanted to see our brother and son drafted into the war. We did not want any of it. Most women do not want any of it.

As Virginia Woolf writes in her classic *Three Guineas* (1938/2006), women do not share the 'benefits' of war and there is no need for men to protect 'our' country and its women. As she notes:

> Therefore if you insist upon fighting to protect me, or 'our' country, let it be understood, soberly and rationally between us, that you are fighting to gratify a sex instinct which I cannot share; to procure benefits which I have not shared and probably will not share; but not to gratify my instincts, or to protect either myself or my country. 'For', the outsider will say, 'in fact, as a woman, I have no country. As a woman I want no country. As a woman my country is the whole world' (p. 129).

Reflecting on the First World War, the novelist Erich Maria Remarque wrote extensively about the destruction and senselessness of war. But he also emphasised that even in the chaos of war there is always space for some humanity. In the face of death, some soldiers can and do try hard to keep their sanity and empathy, and behave humanely. In his classic *All Quiet on the Western Front* (1966), Remarque talks about the pressure to go to war, and the realisation that the people on the 'other side' are humans too:

> But now, for the first time, I see you are a man like me. I thought of your hand-grenades, of your bayonet, of your rifle; now I see your wife and your face and our fellowship. Forgive me, comrade. We always see it too late. Why do they never tell us that you are poor devils like us, that your mothers are just as anxious as ours, and that we have the same fear of death, and the same dying and the same agony? Forgive me, comrade; how could you be my enemy? If we threw away these rifles and this uniform you could be my brother ... (p. 140).

Remarque reminds us of the universality of pain and suffering: all bodies in war suffer injuries regardless of their allegiance.

Likewise, Elaine Scarry, in her ground-breaking work *The Body in Pain* (1985), studies the politics of pain and analyses physical suffering in the context of war and torture. She argues that although pain is inexpressible, there is "the incontestable reality of the body—the body in pain ... —separated from its source and conferred on an ideology or issue ..." (p. 62). Her argument is that no matter what the political affiliations or beliefs, all injured bodies in war are the same:

[I]f the wounded bodies of a Union and a Confederate soldier were placed side by side during the American Civil War, nothing in those wounds themselves would indicate the different political beliefs of the two sides, as in World War II there would not be anything in the three bodies of a wounded Russian soldier, a Jewish prisoner from a concentration camp, a civilian who had been on a street in Hiroshima, to differentiate the character of the issues on the Allied and Axis sides (pp. 115–116).

As in any civil war, my brother was expected to fight and kill his friends from childhood, and the neighbours he grew up with; those who found themselves on the 'other side'. Overnight, they had become his fiercest enemies and targets for killing. To consider yesterday's friend as today's enemy must have been devastating. I can only imagine what was going through his mind, as we, his family, do not know anything about his war experiences. I remember he mentioned that once he had to eat grass because he was so hungry and there was nothing else. That is all he has ever shared with us. We did not encourage him to tell us more, not because we did not care, but because our daily lives were already filled with so many stories of evil, and we could not bear the thought of hearing such tales from someone we loved. We did not realise how the retelling of his stories might have been crucial for his own healing process and future ability to deal with the trauma. I keep thinking that my writing might be inflaming his wounds that have never healed. He survived the war, but has been changed irrevocably. Like many of his peers, he hid his trauma from his family once he returned home. As Kathleen Barry points out in *Unmaking War, Remaking Men*,

> ... the violence of war is obscured; we cannot see how it reaches deep into our society and silently but surely shapes all of our lives ... The violence of wars turns against soldiers, if not during the war, then when they return home, where too often their trauma is not understood, their stories are left unheard (2010, p. 188).

Besides losing their lives, limbs and spirit, soldiers become good actors, pretending that they have no emotional scars, that their mental well-being has remained unscathed. We all know that this is impossible. But soldiers, as civilians, often do not tell their stories at all. If they do, they might be ignored or dismissed as the stories of either perpetrators or victims. Yet after going through an abnormal experience such as war, is it not normal to have trauma and to seek help? Unfortunately, many ex-combatants do not do so. Those who survive feel lost, betrayed by their community and government, and often harm themselves or take their own lives. Such actions take a terrible toll on their family and friends.

In 2011 in the United States, almost 6,500 war ex-combatants were recorded to have committed suicide, more than the total number of soldiers killed in the Afghanistan and Iraq wars combined (*PressTV*, 2012). The suicide rate was almost 25 times higher than the fatality rate on the battlefield. It seems that for many soldiers peace is worse than war. It can be even more dangerous if we ignore and show no understanding towards the men and women who come back from the combat zone. In his 2008 book, *Ratna Psihotrauma Srpskih Veterana* [War Trauma of Ex-Combatants in Serbia], Željko Špirić, a neuropsychiatrist from Belgrade, analysed the psychological consequences of war in relation to ex-combatants. He argues that they can lose much more in peace than in war if their experiences are not valued, when they are haunted by their memories and feel reluctant to talk about their experiences (p. 95). The soldiers' scars are invisible and intangible, and this is what makes them emotionally vulnerable and potentially dangerous to themselves and to others. The scars are there, but well hidden from friends and families, from partners and children. Ex-combatants hide behind smiles and false happiness, but in reality they might be 'ticking bombs' waiting for someone to press the button. My brother is fortunately not among those 4,000 Bosnian ex-combatants who killed themselves after the war (Dzidic, 2012). I don't know how he copes with his nightmares. We never speak about it.

The two of us have never had a real sense of kinship again, nor repaired the bridges burned by the war. He was in the army, while I was a refugee. I am convinced that I could have had a genuine relationship with my brother if it hadn't been for the war. We became strangers, never again able to connect. We lost each other somewhere in the mayhem of war and we have no language or ability to find our way back to each other again. War has disconnected and silenced us, leaving our relationship in tatters.

War destroys everything. As Ivo Andrić (an author from Bosnia and Herzegovina, and winner of a Nobel Prize in Literature) said in his short story 'Destruction' (1960):

War which produces large-scale destruction of visible objects, does so even more with humans. Only some individuals, and only gradually, become aware of this type of destruction. It takes off from our faces the last mask of humanity, turns us inside out and brings to the surface some unexpected qualities, radically different from what others believed us to be and what we believed we were. Moreover, it transforms the family system and produces changes of the sanctified rules and relations, including those deemed eternal and immutable ... (p. 131).

War experiences often permanently change the lives of ex-combatants and their families. As Andrić argues, war transforms their relationships into something they often struggle to understand. During war soldiers are primarily in physical danger, but in peacetime it is their psychological well-being that can be most at risk. Johan Galtung argues that after war, traumatised people have two basic choices: one is to relive and recreate trauma; the other is to embark on the path to transcendence (Galtung, Jacobsen, Brand-Jacobsen, 2002).

Richard Tedeschi and Lawrence Calhoun identify three categories of perceived benefits amongst survivors of individual and collective trauma. These include "changes in self-perception, changes in interpersonal relationships, and a changed philosophy of life" (1996, p. 456) Perceived changes include "emotional growth," becoming a "better person," feeling more experienced about life, feeling stronger and more self-assured, as well as potentially more self-reliant, and more confident when dealing with new challenges (p. 456). Earlier traumatic situations, in which "fundamental assumptions are severely challenged, can become fertile ground for unexpected outcomes that are observed in survivors: [a form of] *posttraumatic growth*" (p. 456). Due to such profound and life-changing experiences, ex-combatants have great potential for peacebuilding processes. But for this to occur, recognition and acceptance of their war experiences is necessary. They need to engage with other survivors and their communities in order to arrive at social transformation.

My hope is that my brother and his peers will speak up about their experiences, acknowledge the role they played in the war, and condemn the crimes committed in their names. I believe this is the only way to move forward and prevent future destruction.

Truth Seekers

I often find myself blaming the war for all the things that have happened to me. I blame the war for my lack of sleep, for nightmares, for lost friendships and lovers, for lost innocence; for the fact that my life has itself become a war. I blame the war for my life in exile and the ongoing challenges of living in a country that is not *mine*. I'm angry at the war. I quarrel with the war. I often wonder how my world would look if there hadn't been a war, and I try to imagine that I did not live through it. The fantasy of such a life is always dangerous because it takes me to the bottom. I sink below the earth to imagine a world that will never be real. These imaginings are filled with frozen memories that won't go away. All those memories of my life before the war are ideal, bright and light, almost perfect. The past is so present in my life that I sometimes think the present doesn't really exist. And I don't really think much about of the future. I only think clearly of future writing.

Despite the fact that some people (including members of my family) consider me a 'traitor', I must write. Writing about war comes easily to me, but is that a good or a frightening thing? It is paradoxical—to say the least. I have built my academic track record on the misery of events in my home country. My career is progressing because I am producing papers that talk about war and the courageous people it left behind, dead or alive.

On a daily basis I read news and blogs about past atrocities, newly-discovered mass graves, concentration camps, fugitives on the run, and human rights activities undertaken across the former Yugoslavia that aim to deal with the past. I don't *have* to read about these things, but I am drawn to what I fear most and what I am anxious about. I tell myself that I need to make sense of these atrocities, otherwise my life will be a senseless waste. I feel this is my calling and I need to respond to it; to find out the truth.

I often ask myself whether a time will come when I will be tired of writing about war. But can I be tired of myself? I love my non-existent land, shattered to pieces, yet still kicking. The land of my birth is my pain and sorrow, but ultimately it is also a source of inspiration and love. It is in my blood and never stops circulating through my veins. Writing about its death is a journey that my family, although unwillingly, has had to take with me. We are all part of it; we are all struggling to come to terms with what is left of us and our past. Writing and reflecting on it will eventually save us, or tear us apart. And not only us. There are many families like ours walking the thin line between love and hatred. There is a woman who made many sacrifices for the sake of rediscovering and retelling the truth. Her name is Radmila.

Paying a High Price

Radmila Karlaš is a middle-aged, single woman of Serb ethnic origin, who writes about, and publicly calls for, truth and accountability for the crimes committed in BiH during the war. Radmila tells a poignant story of life spent in constant physical, psychological, and what she calls 'existential' danger. She is one of a few 'lone warriors', a Bosnian woman in transition who keeps searching for the truth about the past and demanding justice. A writer and former journalist, Radmila left her profession because she refused to write along party lines. She decided not to compromise her principles, but instead, to earn a living from independent writing, which is a struggle anywhere, let alone in BiH. After reading Radmila's novels, *Four Leaf Clover* (2009) and *The Silence of Mestizos* (2010), I felt the urge to meet her and discuss her life, and how it felt to live in BiH 16 years after the Dayton Peace Accord had been signed on 14 December 1995. Her novels deal with the direct experience of war in BiH and with the phenomenon of evil in human nature. She attempts to demystify the process that has led her homeland into its current situation. Her writing analyses war crimes committed against the non-Serb population in Radmila's (and my) home town, Banja Luka, and in Prijedor, a town in the north-western part of BiH (both now situated in Republika Srpska).

In December 2011, I met Radmila several times over coffee in Banja Luka, to talk about her books, her life, and the difficulties of survival in BiH. I was intrigued by this tall, blonde woman who smokes her cigarettes exclusively with an elegant cigarette holder. I was impressed by her courage. She is well known for her honest journalism and sharp tongue. She says what she thinks and never backs down. Radmila is often invited to be a guest speaker in the Bosniak media and she writes occasional short essays and articles about politics and transitional justice in BiH. She and I forged a connection immediately and have been exchanging our thoughts about the war and its aftermath ever since.

Because of her work, Radmila continues to be criticised, as she puts it, as 'a traitor of her own people', accused of attacking only Serbs and of 'being paid' to say the things she says. This assessment of her is not surprising since those who criticise the Serb government and its politics as being rooted in the denial of crimes, are often accused of being traitors and Western spies. As Sonja Biserko of the Helsinki Committee for Human Rights in Serbia argues, "'Western agents' have been all those, especially women, who advocate for the respect of human rights and raise the question of war crimes. They have been 'criticized, hated and attacked'" (Women in Black, 2005).

Despite ongoing threats and attacks, Radmila refuses to be 'put in a box' with the masses who allowed war crimes to be committed on their behalf. She is representative of those in post-conflict BiH who dare to speak the truth while risking ostracism and marginalisation. The culture of denial is prevalent among her fellow citizens in Banja Luka, which has become the place where she often has "no one to talk to" (pers. comm., December 2011). Instead, she must turn to writing and "write till unconsciousness" because "writing is saving [her] life." Her first novel emerged from this "loneliness, pain, and a painful life" which was marked by the destruction of the country which "destroyed [her] too." Radmila's tale—a portrayal of a woman who refuses to think along mainstream lines and who dares to say what she thinks—shares a plot with other similar stories of transition from war to peace. She 'walks and talks' her ideology, and as a consequence, lives below the poverty line and in constant fear for her own life and the lives of her family members. Her account is a living example of the dangers of not toeing the line and of working in societies where competitive truths about the past still co-exist.

Radmila earns very little money from her writing, and thus, although she is in her late 40s, she must live with her parents. She shares a modest two-bedroom unit with them and with her beloved German Shepherd dog, Toto Vuk. She is not only an outcast in her community, but she and her family are under a constant threat. Recently, her dog was attacked and almost killed. Someone had broken his jaw in three places to punish Radmila for being outspoken about war crimes committed by the Serb army. As Radmila recalled:

> Toto Vuk is a special dog in many ways, and I never doubted that he would win over this human malice. The veterinarians who treated him said that, in their practice, they had never come across a case where a dog had survived such an attack—or even much more minor injuries. But he did. I have no idea who attacked him. People are constantly telling me to shut my mouth. Before this attack, in passing, someone told me to take care of what I was saying, because they will kill Toto Vuk. But we move on. They won't beat us (pers. comm., December 2011).

This act of violence was committed in order to show Radmila what could happen to her, and how those she loves most will be punished, if she continues to write. This was the first time that criminals had acted on a verbal threat and almost killed someone she cared so much about. A month beforehand, an anonymous caller had asked whether she liked her dog, implying that Toto Vuk could be hurt. Also, a few days before the attack, an unknown man had warned Radmila, while she was walking through the city centre, that she and her dog would be killed if she did not shut up. Radmila's sin, like mine, is that she writes about Serb crimes against Bosniaks and Croats. Like me, she despises all war criminals, but feels a responsibility to write about those who belong to her 'own people'. She is deeply affected by the war and the destruction it brought to past and future generations. The war in BiH has broken generations of people who were once proud to be called Yugoslavs. As Radmila explained:

> The war in the former Yugoslavia, especially in Bosnia, is something that marked me deeply, wounded and nearly killed me. It drove me to immerse myself in the issues and questions of our being, human nature and the like. I did not have to see Sarajevo to be hurt, everything around me was bleeding. My writings reflect the need to penetrate into the essence of things, and to circumvent a skilfully laid trap of illusion (pers. comm., December 2011).

With the dissolution of Yugoslavia, BiH lost the multi-ethnic social form of which it was once proud, with guaranteed social security, and close ties among people, and became, according to Radmila, "three nations, three herds of sheep." The old BiH is "gone for ever." After four years of war, in today's 'dirty peace'[10] Radmila, like many of her fellow citizens, is threatened by what she calls "the existential collapse." She is one of the few people in RS who—from the very beginning of the war in the former Yugoslavia in 1992—were publicly outspoken in condemning nationalist politics, persecution on ethnic grounds, and similar crimes. Radmila was aware that by doing what is "the essence of her being"—writing and speaking the truth—she would "have to pay the price" (pers. comm., December 2011).

And she is paying the price now for not allowing nationalists to mould her thinking, and for following her own beliefs and principles. In her own words, she has found herself "on a windswept island, alone." Radmila described this loneliness in *Four Leaf Clover*, and told me that "it is terrible to be in the tunnel, yet I continue to believe that there is a light [at the end]" (pers. comm., December 2011). In *Beyond Tribal Loyalties* (2012) Avigail Abarbanel writes about how it takes courage to protest against something that is still well-established and accepted mainstream ideology or practice (p. xviii). There is no doubt that by being publically outspoken Radmila practises courage in its most literal sense.

Although we both write about transitional justice and the legacies of a past that still haunts our homeland, the difference between us is that Radmila continues to live and work in Banja Luka where, of its approximately 200,000 inhabitants, almost 90% are now Serbs. The city was 'ethnically cleansed' of the minority Bosniak and Croat population, with many being forcibly expelled and others killed. In a Serb-dominated city that is the heart and mind of RS, Radmila dares to write and publicly speak about the crimes committed against the non-Serb population during the war. I, on the other hand, live and work in a country where my life is not in danger because of my research and critical writing. I might be worried about my family back home, and whether they could experience problems as a result of my writing, but I don't risk being killed on a daily basis. Radmila has put so much more on the line.

When my mother came to visit me in Australia for a few weeks in January 2012, I told her about Radmila and showed her the books

---

[10] Bosnians call the peace they live in 'dirty', 'unsustainable', 'poor', 'weak', 'intoxicated with ethnic hatred', or 'bad'.

she had published. In fact, my mother was present when a shipment of Radmila's books arrived on my doorstep. There was not much point in trying to hide the fact that I was helping to sell her books in Australia to the Yugoslav diaspora. At first, my mother did not say anything about it. But then one night while I was making dinner, she hissed at me, her voice coming from nowhere:

"Why do you want to help Radmila Karlaš?" She looked at me with her tense, dark eyes, waiting. My heart began racing. I felt breathless and noticed a sudden heat in my chest. I downed my glass of water in one gulp.

"Because we do the same things." I looked over at her then lowered my eyes.

She paused until I looked back at her. "And that is?"

"Write about war crimes." I rubbed my face nervously.

She dropped her arms in frustration and looked at me. "Why do you write about the war crimes? And you write all against the Serbs. Aren't you afraid?"

"No, I am not." I looked directly at her.

She raised her eyes, staring as they met mine. Finally she said: "You know that we could all be killed because of your writing."

It was a moment of truth. I had always felt guilty and scared about what could happen to my family as a consequence of my writing. But this was the first time a close family member had looked me in the eye, pinned me to the wall and directly put all the responsibility on to me. I had always known what was behind my father's anger and disagreement with my work: the embarrassment of having a daughter who was a 'traitor', but also the fear that someone might hurt him, my mother or my brother. While serious physical harm to any of them is unlikely today (I truly hope so), there is a legitimate fear of them being bullied and ostracised. For them, that would be an act of social death, as they live in a micro-community in which people rely heavily on one another. I obviously do not want to contribute to that possibility. But, the reality is that I do. I already felt guilty—for being far away at a time when my parents were getting older and needed the support of their child. I felt awful. I felt sick. I wished she had never said that, but she did, and there was no way back.

I searched my mind for something to say in response that would make sense, but could think of nothing meaningful. I didn't try to explain. I saw no point. She did not understand where I was coming from, why the writing about the past had become the essence of me. Whatever I said, it would have been an inadequate justification for my conscious decision to write about the crimes 'my people' had committed. So, I looked away and said nothing. I knew she was right from her point of view. I understood her anger and genuine concern. Still, I could not say to her that I would stop writing. She was asking the impossible, just as my father had. It was like asking me to stop breathing. My hands were shaking while I made mashed potato.

My mother folded her hands and looked at me. I felt threatened and vulnerable; betrayed. I assume she felt the same. I looked around the kitchen, searching for milk. I made two steps to take it from the fridge and came closer to her standing there in the doorway, following every step of mine. From the corner of my eye, I could see she was waiting for me to say or do something. Finally, she gave me one last look, sighed and disappeared into her room. I heard her pacing. I felt upset that no one in my family understood the inner necessity for the work I do. But I knew she was hurt and felt scared too.

We were tense for days after that conversation, but we never raised the matter again. At least Radmila has support from her family, and I envy her for that. Yet, it is not enough to keep her safe. She is paying a high price for being honest and loyal to her principles. I feel for her enormously. Surviving on her parents' meagre pension, Radmila is still determined to continue writing. The ostracism is great and her life is in constant danger. I feel utterly helpless and this is the feeling that I hate most. I can see that my life could have been like hers had I stayed in BiH. Still, although physically far away, and in exile, I am closely judged and critiqued for my work by my fellow compatriots and family. But I am quite certain that I would not be able to write about the things I am writing now if I had remained there.

This acknowledgement makes me realise (once again) how privileged I am to be able to sit in the safety of my new home in Australia, and write about justice, peace and war with no direct threat on the horizon. "Each day I awake to security; each month my delight in being alive is enhanced" writes Craig Jurisevic, a surgeon from Adelaide, in *Blood on My Hands: A Surgeon at War* (2010, p. 7). In 1999 Jurisevic had temporarily exchanged his peaceful life in Australia for war-torn Kosovo to help wounded civilians. He knows that in

Australia many of us take for granted the peace that we live in, but that such security does not exist for many people in the world.

But there is 'peace', and there is 'dirty peace': a peace in which the shooting is over and the killings have stopped, yet 'war' is fought by other means and continues to live in people's minds and memories. Radmila's 'peace' is not the peace she envisaged for herself and her family, nor anything comparable to peace experienced in countries such as Australia. Concerned for my safety, another close friend from BiH (who wishes to remain anonymous) told me that it would be good for me to 'slow down' with my writing and to talk about other things too, "to find a balance between writing about the crimes committed by the Serbs and against them" (pers. comm., 2010). But after hearing stories such as Radmila's, I am even more determined to continue on my path. I owe that to myself, to Radmila and to other people who risk their lives by telling the truth and righting the wrongs through words. Unfortunately, Radmila's story is all too familiar. So many journalists and writers have been persecuted or have lost their lives because they were determined to live according to their principles and belief in the necessity of justice and truth.

Slavko Ćuruvija was one of them. Ćuruvija, a Serbian journalist and newspaper publisher, was brutally murdered in the centre of Belgrade (Serbia) in April 1999. He was shot dead by two masked men in front of his house. It is still not known who carried out the assassination, nor who ordered it. Ćuruvija's murder has become one of the widely cited examples of the Serbian government's alleged brutality. In October of the same year, another Serb journalist and newspaper editor from Banja Luka, Željko Kopanja, was also attacked. He lost both legs from a car bomb in apparent retaliation for his reporting on war crimes by Bosnian Serbs. Of course, such incidents have not been limited to Serbia or BiH. Anna Politkovskaya, a Russian journalist and human rights activist, was well-known for her opposition to the Chechen conflict and the then President of Russia, Vladimir Putin. On 7 October 2006 she was shot and killed in the lift of her block of flats in Moscow, in an assassination that has never been solved. Anna had continued to speak out in spite of a number of death threats before she was killed.

My parents are all too well aware of these tragedies both abroad and at home. They know that it is dangerous to speak and write about crimes committed by members of one's own ethnic group. People who do so are made unemployable, bullied, physically attacked, or killed. What makes my parents particularly opposed to speaking out is their conviction that it won't change anything for the better. They are certain that it will only provoke anger and revenge with fatal consequences, so the risk is not worth it. Perhaps this outlook is common among parents whose children work for social justice. But I see writers like Radmila and others as committing acts of courage.

Choosing between the people you love most and what you must do is an impossible task. Almost 20 years after the war officially ended in my country, little has changed. People are still not free to say and do what is right. The peace they live in has not brought them justice or relief. They still have to be on the lookout for danger, but now the danger emanates from their own people. In today's BiH, people have to struggle not only for food, work and shelter but, in some cases, for life too.

In *Courage* (2007), Melbourne-based writer and historian, Maria Tumarkin, raises the complex question about the meaning and sometimes impossibility of defining an act as one of cowardice or one of courage. She points out that "living in a world where you are confronted not only with the possibility of your own death but those of people you love as a direct result of your actions and choices turns our ideas about courage and cowardice upside down" (p. 186). What choices do I face? Am I courageous for leaving my home town and putting on the line the lives of the people I love the most? Or am I a coward because I do not have the courage to return there and write as I live? Am I *a traitor* of my own people or a *truth seeker*?

How to Face the Past?

A few years ago, I was invited to a party to celebrate the birthday of an acquaintance, Vladan (a pseudonym). Though I did not know him well, I decided to go. I was new to Brisbane and thought it might be a good opportunity to connect with people. I knew that some of the group would be from 'my' community since Vladan was originally from BiH. As I had expected, that afternoon his house was a mini ex-Yugoslavia, filled with people from all ethnic groups. Vladan, a Serb, had fled the city of Mostar during the war, along with his wife, originally a Bosniak. Like many other ethnically 'mixed marriages', they were forced to flee the country due to the difficulty of finding a safe place where they would be able to live together in peace. After many years of searching for a new home, they settled in Brisbane with their two daughters.

It was a sunny Sunday afternoon and tables were set for lunch on the verandah. On the other side of my table, a tall, blonde woman in her late forties, Boba (a pseudonym), overheard a conversation I was having with the man sitting beside me. We were talking about our professions and I told him that I was an academic and writer in the fields of international law and peace and conflict studies.

"What are you writing about?" Boba asked me in a strained voice.

I instantly knew, from the tone of her voice and the look on her face, that my answer would make her angry. It would not be the first time. I felt a familiar discomfort because I knew that I had triggered something and couldn't go back now.

"About war, war crimes, genocide, reconciliati..."

She abruptly interrupted: "Are you writing about *their* or *our* crimes?"

I stared at her. "Well, so far I've written about genocide, Srebrenica and ..."

"Enough! I don't want to hear another word," Boba shouted as she stormed off.

I never saw her again.

One could argue that those who don't want to look at the past have 'adjusted' and 'moved on', but I believe their apparent contentment is only skin-deep. It is more likely that they have frozen that part of their life. As I see it, they have intentionally repressed and erased the past in order to make it easier to live life in their new country. Sometimes when I am with people from the former Yugoslavia, if any discussion about our homeland starts, it is met with a wall of silence until someone changes the topic. It is as if they have pledged that they will not remember or speak any more of that former part of themselves, of that malignant tumour which they persistently want to remove from their lives.

Talking amongst yet another group—one that reminisces about the 'good old days'—I can easily sink into sadness because these stories are often painful and usually end up with music from our youth being played, and lots of beer or *šljivovica*[11] being drunk. Often stories about 'returning home' and new 'five-year plans' are discussed—the eternal migrant myth.

Almost all encounters with 'my people' are filled with something nostalgic, something precious, and occasionally something tragic too. Although it is not the first time that I have found myself in such a situation, the encounter with Boba has been etched into my memory. There was something difficult and threatening in the way she looked at me. Her gaze stays with me. It seemed like she had wanted to tell me other things that afternoon, but her scorn towards me was so tremendous that she had to leave. Those who had witnessed this scene felt uncomfortable, and only after Boba had left, they initiated a discussion.

It is clear that we have not come very far at all in discussing war crimes, apart from conversations about 'our' victims and 'their' perpetrators. It turned out that Boba's husband Ivan (a pseudonym) was a former war correspondent in Sarajevo who had spent the duration of the conflict in that besieged city. I began to understand where her rage had come from. Anyone who was in Sarajevo during that time (1992 to 1996) went through hell. People from all ethnic groups suffered from the shelling. Serbs were killed by members of the Bosniak paramilitary units that ruled the city with terror. They mostly consisted of pre-war criminals, gangsters and drug dealers. They committed crimes such as rapes, killings and torture on the Serb population as revenge for the Serbian army shelling the city. No one has yet been prosecuted.

The siege of Sarajevo was an unbelievably dreadful time. At the twenty-first anniversary commemoration in 2013, the following sad story was recollected. Named the 'Romeo and Juliet of Sarajevo', the lives of Admira Ismić and Boško Brkić ended with two short bursts from a sniper's rifle on a Sarajevo bridge on the afternoon of 19 May 1993:

> Boško, a 24-year-old ethnic Serb, was killed instantly. Admira, his 25-year-old Bosniak girlfriend, was fatally wounded. She crawled to Boško and, after about 10 minutes, died with him. 'The girl was carrying a bag and waving it. They were running and holding hands. It looked like she was

---

[11] *Šljivovica* is a home-made plum brandy kept especially for nostalgic occasions.

dancing', the witness said. 'Suddenly, I heard the rifle shots. They fell to the ground, embracing each other'.

The bodies remained in the no-man's land of besieged Sarajevo for nearly four days before Serbian forces surrounding the city sent some Muslim prisoners to gather them.

Both sides blamed the other for breaking the shaky cease-fire under which the star-crossed lovers were trying to escape the siege. No definitive conclusions were ever reached (Sandić-Hadžihasanović, 19 May 2013).

Many people suffered unspeakable atrocities, but firmly holding on to only one position, one view of the war that scarred us all, simply escalates and continues that same thinking. These experiences need to be looked at from several standpoints and discussed in relation to other crimes and experiences. I truly believe that is the only way we can make progress towards a better future. Otherwise we will continue blaming one another—with no end in sight. My hope is that more people will come to ask themselves what they did during the war. Did those actions help to stop the war or protect their neighbour? Were they cheering the perpetrators or contributing to denials of mass crimes? Depending on their answers, are they victims or collaborators?

Soon after the incident with Boba, Ivan asked me why I was not writing about the war crimes committed against my 'own people', the same question my father always asks. I feel that the pressure from my 'own people' to write about their suffering is getting more intense. I told him the same thing I tell everyone who poses this question: I think that I should write about the crimes that 'my people' committed in 'my name' against other ethnic groups. I said that I am convinced that I have to 'clean up my own backyard' first before I can criticise the neighbour's. My response was accepted with a half-cynical smile, and a comment that it was obvious I had 'studied in the West'. Awareness that someone committed crimes in 'our own name' is also too often justified by saying, 'but the others did it too'.

I encouraged Ivan to put his sombre war memories on paper in spite of his cynicism and to write about horrors he had witnessed during the war. My interest in 'my people's' crimes comes not only from the fact that I am a survivor, a feminist and anti-militarist, but also because I witnessed crimes committed by Serbs against Bosniaks and Croats. This experience has affected my work and has made me determined to talk about these particular crimes. I am fully aware that my work would possibly look different if I had been a member of an ethnic minority forced to run for my life. But the reality is that I did not have to flee; rather I watched the 'others' being persecuted. Of course, regardless of how we survived this war, ideally we should be able to reflect on crimes committed by *all* warring parties, otherwise, we will never move on from the roles of victim/perpetrator. As Selma Leydesdorff, an oral historian who published extensively on Srebrenica, genocide and war in BiH, points out,

> survivors see the world through a different lens than that used by academics who read about war in armchairs ... For many, it is still too early to acknowledge the suffering and misery of the 'others' ... If an individual is able to admit what happened and to reflect on the fact that both parties committed crimes in the war, I regard that as a sign of great strength and success at growing beyond the role of the victim (2011, pp. 120–121).

Unfortunately, I think we are still far from such general reflection and acknowledgement. We still primarily reflect on 'our' pain and do not have the capabilities to acknowledge the 'other' side without stress and discomfort. Consequently, the lunch and the encounter with Boba and Ivan had turned out to be something none of us had expected: her anger, his testimony about life during the siege in Sarajevo; and my attempt to remain calm and encourage him to write about the things he had told me while smoking one cigarette after another. I vaguely remember that people were dancing around us, that Čola[12] was singing in the background, and people were rejoicing and drinking while I was focused on stories about dead people, torture and the horrors that Ivan had witnessed. I have respect for anyone who survived horrific experiences, however, as long as everyone only talks about their own suffering, it will be hard to understand others; to perceive, respect and share their pain. Sadly, while people in BiH coexist and share physical space with one another, they still lack empathy for one another's suffering. As Kathleen Barry says, it is only "by putting oneself in the place of the other and feeling empathy, [that] we experience our own humanity" (2010, p. 193). Likewise, as Martina Fischer maintains,

---

[12] Zdravko Čolic Čola was one of the most popular singers in the former Yugoslavia.

giving people a chance to hear what it is like for the *others*—Croats, Bosniaks, Serbs (*'them'*)—what their problems are, their fears and hopes, is a very important step towards mutual understanding ... These stories are often very much alike, they tell mostly of hardship and are very human. They inevitably initiate compassion and feelings of solidarity, de-mystification and humanisation of *the enemy* (2006, p. 439).

In *Sympathizing With the Enemy* (2009), Nir Eisikovits claims that coexistence is not a sufficient condition for reconciliation. He maintains that communities and individuals have to "coexist fairly," and "begin sympathizing with each other" (p. 10). Eisikovits defines sympathy as "a conscious attempt to put ourselves in the place of others before we make up our minds about them" (p. 11). As he sees it, sympathy "requires specific, detailed knowledge about the lives of others" (p. 11). Yet this is what many of us lack and remain ignorant about: the lives of *others*; empathising with their pain.

But there is hope. I know a dozen people whose family members were killed or wounded during the war but they do not blame and hate entire ethnic populations. My acquaintance Filip, a Serb, whose aged father was slaughtered in Sanski in 1995 by members of the Bosniak army, confided in me:

> My father was murdered by the Bosniak army when they ran over our village just before the end of the war. The village was burnt down and mostly aged people who did not want to leave their homes were slaughtered. But I don't hate Bosniaks. I was a soldier in the Serb army and I know what we did during the war to them ... [W]e did crimes towards Bosniaks across that region and then they came for a [*sic*] revenge. My father knew that he could easily be killed one day, but he did not want to leave his home. He died a terrible death, but it was a time of war and killing ... (pers. comm., November 2011).

Stories such as Filip's tell us that it is possible to empathise and that there is hope for a brighter future. But these voices are still in the minority. Boba and Ivan were neither the first nor the last who do not wish to speak of the suffering of others but only about their own people. When I published another paper about Srebrenica in 2011 a good friend of mine advised me to stop writing. Without equivocating he told me: "Stop writing about Srebrenica. Why not write about Bratunac and other places where Serbs were killed?" It may be that his advice came out of shame, fear, despair or disappointment. I was deeply affected by his remark because I considered him a close friend with open and liberal views. Although I am well aware that some people have a problem with my writing, it is always hard to hear it from those closest to me, and from those I consider to be anti-nationalists.

I am not sure what is the right way to face the past (or whether a 'right' way exists at all) but I know that we all have to find it and deal with it the best way we can. In *Regarding the Pain of Others* (2004), Susan Sontag suggests that "[t]he memory of war ... like all memory, is mostly local." She is correct. It is local and it is individual too. All of us from the former Yugoslavia have our own memories of the recent war. It is grounded in our political beliefs, ethnic identification, and our personal experiences.

CHAPTER THREE

Moving From War to Peace

The sun that shines in a foreign place,
Will never warm you like the sun in your own;
The bread has a bitter taste there
Where one has no one, not even a brother.

—Aleksa Šantić, 'Stay here' (1896/2006)

"How close have you been to death?" she asked me while I was
drinking a cocktail at her house-warming party in tropical Queensland.
I remember clearly that hot summer night two years ago. I was taken
aback and just stared at her, not knowing how to respond. I was
sitting on a verandah, happily chatting about ordinary things, when
the question abruptly interrupted the conversation. I didn't respond,
but was instantly drowned in painful memories of the past. Unwanted
images burst through from my subconscious and I found myself miles
and years away from the hot Brisbane night, back in the familiar,
beloved and shattered places where I grew up, surrounded by friends I
had not seen for ages and by those who had lost their lives. This wasn't
the first time I had been asked such questions. *Where was I during the
war? What happened to me? How did I survive the war? Which ethnic group
do I belong to?*

Once people learn where I am from, they often ask me something
about my personal experiences in the war. But the fact that I am from
a war-torn country does not necessarily mean that I am eager to share
my own stories of survival all the time. Milan, my friend from Serbia

61

who works with ex-combatants and collects their stories of surviving peace, reflects on their willingness to answer questions, such as 'What do you now think of the people you fought?': "Some questions are answered easily; others are much harder. Some they choose not to answer, for different reasons. Some questions, regardless how many times one answers them, do not get easier with time" (pers. comm., 16 December 2011). I have worked hard to be able to write and talk about the most difficult things in my life: the loss of my country, friends and language. When I asked journalist and novelist, Radmila Karlaš, who comes from my home town Banja Luka, what losing her country meant to her, she replied: "My country is a part of myself. It is my root, my essence, my tissue. Simultaneously with the destruction and bleeding of my country my soul was torn apart too (pers. comm., 13 November 2011).[13]

Because of our profoundly distressing experiences during the war, in peacetime survivors need distance, time and space to decide whether they want to share any of their experiences and, if so, under what conditions. Like me, many of them had waited many years before they were able to write and talk.

The NATO Bombings

I studied law as a refugee in exile in Serbia while wars raged in Bosnia and Herzegovina (BiH), Croatia and, later on, in Kosovo. I sat my final law exam on 24 March 1999, the same day the North Atlantic Treaty Organization (NATO) started bombing Serbia. I had organised a party with friends to celebrate the end of my studies at my house in Niš (where I had lived since moving from the refugee camp in 1995). But within hours we witnessed firepower greater than anything we had seen before. NATO had an air bombardment capability that was well beyond the miniscule Serbian air forces. After the initial shock had subsided my home became a prison for my friends who had to remain locked inside with me for a couple of days.

The war on Serbia was waged by a coalition of the most powerful forces in the world who remained invisible to us. The NATO planes dropped their bombs from around 10,000 metres—or alternatively

---

[13] In 2012, I published a paper on Radmila Karlaš' work: 'After the war in Bosnia: Radmila's life under handbrake' (Simić, 2012a).

they were dispatched from far away military bases in various parts of the world. It was hard to believe that someone could press a button somewhere in Aviano in Italy, or in Texas, and deploy a bomb that would destroy our local bridges, trains, television stations and hospitals, and 'accidentally' kill humans.

During this period there was destruction on a massive scale. I saw the country in flames and thought that this must be the end of the world. I recall one night in May in particular. My friend Dragana was visiting and we were standing near a window, looking out at the sky and the city before us. The house was situated on a hill, close to the Serbian military airbase which was considered a 'legitimate' NATO military target. Suddenly there was a flash of light and we found ourselves plunged into total darkness. Panicking, I said, "They've dropped an atomic bomb for sure. This is it." We were certain that we would all die. It was surreal and frightening to see the entire city blacked out in a split second. In reality, this was the first of many nights to come during which NATO used graphite bombs[14] to disable the power stations, resulting in power shortages across the country.

For 78 days (until 10 June 1999) local residents spent their time dashing between their cellars and garages, bedrooms and kitchens. We never knew when to expect the next attack or how close it might be. I was living in a permanent state of fear and anxiety. I tried to block my ears and shut my eyes in order to avoid the distinctive sound and flash of light that bombs produce. My whole body was exhausted, I suffered from insomnia and could not rest. I was angry at the whole world for allowing this to happen. I felt helpless, and kept thinking that Serbia was being used by the big powers as merely an 'exercise field' to test their latest weapons. In saying this I am not in any way excusing the Serb crimes in Kosovo, and the war crimes the Serbian military forces committed against the Albanian population. But the answer to violence can never be more violence. There must be other ways. Too many innocent people were injured and killed during these bombings.

---

[14] "[A] carbon-graphite bomb ... sprays electrical power stations with a dust that sparks instant short circuits ..." (Walker, 4 May 1999).

NATO air forces occasionally dropped cluster bombs[15] and we would sometimes see unexploded devices around our houses. They were usually bright yellow, making them particularly attractive, and extremely dangerous, to children. Depleted uranium munitions[16] and cluster bombs were heavily used during the NATO bombardment although they had already been 'officially' banned because of their long-term health effects. The NATO bombing was dirty and dishonest, asymmetrical and disproportionate to the capabilities of the defending Serbian air force which was in poor shape due to lack of maintenance and equipment. It was an unprecedented unleashing of violence against the infrastructure and the people of Serbia; it was carried out with the newest military technology, and warfare strategies designed to exert sustained psychological stress and fear throughout the nation. The war resulted in the killing of between 500 and 1,000 civilians, classified by NATO as 'collateral damage'.

Jamie Shea, a NATO spokesman, was reported as stating: "There is always a cost to defeat an evil. It never comes free, unfortunately. But the cost of failure to defeat a great evil is far higher" (*BBC News*, 31 May 1999). He insisted that NATO planes had bombed only "legitimate designated military targets" and if civilians had died it was because NATO had been forced into military action. However, NATO also attacked civilian targets. For instance, on 12 April 1999, it bombed a passenger train in Grdelica (a town 300 kilometres south of Belgrade). Fourteen people were killed and 16 were injured. On 7 May NATO air forces dropped two containers of cluster bombs on the hospital and the large, lively marketplace in the centre of Niš (the town in southern Serbia where I was living at the time). My friend Aleksandar and several others were wounded, and 15 people were killed. NATO admitted that it had made yet another mistake; that bombs had "missed the target" since they were aimed at Niš

---

[15] "A cluster bomb, or cluster munition, is a weapon containing multiple explosive submunitions. These containers are dropped from aircraft or fired from the ground and designed to break open in mid-air, releasing the submunitions and saturating an area that can be the size of several football fields" (Cluster Munition Coalition <http://www.stopclustermunitions.org/the-problem/what-is/> accessed 30 December 2013).

[16] "DU [depleted uranium] is a chemically toxic and radioactive heavy metal produced as waste by the nuclear power industry. It is used in weapons because it is an extremely hard material capable of piercing armour. However, it can contaminate the environment, and has been linked to health problems in civilian populations" (Edwards, 6 March 2013).

airport (*BBC News*, 7 May 1999). On 19 April 1999, NATO bombed Albanian refugees near Đakovica after a pilot mistook the civilian vehicles for Serbian military units. It admitted this mistake by reporting that "[s]ometimes one has to risk the lives of the few to save the lives of the many" (*BBC News*, 15 April 1999). The tragic bombing of the state television station in Belgrade on 23 April 1999 resulted in the deaths of 16 journalists and support staff, and the wounding of a further 16. The employees had received an instruction from the Serbian government that not coming to work would be considered 'defection', despite an open threat by NATO that the station would be attacked by missiles. The British Prime Minister at the time, Tony Blair, reportedly claimed that the bombing of the television station was "entirely justified" (Norton-Taylor, 24 April 1999).

No one has ever been prosecuted for any of these crimes. It appears that NATO is not accountable to anyone for its actions, and places itself above the law. It's 'mistakes' were excused because of the 'greater good' apparently achieved by the bombing. Even the International Criminal Tribunal for the former Yugoslavia (ICTY) reported that as long as the attack on the television station was aimed at disrupting the communications network, it was legally acceptable. The ICTY Committee in charge of assessing the allegations against NATO suggested in its final report that the Office of the Prosecutor (OTP) should "not commence an investigation related to the bombing of the Serbian TV and Radio Station ..." (United Nations ICTY, 2000, paragraph 79). It is interesting to note that while NATO killed many civilians 'by mistake', apart from an occasional apology, it never offered any compensation to their families. However, when it hit the Chinese embassy 'by mistake' it formally apologised to the Chinese government, and agreed to pay $US28 million in compensation to the government, and $US4.5 million to the families of those killed or injured (United Nations ICTY, 2000, paragraph 84).

In the midst of all this chaos I decided to go back to BiH and visit my parents who were very worried about me. At the bus station I was told that it was not safe to travel, but I made the 800-kilometre trip to Banja Luka anyway. Once there I could not settle and could not sleep. I would lie awake and listen to the NATO planes flying over BiH on their way to bomb Serbia. I felt guilty that I was not in Niš with my friends and partner, supporting one another through this dangerous period, so was constantly on the phone to them. The fact that I was safe kept gnawing at me. Two days later I decided to go back.

I would be returning to uncertainty and potential death. I felt uneasy about this decision, and delayed telling my family. They reacted to my plans with alarm: "You can't go anywhere now. NATO is bombing day and night. They bomb buses and trains." That was true, but I felt I had no choice. I was going crazy. I recall the morning when I departed for Niš. Fear surged up inside me as we crossed the border between BiH and Serbia. The bus driver turned to us and said in a low-pitched voice, "Now we must all take a moment and pray that they won't hit our bus today." I looked at the sky and closed my eyes. I took a deep breath and let it go. Ten hours later we arrived safely in Niš. I only realised much later how stupid (and lucky) I had been. I still feel for my parents who must have gone through a great deal of emotional pain.

During the NATO bombing in 1999, I took part in the civilian demonstrations which saw thousands of people marching each day across the cities of Serbia, demanding that NATO stop the destruction. I would pin my 'target' brooch[17] on my chest and proudly march, and stand on one of the bridges in Niš along with hundreds of other people to create a 'live shield'. I hated Madeleine Albright, the US Secretary of State, and the golden butterfly brooch that she wore on her formal dresses. Her bright face, greenish eyes, and neatly combed hair are for ever etched in my mind as symbols of bombing and destruction. Whenever we had electricity, we would watch the news and her determined face would pop up in front of us. She would always justify NATO's continuing bombing, and say something about the necessity of waging the 'humanitarian war' on Yugoslavia so that Serbia would stop the war against the Albanian population in Kosovo.

---

[17] The 'target' brooches and T-shirts were produced and distributed by the student movement. The plain black circles on white background had a symbolic meaning: we were all potential targets of NATO bombing, and we wanted to send that message to NATO and to the world. We stood at river crossings, power stations, and on main roads which were the major arteries of our country. The brooches and T-shirts were messages of protest against violence and destruction.

Life as a Refugee

From 1992 to 1995 I lived in a refugee camp that was also a home for orphans in Niš. We students in exile from BiH and Croatia, lived with these children for three years. We had very little food, no heating and no normality in the refugee camp. Some nights I cried from hunger. I had no money to buy food and I hated the meagre rations provided at the camp.

In 1993, I suffered an attack of appendicitis in the middle of the night. I was in so much pain that I could not move. I had no money for a taxicab and there were no buses. I could not walk. My best friend Mišo, who lived with me in the camp, took me in his arms and walked almost two kilometres to the hospital. He carried me the whole way. When we finally arrived at the emergency department I was examined and admitted, but the doctors decided not to operate because they did not have enough anaesthetic. It was being kept for urgent cases and I did not fall into that category. After a few days I was discharged, feeling better but terrified that this could happen again at any time, or that my appendix might burst.

I had been struggling financially for some time and tried to think of ways to earn some money. Through a mutual friend I met a local woman who sold a variety of items at the market. She offered me some weekend work selling fruit. I also volunteered to smuggle some goods for her from Bulgaria. It was very popular back then to go to Bulgaria's black market and bring back cigarettes, coffee and other items. For reasons I could not understand, juice makers were also in demand on the Serbian black market. One day she came to me with a proposal. "We leave tomorrow at 4 am to go to the Sofia market. Do not bring anything with you. I will give you some money to buy cigarettes and juice makers." I nodded. She continued, "I want you to follow my instructions once we get there." It was tempting and scary at the same time. I had just agreed to go with a woman I had known superficially for only a few weeks to a country I had never visited. I was young, and foolish. I thought I had nothing to lose, and could earn some easy money.

I woke at 3 am excited and afraid. It was a big adventure; something unknown and risky lay ahead of me. I was supposed to travel by bus from Niš to Sofia with other smugglers. I was the youngest on the bus, with no experience of smuggling and not sure of what I was doing. Most of my co-passengers were middle-aged or older. They all seemed to know one another. These tours had become regular trips for many of them over the last year or so due to the high level of unemployment and poverty that engulfed Serbia. We travelled for about three hours and arrived in Sofia just as the market was opening. I had never seen anything like it. It was the biggest black market in the region, packed with people from the Balkans and Eastern Europe negotiating and trading. After hours spent buying cartons of cigarettes and juice makers it was time to go back to Niš. We boarded the bus, and just before we reached the border with Serbia one of the passengers bribed the driver. The bus stopped in the no-man's-land zone and we were asked to get off the bus. I did not know what to expect. I was afraid. The woman I now officially 'worked for', my 'boss', came to me and muttered, "Take off your track pants." I glared at her but said nothing. She had a carton of cigarettes in one hand and sticky tape in the other. She was short and rounded with medium-long hair that was tied back from her pale face. There were dark circles under her eyes. She was in her late 30s and single, trying to survive the enormous inflation that had hit Serbia. Her hands were full as she looked at me impatiently.

I looked around and saw that everyone was stripping off parts of their clothing and tucking the smuggled goods under shirts or pants. My mind was racing. There was no way out. I took off my track pants and stood there in my underwear. I looked around again but no one seemed to care. Everyone was busy taping their own items. I watched as my boss taped packs of cigarettes around my legs and arms. I felt the tape tighten on my skin. I looked down at her while she worked on me. I was amazed to see that she had managed to tape almost four cartons of cigarettes around my body. Once she had finished I struggled to pull my pants back on. I looked huge. But this was not yet enough. She also tucked a juice maker under my top. She said, pursing her lips, "If the security guards on the border ask you what is under your shirt you will tell them that you are eight months pregnant." I indeed looked like that. I was enormous, as was everyone else around me. I looked up at her. There was no point in arguing. I knew I had no power.

Smugglers routinely bribed guards and immigration people on both borders. They knew what we were all doing. Once we came to the checkpoint we were told to leave the bus and form a line holding our passports. I stood, sweating with fear that they would find the goods on me. The border security guards began checking our documents. One of them, while inspecting my passport, glanced down at my belly, raised his eyebrows and asked me: "Are you expecting soon?" The colour drained from my face and for a moment I was frozen with fear. I imagined myself being imprisoned as a smuggler. I felt ashamed, wondering how I could ever wash such a stain from myself. Here was I, a law student, smuggling goods from the notorious Bulgarian black market. It did not make sense. But my life at that point in time did not make much sense anyway. It was pure survival. I forced myself to fake a smile and with one of my hands on my belly I heard myself saying, "Yes, I am. I have only six weeks to go." I felt the juice maker scratching my skin under my clothes. I wanted to vanish into thin air. "Make sure you get some time to rest before delivery," said the young officer with a half-smile while returning my passport. I hurried back to our bus loaded with black market goods: coffee, jeans, cigarettes, shirts, underwear, rice, oil. And juice makers.

Once inside, I sighed with relief. As I steadied my nerves, I looked out through the window. I saw dozens of people doing the same thing I had done a minute ago: waiting in a queue with their smuggled goods hidden under their clothing and in their bags, waiting to be questioned by bribed border officers. Still, I was nervous and could not relax. I could see that the others on the bus were also eager to move on from the checkpoint as soon as possible. No one spoke. We just sat and waited for the rest of our co-passengers to return. An hour or more passed until the bus finally started up. We headed north. Once across the border it was safe to untape the smuggled goods from our sweaty bodies. I was too young and naive to understand that for my fellow passengers, and the border guards, this was simply a routine game they played. There was nothing to be scared about. Everyone— except me—knew the rules of the game. The young Bulgarian officer knew that I was lying, but he got his share of the bribe, so he did not care.

I could not believe that I had successfully smuggled so much merchandise. It also dawned on me that things could have turned out quite differently. I could just as easily have been trafficked, raped, kidnapped, or even killed. I could have disappeared without a trace. I have never told my parents about any of this. What would be the point? It was a time of war, of huge inflation, of corruption and of criminal activities entrenched in all walks of life. Human life was virtually worthless. It was a time of pure survival. Nevertheless, this was my first and *last* smuggling experience.

Despite the obstacles and hardships, the majority of student refugees who lived in the camp somehow managed to finish their studies. We also worried about the families we had left behind. Even now it is difficult to comprehend how we succeeded while sharing space with so many strangers.

In 1995 I was able to leave the refugee camp. I moved to a house that had hot water and the smell of nice food. I remember calling my mother for the first time from this house and exclaiming: "Mama, can you imagine, they have hot running water *all the time!*" My mother says she will never forget this call because she did not know whether to laugh or cry. Despite the fact that we had already survived three years of war, we were still grappling with the misery it had brought us. It was pathetic to be excited about having access to hot water, something we had always taken for granted, but it was the best thing that had happened to me for some time. In the refugee camp we all had to shower with cold water, even during the winter, which had long-term effects on our health.

After the NATO bombing ended on 10 June 1999, many of us scattered around the world in search of peace, stability and a decent life. I was restless, not knowing what to do next. Finally, I decided to continue my education and, in 2002, enrolled in a Master of Law (MLL) in International Human Rights Law at Essex University in the United Kingdom, and lived on campus for a year. I had a hard time: it was my first degree in another language and away from my homeland. During that year I met some people from the United Nations (UN) and after completing the degree and returning home I began working for the United Nations Children's Fund (UNICEF) in Sarajevo. However, I soon became very disillusioned and thought about leaving. I was an activist and feminist and the UN was anything but that. It was highly bureaucratic with lots of repetitive paperwork. I was bored. I had taken the job in order to help women and children but I didn't get anywhere near any 'live' women or children in the ten months I worked at UNICEF. I had a ridiculously high salary (which I spent on family and friends) but was embarrassed about it, and the 'high life' I was supposed to live.

At one point I found myself in Tirana (a town in Albania) in a 5-star hotel with a colleague from Canada. On the way to a venue where we were to give a presentation on trafficking in children, we had to literally step over poor Roma kids begging on the streets. They were everywhere: sleeping rough and stretching out their hands for money as we passed. They were sitting on large pieces of cardboard which served as beds, living rooms, kitchens. I felt terrible. I felt really angry that I was expected to pay no attention to these children who lived such sad and dangerous lives in plain sight. I stopped in the middle of the street watching the kids around me. My colleague from Canada saw that I was upset. She pulled me by the hand and hissed: "Come on! We will be late." I remained deeply affected by what I had seen, and started questioning the value of my work at UNICEF.

At that time I found out about, and applied for, a Master of Arts Programme in Gender and Peacebuilding at the University for Peace in Costa Rica. After being accepted I decided to resign from my position. The staff in the UNICEF office in Sarajevo could not believe this announcement. Apparently, no one ever resigned from their office; certainly not 'locals', not in poor countries such as BiH. The American Director even invited me to discuss it further with her. She could not comprehend how I could leave 'such a job'. She kept asking me: "Are you sure? Would you like to rethink your decision?" I resigned and left for Costa Rica in 2004.

I returned with the completed degree in 2005. (See Chapter Five for more information about my time in Costa Rica.) After a few months working with a non-government organisation in Serbia, I decided to go back to Sarajevo in BiH to find work in academia (law schools and schools of politics). I had some personal connections, but the people who ran the faculties were pro-nationalist and I was rejected because apparently they could not 'recognise' my three university degrees. In reality they did not want to employ me in their law schools or departments of politics because of my Serb ethnic origin. They did not want to take the risk, as my colleague told me, that I might teach students 'another history'.

After six months of being unemployed I became quite desperate. I tried to find work in my home town, Banja Luka, but a group of conservative people (from the old communist times) were running the universities. Here I was perceived as a threat because I was highly educated, proficient in English, and well-travelled. I was a 'product of the West' whose presence would highlight just how 'old-fashioned' and limited their skills were (especially when it came to being able to speak foreign languages, or use computers and the Internet). I finally came to terms with the realisation that all the doors were shut to me.

It happened (as it always does) that at the same time I was travelling around BiH searching for a job, a large conference on peace and reconciliation was held in Sarajevo, organised by RMIT University (Melbourne, Australia). I attended, and met some doctoral students from former Yugoslavia who were studying at the University of Melbourne. They encouraged me to consider moving to Melbourne and enrolling in a doctorate. I contacted Professor Dianne Otto at the university because I had previously read her work and knew that she had a keen interest in gender and peacekeeping. I was eventually offered a place and a full scholarship, and moved to Australia in 2006. After receiving my PhD in 2011, I accepted a teaching position in the Law School at Griffith University in Brisbane where I now live.

Building Peace

There are common threads in all stories about surviving and working for peace, no matter where it happens: the desire is for a peaceful community, often pursued among people who are themselves survivors of war. No one can have a greater stake in finding peace than the people who live in a country that has been affected by war. They are the ones who have dealt with all the consequences of war: destruction of life, property and social fabric. They are victims, but also survivors. They carry the burden of war, but also the difficult task of building peace. They are traumatised and exhausted. They want to move on, to forget about it all. Such is the case with many of my family members and friends. My mother does not want to talk about the past, about the war, about her feelings. She has never really dealt with the trauma of war. As soon as she starts to talk about anything related to the war and the past, she begins to cry. Like most people she just wants to 'catch up' with the rest of the world and get back to a normal life.

I often feel that I lost those years of my life when I lived in the refugee camp. I was angry that I had to spend my youth, my student days, sharing a room with four women I had never met before, not having hot water, being hungry, being removed from my family for the first time. I felt trapped while I waited for the war in BiH to be over. Although I was lucky to move into residential accommodation in 1995, I was still in exile. In 1999, I waited for the NATO bombing of Serbia to be over, then for other people to build peace for me so I could safely return home. I was eager to embrace normal life as soon as possible. I didn't realise that peace in my country had to be built by people like me, and that no one else could do it for us. I was also unaware at that time that all those years of hardship would make me what I am today, and that the misery of those times would be a powerful energiser for my current work.

But I was not yet ready to seek the truth, to explore war crimes committed in 'my name', to talk about war and my experiences. I needed time to recover, to find work, and escape the state of numbness and emptiness.

Surviving violence and war marks a person's life for ever. You carry it with you wherever you go; only the intensity changes. Sometimes it is overwhelming; and sometimes it is just there waiting in a familiar touch, smell, or sound, that turns your peace of mind upside down in a split second. You become oversensitive and sometimes expect too much from others.

In 2008, as part of my doctoral research I interviewed women who had dated peacekeepers during the UN mission in BiH. In answer to my question about whether local women were particularly vulnerable immediately after the war, one woman stated:

> We all experienced the war and we all have traumas. People here think that they deserve credit just because they are survivors. They also think that people will be more caring and gentle towards them. I think that should be what happens, but I doubt the world sees it that way (pers. comm., 11 November 2008).

There is disappointment in this statement, but also the important realisation that one should not expect too much from 'them' or 'the world'. You have to rely on yourself and your own personal strength. Rather than being buried in victimhood, we can recognise ourselves as survivors. We should feel responsible for the past, present and future. Besides bringing great hardship, such devastation also creates opportunities for people to look at new ways of working together, and to rebuild human relationships. It also teaches us to appreciate the things we took for granted before the war, such as life and peace. Material things are of little relevance during war, but spirit, friendship and kinship keep you moving, keep you surviving.

After the war, I found I had become a 'representative of a war-torn country'. By the mere act of surviving, I unwillingly acquired the identity of a 'war survivor' who has become an 'expert' on war. The first time I was confronted with this new identity was during 2004 and 2005, when studying in Costa Rica. I was the only person from BiH and every time my homeland was used as a case study, everyone would look at me, expecting some comment, some 'words of wisdom' from me as the 'authority' and 'expert' on BiH. The fact was that, in one sense, I knew less about what had really happened there, while in another, I felt the experience of war under my skin. But I was not yet ready to talk about what the war had done to me personally, and to my country generally.

There is fear in speaking up when we are faced with the hard questions. How do we live together after the horrible atrocities perpetrated against 'my people' and, most importantly, those committed *by* 'my people'? How do we live among those who committed atrocities and still walk freely around their communities? Muniba, a woman who survived the genocide in Srebrenica in 1995[18] asked me some years ago: "How do I know that a man sitting next to me in the bus is not the killer of my sons and my husband?" Šuhra, another survivor from Srebrenica, shared her story with Women in Black, a non-government organisation from Belgrade which has been working for peace and justice since the early 1990s:

> I have lost two sons, three brothers-in-law, five nephews, and two sisters-in-law; my sister was burned in the municipality of Bratunac in her house with a lot of other women ... [W]e survived this catastrophe that we can never forget. We keep encouraging each other to walk with our heads up, confidently. Our sons, husbands, brothers, fathers, fathers-in-law and brothers-in-law were never criminals. That's why I am telling this proudly. I am having a very hard time, but I want to speak out for myself and stand firm (Women in Black, 2007, p. 217).

[18] In July 1995, Srebrenica, a small town in the east of BiH, became the site of a genocide that occurred in just four days when approximately 8,000 Bosnian Muslim men and boys were slaughtered by members of the Serbian forces (*BBC News*, 9 June 2005).

Peace is a time to look back, to realise what you lost, to mourn, to make sense of senseless violence and the time of war; but it is also a time to learn how to live in peace after living for such a long time in the violence that is war. I needed time to look back, to absorb the past and to be ready to work for a better future. I needed ten years to be able to speak up, to write and to look myself in the eye. It takes time and it takes trust. I am still uneasy about trust.

Finally, after a long time, during the last 10 years I have started to write about the war in my country and talk about it. In fact, I have been driven to undertake research on the war crimes that have been committed in 'my name', and have started to teach and give talks about my findings in Australia, BiH, and Serbia. Because of so much interest in the Yugoslav wars, many of my friends and colleagues, young academics from the former Yugoslavia, have found themselves suddenly in a position of being 'experts' simply because they were born in the region. My colleague, Helena, has had this experience. She wrote:

> I am from Belgrade, Serbia. As I finished primary school the wars in the former Yugoslavia started and my life since then has been marked indelibly by the conflicts. When I enrolled at the university, in the USA, one of the main markers of my identity was being from a 'conflict-ridden' country. Many people considered me an 'expert' just because of this fact; however, I felt the need to understand the conflict, not just feel it. Thus, my curiosity for understanding conflict and identity dynamics led me to pursue an academic and professional career in peace and conflict resolution (pers. comm., April 2009).

Between 2007 and 2010, I was a visiting lecturer at the University of Sarajevo, teaching courses on gender and war. As part of that course I discussed reconciliation with my students (many of them survivors of the nearly four-year siege of Sarajevo by Bosnian Serbs from 1992 to 1996): *When is the time to reconcile? Is there a time to reconcile? Who should initiate reconciliation?* Teaching survivors about war and peace is a challenging task that itself needs a lot of negotiation and care. During one of our heated discussions about reconciliation and forgiveness, Senada, one of my students said:

> *I* don't want to be reconciled. *I* did not fight with anyone. The foreigners came here one day after the war was over and the next day started their

reconciliation projects. *I* don't want them to tell me when and where and with whom *I* should reconcile. *I* will choose if I want to reconcile at all and, if so, when *I* will do it (pers. comm., 13 December 2008).

Other women feel more ready to forgive when the time comes. As Bala said: "Now I am waiting for myself to start forgiving. But I am afraid that I will not be able to forget what happened. Sometimes I have nightmares. It is hard to continue life here, but it would be harder to start a new life somewhere else" (Women in Black, 2007).

Tamara Šmidling, a peace activist from Sarajevo, believes that the readiness for self-critical questioning of your own responsibility is one of the most fundamental preconditions for reconciliation (pers. comm., November 2010). In *Trauma Trails*, Indigenous Australian writer, Judy Atkinson, writes about the trauma that Indigenous people experienced at the hands of their white colonisers and about their healing processes. She suggests that while trauma has shaped the lives of many in Australian society, "healing is possible" (2002, p. 262). Atkinson describes healing as a journey of self-discovery through which people educate themselves. The work of healing is also about transformation and transcendence: "[P]eople change as they work through conflictual and re-harmonising activities with each other" (p. 262). Thus, both self-discovery and self-critical questioning of one's responsibility are necessary preconditions to reconciliation in any society.

Indeed, as Amela Puljek-Shank argues, "reconciliation cannot be created out of thin air and out of nothing" (2007, p. 194). However, reconciliation should also not be externally imposed. It needs to come from within us; our hearts must be ready. Melbourne-based writer and historian, Maria Tumarkin, raises the question of the timing of truth and justice processes. She asks: "How long will it take for experiences of violence and injustice to be lived through and absorbed, for the forgiveness to emerge, not to be forced out? It will take *as long as it takes*" (2011). That can be years, decades, and even centuries. Still, if people wait for society to repair the damage it has created for generations, they will wait a long time. As Atkinson says, "[w]e must be about the work of healing ourselves" (2002, p. 256). But trust is something that bothers me. For reconciliation to be lasting, as Trudy Govier puts it, some kind of trust "for sufficient sustainable co-operation" must be built (2002, p. 144). The aftermath of conflict is a difficult and often dangerous time for people who dare to demand justice and expose war crimes, in particular war crimes committed in their own name, carried out by the ethnic group to which they belong.

Learning to live in peace, to face the past and appreciate the present, is not easy because "[t]he past is never quite over ... Years, decades after the event, the past is still unfinished business" (Tumarkin, 2005, p. 12). It will always be present, no matter how hard we try to erase it. War marks one's life for ever, but as well as being damaging, it can also be inspirational. Survivors write, paint, perform and tell stories. After speaking about their own recovery from traumatic events, victims often move on and become survivors who integrate their trauma into their lives (Bartsch and Bartsch, 1995).

Surviving war is tough, but surviving peace can sometimes be even tougher: torn between war and peace, between the wish to live a normal life and the pressing impulse to look back. 'Surviving' means finding the balance between two states of mind because neither of them will ever let go.

Where Are You From?

As Vladimir was helping himself to a bottle of cold Mexican beer, looking for salvation from the fiery Australian sun, Michael (a pseudonym), an Australian who was sitting next to him, decided to pose a seemingly simple question: "Where are you from?" Vladimir knew from experience that the brief answers to questions such as 'Where are you from?' and 'What language do you speak?' rarely satisfy an interlocutor's curiosity, but almost inevitably lead to further questions of ethnicity which some of us do not wish to discuss.

Since I moved to Australia eight years ago, I have been in the same situation as my friend Vladimir many times. Some Australians are very curious about who you are and where you come from, which is fine, as long as those questions do not become a prelude to unpacking your ethnic and religious identities. In Australia, there are around 4 million migrants from all over the world, constituting 22% of the population. There are around 150,000 former Yugoslavians and, according to the 2010 population census, around 40,000 people from BiH alone (Australian Bureau of Statistics, 2011).

Although many people migrate to Australia and other parts of the world, there is a difference between those who voluntarily migrate and those who are forced to live in exile. Zlata Filipović was ten years old when she started to write her war diary (which was first published in 1994). An international bestseller, *Zlata's Diary* records her daily experiences of the siege in Sarajevo, where she was born. At the beginning she writes about the typical concerns of a girl her age: birthday parties, grades at school and her friends. As war engulfs BiH and Sarajevo the topics change: the deaths of her friends, the shortage of water and food, days spent waiting in her house or her nearby neighbour's cellar. Zlata talks about her forced exile with her family to France, and later to Ireland:

> I know lots of people end up living outside of [the] city or country of their birth, some people even move around a lot, but for those who escaped war or poverty, it is different—we never left in search of a better job or nicer climate—we left because we simply had to leave, and we were lucky that an opportunity presented itself for us to realize this. Starting again, adapting, learning about belonging and identity are other stages in the string of experiences of war, something we perhaps forget about for those people who were lucky enough to have survived and escaped (2006, p. xvi).

Forced exile brings other emotions: sadness, nostalgia, depression and distress. It may also divide communities along ethnic and religious lines, as happened in the former Yugoslavia. Our exiles are often divided into 'communities' that are ethnically defined. Despite these divisions, both diaspora and citizens resident in BiH regularly socialise with one another, transcending ethnic boundaries for the sake of personal friendships.

Indeed, many couples and families who migrated to Australia were issued visas because of their mixed ethnic origins. For some time, one of the conditions to receive a visa and resettle in Australia was to prove that partners had different ethnic origins; that they were in so-called mixed marriages. Paradoxically, ethnic communities who could not live together in Yugoslavia have found themselves living side by side in Australia. They mingle and often organise collective birthday parties and New Year's Eve festivities. They socialise, celebrate, drink home-made brandy, eat baklava and home-made scones; but they avoid topics like war crimes, and any discussion about 'winners' and 'losers', victims and perpetrators. They rarely talk about the past war and politics, except within their own ethnic group so that they can be certain that the majority will agree that *others* are to blame for the war and their forced exile. Most people are tired of war tales and stories of misery. They wish to live in the present and enjoy the benefits of this 'lucky' country. They wish to make an ordinary life from their exile, to blend in, to adopt this new place, to slough away the past.

But try as they might to run away from memories, from themselves, from unfinished conversations and numerous unanswered questions, and from encounters with one another, 'harmless' enquiries by Australians (and others) keep bringing it all back. While I observed Vladimir's frozen expression that day at my birthday party, I felt flustered and guilty because one friend was being made so uncomfortable by another.

In answer to Michael's question: "Where are you from?" Vladimir replied briefly, "I was born in Belgrade, Serbia," and then went quiet. His body language and demeanour conveyed that he was not in the mood for a discussion about migration and his origin.

Michael turned to him with a half-smile: "What does that make you then?" I held my breath when I heard this question.

Vladimir looked him in the eye and snapped, "Former Yugoslavian." I felt butterflies in my stomach.

But this was not good enough for Michael, so he stated rather determinedly, "Well, the former Yugoslavia does not exist any more."

I looked at Vladimir as my birthday celebration began disintegrating into a nightmare, spoiled after only one sip of cold beer. He was already tired of this random encounter with a stranger. I wanted to hug him, to protect him from the pain written all over his face.

With his teeth grinding and without looking at Michael, he calmly said, "Maybe we could finish this conversation."

The conversation was in fact over before it even started. I felt awkward and unsettled because I knew why Vladimir had responded in that way. I knew only too well how he must be tired of being asked where he was from while he was relaxing at parties and during coffee breaks, or in shops and restaurants, or presenting papers at conferences and seminars. How many times has this question been asked? It happens so often to people with 'different accents', or 'different skin colours', that even those with a strong constitution start to get weary after some time, and become annoyed when they are asked—yet again—to explain where they come from to strangers. I am also asked these questions on a regular basis and often, depending on my mood, play with the answers. When I say, "I am from Brisbane," that does not work. I am pushed to reveal where I am *really* from. Still, if I am not 'allowed' to be from Brisbane, how can a migrant ever adapt and 'become' a *real* Australian?

I wondered if it might ever be possible for us to have just one gathering without questions, without picking through past affiliations. I also felt bad because those questions were coming from my friend Michael, an esteemed intellectual who I had thought would be well aware of the underlying difficulties relating to the bloody war and its consequences regarding identity. I was convinced that Michael knew more than the average person about the issues that affect people who come from war-torn societies, but this less-than-a-minute exchange showed me that he did not. I experienced this brief exchange between him and Vladimir as a personal defeat, wondering why he hadn't learned anything from me.

Surrounded by my friends from Australia, Greece, Poland, Serbia and BiH while enjoying an exotic cocktail made my friend Slavko, I tried to explain to Michael why Vladimir's response had, according to him, been 'weird'. I told him that we are all more or less 'weird' because the tales of ethnicity are painful, and some of us simply do not want to revisit them. Some people want to elevate themselves beyond an ethnically-defined or racially-defined milieu, and to identify instead at a human level.

It has become almost impossible to talk about the former Yugoslavia without falling into the ethnic matrix and interpreting things based exclusively on it. I told him that some of us were sensitive and tired of that kind of questioning and that consequently people may not be willing to answer his questions. I also said that some people at my party were ex-combatants, some had lost close family members, some of them were in 'mixed marriages'; they simply wanted to be accepted as Australians (as they all are now) and not constantly reminded that they cannot be from Australia because they have an accent. Having an accent should not be a licence to inquire and ask for a clinically precise determination of other people's origins.

I thought of my friend Ervin who was asked where he was from at our friends' wedding reception. After replying, "From Brisbane," the unknown man stared at him. "No, I mean, where are you *really* from?"

Ervin became agitated. Recollections of similar situations swarmed through my head as I tried to explain to Michael. I told him that I think many Australians know what happened in our country and that they can presume that people do not necessarily wish to be pressed about their ethnic identities. He raised his eyebrows and said with a grim expression on his face, "Olivera, many people *don't* know and aren't interested in your people's problems. They simply want to know where you came from."

For a brief moment I thought Michael might have a point. Sometimes we are totally preoccupied with 'our problems' and so focused on our country—perhaps even more so than the people who actually live there. The fact that some Australians or other migrants are not interested in knowing what happened in the former Yugoslavia, or how we relate to our past, does not bother me, however, they should then respect our right to declare or not declare our ethnicity. I felt defeated by Michael's conclusion that he had every right to know who Vladimir was, and to be dissatisfied with his answer that he was simply 'ex-Yugoslavian'. After this incident, I realised that it is hard to explain that ethnicity is not the only identity (or isn't one at all!) by which individuals from ex-Yugoslavia (or, indeed, any other country) want to be recognised; and that there is another human dimension, that thread of common humanity that crosses ethnic, religious and racial borders, by which they would rather be known and remembered.

This anecdote is an example of the behaviour of a powerful dominant group towards a powerless minority group. As Susan Hawthorne argues in *Wild Politics*, the powerful normalise and "control the game" and "constantly invent new and random rules which the powerless are obliged to obey" (2002, p. 78). Michael who is a member of the powerful group (white, heterosexual, well-educated Australian men) insisted on a prescriptive mode of behaviour, while expecting Vladan to fit the norm. Hawthorne argues that the dominant group is often unaware of the power it wields and of the pressure it puts on the minority group to conform to what they perceive as acceptable behaviour (p. 77). Thus, seen as the 'other', the minority group, the migrants, do not enjoy the privilege of a private space. As Gillian Bottomley notes, the ability to delineate a private space is an attribute of social power; lacking such power, the private space of the powerless may be minimal (1992, p. 156).

Those who do not belong to the dominant group (for example: Indigenous Australians; straight and lesbian women; gay men; people with disabilities; migrants; and other 'minority groups') are expected to readily provide answers and explanations to all kinds of private questions, regardless of whether they are willing to do so or not. Minority groups can be defined by their bodies, skin colour, accents and their 'foreignness'; and they are often treated as a monolithic group—homogeneous as well as powerless and inferior. While many migrants come to what is perceived as a 'modern multicultural society' with a hope to escape divisions based on ethnicity, paradoxically in Australia they experience further classification based on race. Some Australians are re-erecting ethnic demarcations that many migrants had worked hard to dismantle on their arrival in Australia. Many who come here hoping to be seen as other than their 'ethnic body', find themselves pinned to the wall with these persistent questions. Their identity, in other words, has been reduced to their ethnicity. Vladimir and Ervin were both under pressure to talk about painful, personal issues to total strangers. What I find most disconcerting is that none of their interlocutors had any understanding of the complexities that lay behind what, on the surface, seemed like a straightforward question.

But it should also be understood that refugees from the former Yugoslavia are not a monolithic group. For some there is pride in, and defence of, the Yugoslavian and Bosnian identity but also a desire to escape a contentious meaning of national or ethnic identity. For many, being reduced to one's ethnicity by others was one of the main reasons for resettling in a foreign country. Of course we must remember that one person's identification with a particular national, ethnic or religious group is a matter of their personal choice. Indeed, any attempt to deny an individual the right to freely identify herself or himself as a member—or, as in Vladimir's case, a non-member—of a particular ethnic or religious group is a serious breach of their freedom of expression and conscience.

This does not preclude that some people are very proud of their ethnic traditions and want to embrace them. Multiculturalism does not mean wiping away ethnic identities but celebrating all of them. These contradictions are perhaps at the heart of moving from war toward peace.

CHAPTER FOUR

The Past is the Present[19]

"How are you?"
"Today, better than tomorrow."
This is a new, dark joke I heard in Bosnia.
Once the reply to this question was:
'Today, better than yesterday',
but not any more.

Sarajevo, 12 December 2011
Olivera's Letter to Maria Tumarkin

Dear Maria

Sarajevo has changed. There are many street beggars—mainly women and young children—in the heart of the city. It is winter here, below zero, but many of the beggars are barefoot and in T-shirts. Large packs of dogs wander through the city. I have never seen so many hungry, dirty, beaten and sad dogs in Sarajevo. I saw dogs with broken legs, with only one eye, with large patches of skin missing. I heard dogs whining and howling. People here do not pay much attention. I guess they are used to it and are preoccupied with their daily struggle to survive, but I found myself on the verge of tears much of the time. I felt sick and in constant fear of what I might see next.

---

[19] An earlier version of this chapter, written by Olivera Simić, Elma Softić-Kaunitz and Maria Tumarkin, first appeared as 'Letters from Sarajevo' in *Griffith REVIEW 37: Small World* (2012).

My friend Selma told me that some of the dogs and cats on the street have a pedigree because they were pets once, kicked out of their homes by their owners who did not have enough money to continue feeding them. These former pets are left on the streets to survive on their own, or to die. Someone else told me that the city no longer provided the service that we all knew as *šinteraj*, which once arranged the collection of street dogs and euthanised them. I guess Sarajevo and the rest of the former Yugoslavia decided to change their treatment to follow the standards of more civilised countries around the world. They decided to abolish *šinteraj* and spare the street dogs' lives and treat them with care; however no care has been provided so far.

I have been told that the city plans to build a shelter for street animals. In the meantime, the dogs and cats wander among the people. A handful of organisations try desperately to protect the animals but there is only so much they can do. They have no financial means to undertake projects for animal protection and the staff who work in these organisations often have no choice but to shelter animals in their own homes or offices. Their meagre financial help comes from a handful of foreign animal welfare organisations while authorities in BiH remain indifferent to the problem. Like many laws in my country, BiH's legislation protecting animals is a paper tiger.

Beggars too are ignored and neglected, and must fight to survive cold and hunger. I saw young kids sitting on cardboard boxes, singing, with one hand out begging for money. It seemed that a number of the beggars were Roma people, but not all. Late one evening when the temperature was below zero, I saw a beautiful young girl with a long dark hair, maybe six years old, in a shirt without sleeves. She was running after a group of older foreign men, shouting that they had given her money that she could not change into Bosnian currency. The men were dressed in business suits and spoke in a foreign language; they were amused by the girl's panic. I have seen too many heartbreaking scenes like this. When I told this story to one of my friends, he said in a flat voice, "But we had beggars before, this is nothing new." My friend was taken aback by the fuss I was making. Still, for reasons I cannot explain, I am convinced that it was not 'like this' before. It may be that these days I can only recall good things from the past; that I have 'forgotten' all the bad things that make one feel embarrassed and not proud of one's country.

Do I see things differently now? Do I notice more? Is it because I live in Australia now? Or, as you, Maria, write in your memoir *Otherland:A Journey With My Daughter:* "I never paid attention to this kind of stuff before, it was the way things were and it never used to matter. Now, all of a sudden, it does" (2010, p. 48). Of course Sarajevo had street dogs before but never as many as there are now. The difference is maybe the sensations I feel. I notice things I would not have noticed before or which my Sarajevo friends are used to living with. I complained to a few of them about the appalling conditions of the street dogs in the city and then immediately felt ashamed. How dare I make a fuss about the dogs to my friends who have no jobs, no money and a pretty bleak future ahead of them? Do I care more about the dogs than the people? How arrogant must I appear to be, worrying and looking desperate just because I cannot save the Bosnian dogs?[20]

People here are preoccupied with their own survival, so I understand that they have different priorities. (Still, this does not excuse the torture of animals!) Literally everyone I meet is in need, financial or psychological. Every second citizen is unemployed. The average salary for the lucky ones who have some sort of job is the equivalent of around 600 Australian dollars per month. In Bosnia, it is hard to survive on this amount of money, but the real issue is unemployment. Young people, walk around without jobs and without plans for either the present or the future. I don't dare ask my friends where they are going for Christmas or the New Year holiday. I know that many have not been anywhere on holidays for years.

Despite 'being aware' of such circumstances, I ignorantly made a comment to my friend Alma recently over a coffee: "You are so lucky here. You can easily go back and forth to the Adriatic coast; just two hours' drive to paradise. I envy you for being that close to those beautiful beaches." I thought this was a compliment of sorts, and was all smiles. She took a sip of coffee, brushed her hair away from her face, and said pointedly:"I haven't been to the Adriatic coast for eight years

---

[20] Sadly, this situation remains unchanged in 2014. According to Bosnian media reports, almost 11,000 stray dogs wander through Sarajevo. They are destined to die either from hunger or torture. It is indeed impossible not to ask oneself, as Slavenka Drakulić does:"What kind of people torture dogs, and allow their kids [to] do the same? What kind of society allows such people to get away with such acts scot-free, while witnesses to their criminal behaviour are forced to leave the country?" (14 January 2014).

now. I cannot afford it." I blushed and wished the earth would open up and swallow me. How could I make such an arrogant comment to someone so dear to me, whom I know so well? Alma's husband lost his job during the war and has remained unemployed since then. She is the only breadwinner and her monthly salary of 400 euros would certainly not allow her to take her four family members on a holiday.

Many of my friends do nothing because there is nothing to do. I wonder sometimes how they spend their days. What can you do the whole day if you do not have a job or money? "Nothing. I watch TV, cook something and babysit for my sister and friends. I check my emails and sit around the house," my friend Aldijana told me in a matter-of-fact tone. She is in her early thirties with a Master's degree in Gender Studies and has been unemployed for a year.

It is vital to have a job here, any job, and parents will do anything for their children to be employed. The mother of a friend told me: "She [her daughter] has a job: that is important. It does not matter that her salary is four months late. She will receive it one day, hopefully." In *Worlds Apart: Bosnian Lessons for Global Security* (2011), the former American Ambassador Swanee Hunt (who served in Vienna during the war in Bosnia and Herzegovina [BiH] and was intimately involved in American policy toward the Balkans) reflects on her life and work in BiH. She made many trips throughout the country, and the rest of the former Yugoslavia, attempting to understand the costly delays in foreign military intervention. Writing about Bosnian people and the aftermath of war, she notes that "most Bosnians had been working without wages for several years. Life had been simply a matter of surviving at the most basic level" (p. 21). Not having a job with its attendant income, sense of purpose and meeting of expectations can lead to stress, alcoholism, drug abuse, disillusionment and a desperation that may lead to illness and suicide. Nevertheless, it is difficult for many to comprehend how someone can be satisfied with having any job when payment is several months or, in some cases, years late.

Some of my unemployed friends suffer from anxiety and other mental health problems. They are qualified lawyers, doctors, or tradespersons, in their mid- to late thirties, with or without children. Many of them are stressed, angry, and helpless. Some are bitter about those people who lost close family members in the war and are now eligible for a pension and other benefits from the state because of it.

One of my friends said to me:

> Does it mean that my father needed to be killed in the war so my family has a meal today? I am sick of the people who lost someone close because they have more benefits than I who did not lose a close family member. Even during the war, these people got two cups of flour and my family got only one because no one died in my family.

When I told my friend Elma about this complaint, she told me a war joke that had circulated in Sarajevo during the siege: Little Mujo asks Huso who is eating a big sandwich, "Huso, give me a little bit of your sandwich, I am hungry." Huso replies, "I don't want to. My *babo* [father] is a *sehid* [martyr] and I deserve this sandwich." Mujo tells him, "Oh, Huso just wait and you will see. My *babo* will be a *sehid* too and I will eat such a sandwich and won't give you any."

In Sarajevo, images of poverty exist in parallel with new buildings, large Western-style shopping centres, coffee shops and pubs with wireless internet connections, fancy bookstores and expensive handmade souvenirs. None of it is for the local population, but for the foreign tourists and researchers who still flock to the city: temporary visitors and academics like myself. I am a Bosnian, but I am a foreigner too. As Suada, the mother of a good friend in Sarajevo, told me, "I have a homeland, but no home any more." In this one sentence, she has captured the essence of the aftermath of war. Indeed, this is exactly how I feel too. I used to have many friends in Sarajevo, but each year there are fewer. There are now only a couple of friends that I call on when I come here, and one of them is the very Elma Softić-Kaunitz to whom you have written a letter for me to hand deliver. I met Elma ten years ago at an international organisation where we both worked. Although I have been living in different cities (and countries) over the past decade, I have always maintained a close connection with her.

As you are obviously aware, Elma is best known for the war diary she wrote during the siege in Sarajevo. *Sarajevo Days, Sarajevo Nights* (1996) was published as a book and instantly became a bestseller. Elma never left Sarajevo, the city she was born in. She could have left during the siege, but chose not to. This choice is what made Elma's story so unusual.

Still, Elma was not the only one who chose to stay in her beloved city. The cellist, Vedran Smajlović, has become world renowned for his daily recitals on the sidewalks of Sarajevo and in ruined buildings, even during shelling. A member of the Sarajevo Opera Orchestra, Smajlović, known as the 'Cellist from Sarajevo', wore formal tails for his pavement performances. On 27 May 1992, several Sarajevans were hit by a mortar shell while waiting in line at a bakery. Smajlović was appalled by what he saw, took his cello, sat in a crater made by a shell, and played for 22 days straight—one day for each neighbour killed (Hunt, 2011, p. 173). As the reports of his performances spread, a journalist questioned whether he was crazy to play his cello in the midst of a war zone. He countered, "You ask me am I crazy for playing the cello, why do you not ask if they are not crazy for shelling Sarajevo?" (Buttry, 2011, p. 306).

This was the spirit of Sarajevo during the siege. Now, 16 years later, Elma reflects on her life during the 'bad peace' (as she calls the peace she lives in now). She told me that the spirit of the people is destroyed, and the energy that many people like her invested in Sarajevo by staying behind has gone. "When your life becomes everyday life, then it is not life any more. What sort of life is your life if it is just 'everyday life' and nothing else? It is not *a life*." Although she stayed in her beloved Sarajevo during the longest siege of a city in modern history, Elma's advice to her two children, Hannah and Ivo, who were born in the middle of it all, is that they should leave the Balkans altogether.

A few nights ago, Elma and I met in a famous Sarajevo beer house. It is a large pub and restaurant where international visitors and a few high-income locals like to come, eat, drink and socialise. I do not smoke in Australia, but when I am in Bosnia I smoke and like to drink *šljivovica* with my friends because this is a part of our ritual and bonding. As a migrant, you change language, friends, residence, your way of thinking and consciousness, and often live in a political and economic system different from the one you are used to. Once you return home, you instantly reconnect with who you were before leaving: a local person immersed in familiar rituals, traditions and culture.

I am transformed from the moment I step off the plane in Bosnia. I start to speak my language, switch off my Australian mobile and turn on my Bosnian phone (I have kept the same number all these years). I have a valid Bosnian identification and passport, and occasionally I still receive letters addressed to my home in Banja Luka. My parents keep the mail for me and each year when I visit I go through it. It all seems surreal, like my life in Bosnia has been frozen in time and my life in Australia is just a dream. It often seems that I live in two parallel universes. The fact that I usually come to Bosnia in winter makes it even more surreal and distant from my life in Australia, a country with little snow and temperatures that rarely dip below zero (at least in Queensland). In BiH, I still have my dentist and a family doctor whom I always visit during my stay. While there, I always have to confront my emotions, as you did when you were visiting your homeland after a long time. Like you, I have to face "tenderness, nostalgia, longing, disgust, and something closely resembling survivor's guilt" because I was lucky "to cut and run while others were not" (Tumarkin, 2010, p. 49).

My mind was buzzing with these thoughts on my way to meet Elma at the pub. Knowing that she smokes, I brought a pack of cigarettes. After we hugged and kissed each other, happy, excited, I opened the pack, lit a cigarette and said: "I have a lot to tell you, but first let me tell you about Maria Tumarkin." With these words I opened a Pandora's box of emotions and memories of the war. I told Elma that my colleague and friend Maria had written her a letter, and that in your first book *Traumascapes* (2005), you write about Sarajevo and about her. Elma, with a great surprise, and wide-open, big green sparkling eyes asked: "About *me*?" Looking at her intensely I said, "Yes, *you*."

I told her that you had given the letter to me, and while I was taking it out of my backpack, I said that it was up to her whether she wanted to read it now or later, and whether she wanted to respond. She wanted to read it immediately. Around us people were chatting, eating and smoking. The light was dim, so we asked the waitress to light the candle on our table. I watched Elma open the envelope and unfold your letter. She moved closer to the flame and started to read. This image of Elma reading by candlelight reminded me of the war, of how Sarajevans rarely had electricity during the siege. I was thinking of how Elma wrote most of her diary by candlelight. Now, almost 16 years later, Elma was sitting and reading your letter beside a thin candle flame. I could see her eyes immersed in the words coming from across the ocean, from so far away, written by someone who had never met her, but had been moved by her destiny and life.

I was trying not to look directly at Elma because this was an intimate moment, although she had chosen to read the letter in this loud, smoky place. Out of the corner of my eye I saw her shaking, her eyes full of tears. I, like Elma, might not always realise how profoundly we have been affected by the way we experienced or witnessed war, and the extent to which small signs of humanity and attention can trigger painful memories from the past.

Melbourne, 24 November 2011
Maria Tumarkin's Letter to Elma Softić-Kaunitz

Dear Elma

When I read *Sarajevo Days, Sarajevo Nights* almost ten years ago, I felt such a strong sense of kinship with you, such an inexplicably deep connection that to discover all these years later that we have a friend—Olivera (I call her 'Oli')—in common feels to me exactly right. It all makes sense. I wrote about you in my first book called *Traumascapes*. Oli was going to bring a copy for you to Sarajevo, but I got the dates of her departure mixed up and sent it too late. I am really sorry. One day you will have it.

I want to tell you that reading your words written during the siege, the way you wrote them, the register in which you wrote, the need that drove you to write them in the first place, struck me on reading them for the first time—and they have the same effect on me still—as the very essence of what I understand as humanity, of what I understand as courage, of what I understand as the refusal to be broken by fear and suffering. I read your words and wondered what I would do in your place (and the fact that what happened to you in Bosnia didn't happen to us in the Soviet Union after its collapse is a sheer fluke, dumb luck really, it could have so easily been us). I wondered whether I would have had ten per cent of your inner strength, of your fearlessness, of your refusal to be made into something less than fully human. Could I have written as clear-sightedly, as brilliantly, as honestly as you did? I read and re-read your words and felt the deepest kind of admiration, pride and, also, hope.

I want to thank you from the deepest place in me for being the way you are, for your words, for your refusal to leave Sarajevo, for your need to bear witness, for the way in which you put—and continue to put—your life on the line so others like me can understand the world and humanity a little bit better. I want to thank you for your humour too, for the lightness of your touch, for the brilliance of your mind. We all grow taller with people like you next to us.

I wonder if you could tell me how you are now, what it is like to be in Sarajevo, to be you. I would be very grateful if you could tell me what you think about it all more than fifteen years later—the war, the siege, the survival, the aftermath, being a woman in all of this, being Jewish in all of this, having children in all of this. I know that one day we will meet. I hope Oli will give you a hug from me. She is beautiful, Oli.

With the deepest respect and much, much warmth
Maria Tumarkin

"I need to meet her," Elma said through tears, as she finished reading. "How is it possible that my work could affect someone so much, someone so far away?" It was a sincere question. So was my response:

> Because you decided to stay in Sarajevo during the siege. Because you had an option to leave but chose to stay. You chose the option that brought you closer to death with each passing moment, day, week, year. Because people admire courage and are fascinated by your decision and life. I, and other people, think that what you've done is extremely courageous, that's why.

I could see that your letter had reached deep into Elma's soul. There was a sense of disbelief that someone would be thinking of her after all these years; that someone cared enough to write a personal letter to her and express gratitude and admiration for who she was and is.

There are not many people left who still remember Elma's war diary. Even though it was a bestseller it seems to have been largely forgotten by most. Before reading your letter she had thought that her story had lost its meaning. Not many people I meet here now have enough empathy, or solidarity, or even patience, to listen to someone else's story. This is because everyone in BiH has their *own* story of survival to tell.

I have seen Elma each day during my stay here in Sarajevo. On the last occasion we met in a cake shop in the centre of town to say goodbye. She brought a book for you and for me, as a present to take back to Australia. All the sadness and feelings of anxiety I have kept deep down inside me over the last few days found their way out through my eyes. I could not control myself; tears were rolling down my cheeks. Elma was trying to console me. I told her how ashamed I felt to cry in front of her, when her home city had witnessed unspeakable atrocities at the end of last century. Modest and humble as always, she warmly embraced me, saying: "But, look at the city now. It is alive, kicking and beautiful." We kissed each other and parted ways on a cold night. Elma told me then that she would respond to you before I left Bosnia. She kept her promise.

Love
Oli

Sarajevo, 23 December 2011
Elma's Letter to Maria

Dear Maria

Olivera (I call her 'Olja') gave me your letter a month ago when we met at a restaurant in Sarajevo. I always enjoy Olja's company—she is so smart, such a positive and brave person—and she makes me feel how I would like to be. So when she told me she had a letter for me from her friend from Australia—I was surprised. I thought we might have some mutual friend from Bosnia or Yugoslavia (better known as 'ex-Yugoslavia' these days) who lives in Australia now.

But when I read your letter—I knew we three have known each other not from some ordinary physical place, but from a special world which few people inhabit. I like to call this place 'Yuval', which in Hebrew means 'stream' or 'small river'. It would be a really long story to explain why 'Yuval' means something special to me—maybe we can return to that saga some other time, but I must tell you that that special place is the one where I go when I need to look inwards—where I can still recognise the freedom, freshness and richness of my own being. When I am in that place—I am ready to share my soul with other wonderful inhabitants of that world. Unfortunately, such travels take me far from reality and I cannot afford to be out of reality too often, or to stay there too long.

Thank you so much for your wonderful letter. Thank you for reading my book with such affection and benevolence. When I was writing the book it was a time of horrible mistakes, as each time of war is, but the experience I gained during those years is the most valuable experience I have. I realised that destruction and torture really do exist, not just in the past or in distant places, that they are filling up each pore of life here and now. When thinking today about war and life and writing my book, I believe that I put so much effort into writing my diary and letters to known and unknown friends because I was scared to death. I was not so much afraid that I would be killed or injured. Of course I was worried for my family, but I somehow knew, or simply believed, as many others do, that bad things cannot happen to my dearest. I was horrified because I became accustomed to all that horror around me. I believe that the reason why I put so much effort into writing was because I desperately needed to explain to myself that the horror should not be the normal order of the world.

Today I do not write as I used to. It is much too painful when I face my own thoughts. They are so superficial, so muggy and so colourless. I feel that, in some unknown moment during the last fifteen years, I lost the ability to judge the world and myself. Although I can distinguish between good and bad, it is not enough any more to be sure I will do the right thing. When I start to analyse good and evil, I discover that both have the same source, the same argumentation and the same face—the face of timeless despair.

I know my last sentence sounds so pessimistic, but I am not a pessimist at all. I am okay. I love, I work, I am trying to educate my children, love my husband, be helpful to my parents, not to be alienated from my sister who lives in Australia—in a very, very different society. In fact, I am doing my best to convince myself that I am successful in striving to be a good person in an environment in which the conditions are not conducive for the development of a strong and positive personality.

Sometimes I write a poem or a short story. But—I never write the end. You will ask me why? I do not know. I think it is because I know that the end will sadden me. And, I do not have the right to be sad—at least—not yet. There are people who need me to be strong and playful and not sad and blue. And that is how it is being me in Sarajevo today.

Dear Maria, I feel like I know you and I know we will meet some day—not just in my 'Yuval' place, but in this real, somewhat sore, but still interesting world. Until then, I will meet you and Olja and a few other wonderful persons in my precious sanctuary where I go when all the other doors are closed.

With respect and warmest wishes for you and your dearest
Elma Softić-Kaunitz

The correspondence continued between me and my two friends who have never met except through the writing that keeps them alive in the present. I have become the channel between them and they have become my companions in working and reworking the traumas that all three of us shared. The main connection between the three of us is the written words that we use to preserve the past in the present.

Melbourne, 31 March 2012
Maria's Letter to Olivera and Elma

Dear Elma and Oli

I've almost forgotten this about books—that they can bring us together like this. Oceans are nothing for books, and decades gone are nothing, and the idea that most people in the world are strangers to each other is a big fat nothing, too. Here we are, the three of us, connected now in a way that cannot be undone. All because of your book, Elma.

And it hurts to think, dear Elma, that you feel that your book, once heralded as 'an extraordinary document' (those reviews were glowing), read eagerly, passed from person to person, doesn't mean anything to most people these days. For a moment there, when your book came out, it connected you and the unfolding history you recorded to the rest of the world, and the book itself, correct me if I am wrong, only exists because during the 1,395 days of the siege, you refused to allow for the possibility that your people and your city, surrounded from all sides, isolated and unreachable, could simply fall out of history and be forgotten. This is why you kept a diary. This is why you wrote your letters.

I want to tell you that your book is not forgotten. I know this for a fact. I am sure you've read Mikhail Bulgakov's *The Master and Margarita* (1996). Remember that line from the book, the most important sentence in it: "[M]anuscripts do not burn" (p. 55). They don't, Elma. Books do not just disappear. Your book is beside me right now. It still reads as if it was written yesterday. It is urgent and timeless at once. I am still terrified when I read it. I still feel like my heart will break. And your words make me laugh too, Elma. How is it possible?

Dear Oli, you write—about what happened in Bosnia, about crimes committed in your name, about memory and grief, about families, like yours, damaged beyond repair, about peace that has brought no peace to you or to Elma—as if your life depends on it. You remind me of what it is to write. In Australia, people don't talk about Bosnia much these days, do they? Perhaps, they still do in Europe. But here it feels like people have forgotten already, or perhaps everyone is just too relaxed and comfortable, or it's just too much, you know, every month brings a new disaster, a new kind of unbearable pain. I know you understand and I know too that the thought of Bosnia slipping out of people's minds with such finality is unbearable to you. Sometimes I think you write like a woman possessed. I mean it in the most admiring of ways.

Dear Elma and Oli, I come from a country (there are many others like mine, I know) with an unbreakable tradition of which I remain intensely proud, of people bearing witness to the moral catastrophes around them. I know now that without their words, there would be no true documents of what happened in the Soviet Union. Without their words, there would be nothing to stop history being totally rewritten, or forgotten (forgetting happens so quickly, as you know).

There lived at the start of the twentieth century a celebrated Russian-Soviet poet called Osip Mandelstam. Like a million others, he perished in the camps in 1938. His widow, Nadezhda Mandelstam, an extraordinary woman in her own right, decided that the foremost task in her forty-plus years of widowhood was to preserve her husband's poems. She was right. Her husband was a genius. To keep his poems alive, including different variations and drafts of the same poems, Nadezhda continuously recited them at night. She spent most of her life after Osip's arrest and death, on the run. She was next in line without question, but somehow she managed to outfox the henchmen. Between 1937 and 1938 more than 1.5 million people were arrested in the largest wave of mass repressions to engulf the Soviet Union. More than 70,000 of them were shot.

In 1938, in a small Russian village near Yaroslavsky Road, where Nadezhda Mandelstam briefly lived, cattle-trains filled to the brink with those sentenced to spend three, five, ten years in the camps would pass through every night. And of course, everyone in that little village would talk about what happened at night and at least some villagers felt insulted by the fact that they were banned from so much as giving bread to those people trapped inside the heavily guarded trains. One day the woman in whose house Nadezhda Mandelstam was living, managed to throw a chocolate bar, intended as a precious treat for her daughter, through the broken window of a train. In an instant, soldiers pushed her away but the woman was happy all day—she had managed to do something, to connect to the people inside the trains. Mandelstam would write decades later in her memoirs (I'm giving you my translation):

> Will anyone from future generations understand what this chocolate bar with the kiddy picture meant in a stuffy train carrying people to camps in 1938? People, for whom the time stopped, and the space became a prison cell ... a cattle-train carriage filled to the brim with the half-dead human cargo, cast off, forgotten, struck off the list of the living with no names and nicknames ... moving irreversibly into the black non-being of the camps ... these were the people who, for the first time in months, received a message from the other world, which was completely closed off to them—a cheap kiddy chocolate bar, which told them that they were not forgotten ... (1970).[21]

Dear Elma and Oli, to me there is no greater purpose in writing than to write against the non-being of oblivion, to write so as to connect people who feel forgotten to those who refuse to forget them. And the refusal to forget itself strikes me as just about the most important

---

[21] See also Mandelstam (2002), p. 55.

human task there is. This is what you do. This is who you are. All I can say is that I will never forget you, and I won't forget your words. You can count on me.

With love
Maria

Here we are, 20 years later, still connected by words written in Sarajevo during the siege that lasted from 1992 to 1996. The words that helped one woman deal with the horrors of war; the words that helped one woman escape her fear.

From *Sarajevo Days, Sarajevo Nights* by Elma Softić-Kaunitz (1996, p. 87).
Sarajevo, 7 July 1993

Dear friends

It's now forty-five minutes past nine. I'm sitting in the kitchen and using up the last drops of petroleum in a home-made lamp—a small jar that was once filled with Fructal brand baby food now contains diesel with a pinch of salt added—to reduce the smoke—and a wick pulled through the lid. The jar is standing under a cylinder made from a bottle of Meinle egg liqueur whose bottom has been cut out, and the whole thing is standing in a glass ashtray.

First: what does it mean to sit in our kitchen in these times in these spaces? It means taking the risk that a piece of shrapnel from a sudden mortar shell might smash through the tile and Arborite of our improvised kitchen and interrupt the writing of this letter, and turn my life into a death notice [notices bearing the name, dates and likeness of the deceased posted on walls, telephone poles, etc., rather like our lost-and-found signs]—its text typed by the hand of one of my loved ones and photocopied ten times over for the ten corners of this city. There exists, of course, a more fortunate possibility—that I lose a hand or some other trifle of my anatomy. We already have one hole from such a piece of shrapnel in the kitchen ceiling. It is not my wish to frighten you or fascinate you. I'm merely trying to illustrate for you, life in Sarajevo.

   Secondly: what does it mean to use up the last drops of diesel fuel? Most simply put, it means that for the time being we will be groping around in the dark unless I manage to get hold of three litres tomorrow. Somewhere a shell has just fallen, but not close enough to make me withdraw to the 'safety' of a lower floor. But that shell might have landed in somebody's apartment and blown up its safest nook and killed a sleeping family. In Sarajevo there is no safe place. But Sarajevans are now used to that and it is generally acknowledged that one cannot escape fate. Perhaps this statement sounds defeatist to you, but thanks to it, life here manages to flow on.

CHAPTER FIVE

Victims and Survivors

Aren't you just a victim
selling your own trauma?
asked the Harvard blonde
with the brains worth half a million.
I couldn't find the words in English to say:
Do you have any idea how right you are?
Nine deaths, bleeding eardrums,
Dodging bullets—It all fits in the word trauma.
And yes, I was unable to say in English,
I'm afraid
That's the only valuable thing I have.

—Aida Bašić, 'Trauma-Market' (2004, p. 36)

War is an industry, as is postwar recovery and reconciliation. Researchers and academics like me organise seminars, conferences and workshops to talk about war. We receive grants to carry out research on armed conflicts, on genocide, rape and other crimes against women. We travel to places, such as Srebrenica and Kigali (Rwanda),[22] places that we would never have heard of had they not become infamous as

---

[22] The genocide in Rwanda was a mass killing of ethnic Tutsis by ethnic Hutus that took place in 1994 over the course of approximately 100 days (from 6 April through to mid-July). Death toll estimates have ranged from 500,000–1,000,000, or as much as 20% of the country's total population. It is estimated that some 200,000 people participated in the perpetration of the Rwandan genocide. Women were systematically and brutally raped (Des Forges, 1999; United Human Rights Council, n.d.).

the sites of genocides. In their collection, *Dark Tourism* (2000), John Lennon and Malcolm Foley explore people's motivations to board tour buses and visit sites of mass killings as curious onlookers. They argue that horror and death have become established commodities for sale to tourists who have an appetite for the darkest elements of human history (see also Uzzell, 1989).

I have seen, felt and dreamt about some of these places. Still, I don't want to be seen only as a 'victim' but I cannot prevent others from viewing me in that way. Taking on the role of a 'victim of war' can be 'convenient'. It offers compassion and understanding from strangers. They dole out this compassion based on your inherited origin, your place of birth and, of course, your past experience, which might or might not be as traumatic as people imagine. They can feel good about themselves as they pity you.

In his memoir, *The War is Dead, Long Live the War. Bosnia: The Reckoning* (2012), Ed Vulliamy refuses to call those who survived war and torture in Bosnia and Herzegovina (BiH) simply 'victims':

> I try to avoid calling these people 'victims'. They were, of course, but that is not their definition, or who they are. They are traumatised to different degrees, in different ways, but they are survivors. They laugh as well as cry and have made new lives, and many have rebuilt their homes incinerated back where they came from ... This is not victimhood. This is survival (p. xxxix).

I have seen some people abusing the role of victim, profiteering from it and advancing their professional life because of it. I suppose I too should call myself an 'academic war profiteer' since much of my academic career has been grounded in writing about the war events in my homeland. Because I come from a country wretched and destroyed by civil war, because I experienced war first hand, others presume that I am an expert on what it means to lose one's country of birth, to lose family and friends, to be a refugee and to search for—and reinvent—one's identity. This experience has given me, and other survivors, an authority to speak out whether we want to or not. I must admit it often feels good to be perceived as an 'authority', to have this ultimate 'power' of public speech where it seems that everyone listens to you because you are survivor of something 'unspoken' and 'unthinkable'. It gives much needed attention and respect to otherwise voiceless and invisible female survivors in particular. Still, the role of survivor carries with it the burden of collective victimhood and remorse, and a danger of being perceived as a symbol of a damaged 'nation', a representative of past horror. There is an assumption that you must have been a victim of vicious human rights abuses because you belong to a nation that was immersed in war. Even if you were not a survivor of a particular crime yourself, certainly many of your fellow sisters and brothers were, and you are perceived as part of the collective experience rather than as an individual. Your experience becomes not (only) about you, but who you represent.

On the last day of the Women's World Conference 2011 in Ottawa, Canada, I attended a session on BiH and Somalia, and the subject of rape. After the session, a woman sitting in the row in front of me unexpectedly turned and took my hand in hers. I was puzzled by her actions. She was in her late sixties, with grey hair and kind blue eyes. She looked at me with worry etched on her face, and whispered: "Are you all right? It must be hard." I looked at her with bewilderment at first, and then realised that she thought *I* had most probably been raped. She seemed rather surprised when I told her that I had not been subjected to any form of sexual assault during the war in BiH. I was astonished to think that this woman, and probably others in the room, had thought of me as a victim of rape merely because I had introduced myself as a woman originally from BiH. Whenever I had spoken during that session, I had noticed that women looked at me with their eyes wide open and filled with empathy and understanding, and that sort of silent respect we show towards victims. They would occasionally nod at me, wanting to show that they were listening carefully to every word I had to say because I 'deserved' special attention: I was *a victim*. Women were expressing support and comfort with their body language, leaning toward me, eager to hear my voice. I felt loved and safe, but not entirely relaxed about the level of attention I was receiving in comparison to other women in the room. Obviously, some women in the room did not feel comfortable either. A woman sitting next to me expressed her embarrassment about her own origin: "I do not have such an exotic background, I only come from Toronto." While everyone else in the room quietly chuckled at this remark, I felt very uncomfortable, as I always do in such situations. This was not the first time I had heard women express that they were less 'worthy' or competent to talk about war because they had not experienced it. And it was neither the first nor last time that I was simultaneously exoticised and patronised while being empathised with due to my enforced 'victim status'.

One of the paradoxes of experiencing violence first hand is that it can give unconditional power and authority to one's voice, and people who have not had these experiences might feel as if they cannot say anything worthwhile. I have been in several situations where I felt like the woman from Toronto; indeed I have felt incompetent and speechless in the presence of Srebrenica genocide survivors. Several years ago I attended a conference in Sarajevo on truth and reconciliation. Representatives of the Mothers of Srebrenica ('Mothers'), a BiH organisation that gathers survivors of the Srebrenica genocide, were also there. In July 1995, Srebrenica, a small town in the east of BiH, became the site of a genocide that occurred in just four days, when thousands of Muslim men and boys who had sought refuge were slaughtered by members of the Serbian forces. Since 1996, when the first reports emerged about allegations of the massacre, the Mothers have used non-violent actions to find the truth about the events that took place, and bring those responsible to justice.

I clearly recall one of the conference sessions on the possibilities of reconciliation after genocide. The room was small and packed with academics from around the globe, and a few Mothers as well. After one of the conference participants presented a paper on possibilities for reconciliation in BiH, Munira, a survivor of genocide in Srebrenica, stood up and announced in a strong and confident voice: "I don't want to reconcile with anyone. I did not fight with anyone. I lost 32 family members." She swallowed, paused briefly, and sat down. I felt a shiver down my spine. Silence fell over the room and the planned discussion was abruptly terminated. People were speechless in the face of the survivors and their loss. I can't recall who broke the long, awkward silence. How could anyone dare to tell Munira that reconciliation *is perhaps possible*? Or indeed, necessary, if we are ever to move on from this impasse.

How does one argue with a survivor? Munira felt that she needed to say something in this room full of highly privileged academics who tirelessly flock to her country every year to tell her, and her fellow citizens, that they need to learn to live together after committing unspeakable atrocities against one another. The majority of these people live their comfortable lives far away from Munira's war-ravaged country. The presenter who had unintentionally provoked Munira to stand up and speak was the same man who, at the beginning of his paper, had made a remark (which was supposed to be funny) about leaving his wife and four kids at home when he embarked on a voyage to Sarajevo. Munira was sitting just two rows away from me, and I had heard her whisper in a low but audible voice: "Lucky you! I have no family to leave back at my home." She said it in *naš jezik* [our language], so few people would have understood. As far as Munira was concerned, we were all probably seen as 'conference tourists', building our careers on the misery of survivors. A couple of minutes after the presenter had started his talk, she had removed the headphones for translation and just sat there, impatiently waiting for his session to end. Occasionally, she would turn to her colleague and whisper something into her ear.

I was upset by Munira's comment and could sense from her demeanour that there was more to come. I listened to the talk but surreptitiously watched these dynamics and wondered what would happen next. Munira and others who have experienced enormous suffering are often distrustful of, or (over)sensitive to, 'outsiders', to those who have no immediate experience of catastrophe and pain. As Slavenka Drakulić argues, survivors believe that because of their particular experience, they have "sole ownership over it and that they alone have the moral right to tell the world about it" (2012). The survivors know and feel that they have the power and legitimacy to silence any conversation that is outside the scope of their concern or that they find distressing. The questions that keep buzzing in my mind are: Can survivors collude with the perpetrators if they consciously use the authority of suffering to silence any conversation that makes an effort towards reconciliation? Do they have the right to exert a power that makes us feel embarrassed, and that our work is worthless?

I had met with the Mothers in several different settings: public ones, such as conferences and forums; but also more private ones in their office, such as in 2003, when I was working for UNICEF who wanted to find out more about their work. I also met with them as part of a group of academics who visited the Srebrenica graveyard in 2008. These moments were incredibly important to me but also uncomfortable and painful. I often felt anger and helplessness, which was absorbed and muted by the pain I felt everywhere around me. The Mothers have a strong urge to put human faces to perpetrators. Otherwise, they warn us, the whole Serb ethnic group will be alleged as 'the perpetrator', and this is not what they want. "I have no way of knowing if a man sitting next to me on the bus killed my husband and children or not. I need to know who did the killings, otherwise I will see in the eyes of every Serb a potential killer of my family," Munira told me later.

But what about me? Where did I belong? To victims, perpetrators or 'border-crossers'? As a woman with a Serb name, at these meetings I had mixed feelings: admiration for the power of the Mothers' hunger for the truth, but also anxiety. Where can this rhetoric, which is sometimes full of contradictory impulses, lead? To whom do *my* eyes belong? Shall I lower *my* gaze until justice is done and the actual perpetrators are brought to trial? Or should I open my eyes, my thinking and feeling eyes, as wide as possible to see both sides of this historical tragedy while still remaining in the community that gave me life? Do 'my people' and this history define me, or do I define history and the people that I am a part of? How do we open up a space for historical positioning which will allow for new historical meanings about ourselves? To even begin this conversation is a complex, painful and daunting prospect which demands intense honesty, and a safe space to explore a complex truth.

By crossing the borders of ethnic divisions in my homeland and sitting at the same table with women who survived a genocide committed by men belonging to 'my' ethnic group, makes me feel as if I am walking across a thin bridge made of spiderweb, spanning the borders of human division. All who wish to understand these histories and reconcile all sides are implicated in the Srebrenica saga. I can see no future without this effort towards interaction, regardless of the cost, the mutual discomfort. With my small interventions, in the form of writing and speaking out, I and many other women in post-conflict communities are trying to create a space where these often uncomfortable but extremely important conversations can take place.

In her poem, 'Crossing the Lines', Biljana Kašić, a Croatian feminist and peace activist, depicts the importance of women crossing ethnic and religious borders to work for peace. Biljana told me that she wrote this poem in one breath. She felt a need to tell her feminist sisters in Serbia how important they were and how much she loved them despite the destructive war and politics that surrounded them. One morning in 1992, during a period of isolation when communications were halted, she wrote the poem while sitting in her unit and watching over Zagreb in Croatia (Kašić, 1993/2007).

In spaces where borders are crossed, I think about the thousands of Bosniak children who will be brought up on the stories of their Muslim fathers, grandfathers, brothers and uncles being slaughtered by Serbs. I worry about the likelihood of raising future young leaders of BiH who will look at the past *not* as a stumbling block but rather as a foundation for a meaningful and engaged future. It is an extremely hard task facing all of us: to find a way between remembering and forgetting—caught as we are between looking back and moving forward. All those war ravaged communities face the same dilemma and struggle to find a middle ground between retributive and restorative justice; between the reintegration of the former perpetrators into the community, and the compensation for, and acknowledgment of, the suffering of survivors.

From One Disaster to Another

In January 2011 I found myself in the middle of yet another unfolding disaster. This one was caused not by humans, but by Mother Nature. The massive floods which inundated Brisbane and surrounding areas over a period of days triggered my memory of war time and the ways people cope with disasters. After spending two days glued to the television, watching the scenes of devastation, I felt the need to go out and try to forget about the floods, at least long enough to have a drink and eat a decent meal. I was with a group of my friends and we were surprised that so many other people were out and about too. But no matter how hard I tried to enjoy my cold beer, the images I had seen earlier while walking beside the Brisbane River lingered in my mind. I kept thinking about how reality was mixed up with the surreal, and how I was not sure any more what was actually happening. Which was reality? Ordering our meal in a pub, full of people dressed up and laughing, and shouting at each other because of the loud disco music filling the muddy air? Or was it Brisbane under water? People despairing in their flooded houses? I kept watching those around me.

They were having such a good time. It all seemed too much to me, too soon, too indecent in this moment. But then I was there as well. I felt guilty that I was sitting in the pub while others were sitting in evacuation centres, or 'refugee centres' as I called them. While nibbling at the generous serving of food in front of me, I could see on the giant TV screen footage of people lining up to get a basic meal in one of the nearby evacuation centres. Those people, who had lost everything, were less than three kilometres from this pub.

What made me think that everyone should stay home, cry and agonise? And why had I not stayed home myself? As I watched a couple kissing passionately I reminded myself that people had sex during the war in BiH. I have a close friend who lived in Sarajevo during the siege, had sex with her then boyfriend and conceived her son in 1994, an 'unthinkable' year to become pregnant in Sarajevo. But I know of many other babies conceived and born during the war, babies born from love, not rape. I know of consensual sex between women and men belonging to different ethnic groups, people who should have been 'enemies'. At times, having sex seemed to save our sanity during the war. It distracted our minds from death and destruction. Why would it be different during natural disasters?

During the first days of the flood I had not left my house without a camera. But I felt guilty about taking photos of other people's misery. I kept thinking: *Am I a 'dark tourist'? Am I one of those people I criticise in my writing?*[23] I was taking photos of the angry Brisbane River and felt ashamed. Was I turning a tragedy into a spectacle? An exotic adventure? What the hell was I doing and why? There were already too many depictions of tragedy on the Internet, I kept thinking, while holding my camera and zooming in on a tree which was struggling against the river and its powerful energy. I kept watching this tree in the water and taking one shot after another. Would it survive? Would it win this contest of nature against nature?

We humans were deeply saddened but also amused by the horror. We were sitting or standing on the banks of the river taking photos while police were telling us to go back 'where we came from'. In my mind this innocent comment was translated literally. *Where did I come from?* I was not sure. Bosnia? Brisbane? I felt confused and paralysed

---

[23] See Simić (2008) and (2009a) for more on 'dark tourism'.

by my irrational thinking. After a second warning by the police, I called my dog Ugi, packed up my camera and walked back to my car. I felt ashamed.

I kept being connected to and disconnected from this reality, and drifted, as if on a river, through muddy memories and mixed feelings, pretending that I lived another life on another planet in my little unflooded suburb. I thought about the war and our survival during the war. I thought about the loss of my country and its people. The Brisbane tragedy stirred up my old demons, the chain of difficult memories and dreams. I became afraid of the sun appearing at dawn. What would I wake up to see? Would my tree survive the night? Tony, my friend who lived close to the river, and for whom I had been very concerned, told me: "I was disappointed that the river did not surpass the peak of water from 1974. Then I could have said, 'You survived 74?' That is nothing compared with 2011 and what I survived!'" It was a dark humour, but also a bit of 'dark tourism' honesty on his part, admitting to having that rush of adrenaline at the very thought that something bad *might* happen, that the peak would be higher than ever in history. People react oddly to tragedy. They often laugh and make jokes about things they would not dare to joke about in normal circumstances. But survivors have the authority to do so and we readily forgive them. They *have been there* and this gives them the privilege to do and say what others, supposedly, are 'not allowed to'.

After two days of flood paranoia, I disconnected from the Internet and phone. I just could not take it any more. I did not sleep well. I was thinking about the flood peak that was forecast for 4 am but was too afraid to turn on the TV and witness the fate of the city. (Shall I say 'my city'? Is it now *mine*? Was that *my* test for Australian citizenship? Did I pass with distinction because I did not betray the city in its darkest hours by fleeing from it, as I did when disaster struck my homeland?) The next morning I turned on the news at 6.30 am and burst out crying, shocked by the horror in front of me: whole suburbs and the city centre were under water. I could only see the very tops of roofs peeking above the muddy water. The Premier of Queensland, Anna Bligh, had warned us, but nothing could have prepared me for what I was seeing. The city was gone. It had sunk.

My feelings were in a tangle. What reality did we live in? Was it possible that I had enjoyed a U2 concert at a stadium (soon to be under water also), and surfing lessons on the Gold Coast with friends from Serbia, just ten days earlier? While we were enjoying our lives, other plans were being made behind our backs. Our lives had changed in the course of just two days: we could already talk about 'life before' the floods and 'life after' the floods. As my life has changed so many times over the past 15 years, one would think that nothing could surprise me any more. I have survived disaster many times but on each occasion I am still overwhelmed with the same feelings of fear, disbelief, helplessness and shock. I have to wonder if this is my 'destiny': to be followed around the world by these extreme experiences?

I am not religious or superstitious but I couldn't stop thinking about some of the disastrous events that had taken place in my life: the war in Bosnia in 1992, the NATO bombing in Serbia in 1999, an earthquake in Costa Rica in 2004 (see p. 116 for details), and the floods in Australia in 2011 (to name but a few). We live our lives at such a speed that we don't have time to fully absorb what is happening to us. We are expected to, as fast as we can, 'pull ourselves together', 'move on' and continue with our lives as if nothing had ever happened. So, while I was still trying to comprehend the floods, it was time to think about recovery. People were in their boats on the river, and revisiting their homes to face the damage. I saw lots of tears during those days; tears that brought people together, that sparked our human, natural bond. Tears that prompted our neighbours to introduce themselves to us for the first time in the 18 months since we had moved in next door. That was lovely, but why did we *all* need to wait for a disaster to bring us together for a cup of tea?

⌘⌘⌘⌘⌘⌘

Flashback: It is 8 am. I am already in my office, checking emails and reading the latest news. This is my first visit to the United States of America and I am fortunate enough to have secured a legal internship with Human Rights Watch[24] in Washington DC. I have been in the country for less than a month and I enjoy the work, my colleagues and the city. I have my blue backpack next to me and am ready to leave for the train station where I will shortly be catching a train to

---

[24] Human Rights Watch is one of the world's leading independent organisations dedicated to defending and protecting human rights. See <http://www.hrw.org>.

New York City. I am really looking forward to this trip. I am not alone in the office on this morning of 11 September, 2001. A few others are drinking their first morning coffees, slowly pacing and chatting while curling their fingers around their hot cups. The aroma of strong dark coffee wafts around me, lifting my mood, taking me back to BiH and memories of enjoying coffee with my family and friends. I am preoccupied with reading online news but notice others gathering and peering out the window. I hear some commotion but I do not bother to get up and check what is happening. A minute later, I hear cries and shouts. I jump up from my chair and look through the window. I see a cloud of smoke, but am still confused. "The Pentagon has been bombed," I hear a colleague say.

The emergency alarm suddenly sounds and we are all told to use the stairs to vacate the building. I turn away and return to my desk. I am calm, not fully comprehending what is going on. I look around. Everyone is running, bumping into one another and shouting. They are all in a hurry to reach the stairs. Unwillingly and rather slowly I make my way towards an elevator. I am the last to exit the building. For some reason I am annoyed by all the fuss and noise and just want to run away and be alone. When I step out of the elevator my colleagues look at me with astonishment and irritation on their faces. A strong, male voice comes from the crowd of frightened bodies gathered around me: "You should have taken the stairs, not the elevator." A man with curly brown hair stares at me intensely but I say nothing. Words have gone missing. I do not want anyone to talk to me. I walk down a corridor and find myself on the street. I look up and down the road and feel sick. I breathe in and breathe out. I lean against the wall of the building and watch people running in all directions. A breeze is against my skin. I want to scream, wail, slam my head against this wall. Instead, I shut my eyes for a moment. I am numb. I am cut off.

After an hour or so had passed we were able to return to our offices. I was about to leave again when my mother telephoned, sobbing. She had finally reached me from their small flat in Banja Luka. When she heard my voice, she began crying and wailing. They had already heard what had happened; news travels so fast these days. Distressed and tense, I tried to calm her by forcing a smile on to my face while holding back my own tears, "I have nine lives, remember? I am fine, all is good here." That was an utter lie but I did not have the heart to tell her the truth. My voice was muffled in the 'whoosh' of the international line while she kept weeping, "I can't believe this is happening to you again." I had survived a war, the NATO bombing of Serbia and now a terrorist attack in the USA, a place we thought was safe. My parents had watched their TV in horror with the rest of the world as the Twin Towers had collapsed and they knew that I had been due to go to New York City that morning. My friends later joked that I should always let them know my next planned destination in advance so that they can avoid it as, for sure, something bad will happen. How was it possible that I kept being in the wrong place at the wrong time? Of course my story is not that unusual: people are hit repeatedly by events when they least expect it. And in any case, on this occasion I hadn't really been hit, but I was certainly close to the 'action'.

For the rest of the day, I withdrew from the outside world. I retreated inside myself, muffling all exterior sounds and images. I crawled into my inner world; I sank into its darkness. I was constantly on the move, walking with my CD player, earplugs in, volume turned up. I walked with, and into, my past; into another world, the world only I inhabited, and I knew I would struggle to find a way out of it.

At that time I lived within walking distance of my office in a dormitory for international students. That day everyone was glued to the TV news in our common area. Whenever I passed by I would see a dozen students from around the world watching the scenes of planes crashing into the Twin Towers and the Pentagon, over and over again. I did not speak to anyone. I quickly walked through the hall towards the exit. I would leave the dormitory unnoticed, soundless, avoiding eye contact. I wanted to escape all this madness intact. I didn't understand that it was not possible. It was too late. I was already drowning in the chaos.

In the evening, on my way out, the director of the dormitory saw me. She was pale; her brown eyes, hiding behind thick glasses, were full of tears. She knew where I came from and some of the things I had been through. Standing in front of me with shock written all over her face she looked me in the eye: "Have *we* deserved this?" She was breathing heavily. I was taken aback by her question. She asked me to come to her office and then burst into tears. I was stunned. I did not know what to say. "No one deserves to be bombed. However,

I cannot truly answer your question. There are many people around the world who are angry with the USA." She shook her head and said she had never thought about politics before; about the United States' imperialist and militarist policies toward other countries. September 11 made her think for the first time that there might be something wrong with the politics of her government.

I had trouble sleeping. I had flashbacks, nightmares; my mind was occupied with the flashes and fireworks of the NATO bombings in 1999. These recurring images hit me like hammer blows, one after the other. All the fears and panic attacks I had experienced returned. The constant sound of aeroplanes above the city drove me crazy. I just wanted it all to finish.

The USA was not the safest place in the world any more. It felt like I was going back and forth from past to present to past. During the NATO bombing, I lived in a state of constant fear and anxiety for 78 days until the violence stopped. I had to learn to live from one day to the next and to have no plans for the future. Afterwards, I struggled with learning to live again as if there were a future: diaries, daily agendas and duties, and short-term and long-term plans. But in 2001, I stubbornly refused to have a diary while working for Human Rights Watch. I learnt that people in the USA have five-year plans and that they even schedule in when to drink coffee with their friends. That was beyond my comprehension. I came from a place where life was ad hoc, where there were no plans for today, tomorrow or any time after. We existed in the present and our lives and vocabulary were in the present tense. I thought all this planning was nonsense and could not bring myself to write everything down. Instead, I tried hard to remember by heart all meeting and coffee appointments. I would snap at people: "How can you plan days, weeks, months and years in advance? How do you know you will even be alive next year?" I must have sounded crazy. I honestly believed that it was not possible to have plans for the future. For almost a decade I had no plans for anything but to survive until the next day. That was all I craved.

My memories of war overwhelmed me again. I was disturbed by my flashbacks of the 1999 bombings and the feelings of hyperanxiety that had developed during the war back home. But I pretended to be calm. I was afraid and ashamed of my feelings, but did not know what to do with them or who to talk to. I thought I had to 'toughen up' and move on. I was not aware that these were classic symptoms of post-traumatic stress disorder (PTSD). Martina, my boss at the time, had a great deal of experience working with refugees, especially with women who had survived traumas. As a researcher, she was also familiar with the situation in my homeland and had been to BiH on study trips several times. She sensed that I was in trouble and suggested we go for a drink and a chat. I knew that she understood my plight; the loneliness and isolation I felt. She suspected that the terrorist attacks had triggered troubling memories for me. She was right.

It was a wet 13 September morning and people started to arrive at their offices, preparing for another day of work. By the looks on their faces, I could tell that many had not had much sleep the night before. Everyone had been glued to their TVs, too worried to think about normal, everyday life. Martina came to my office and we walked to the nearest coffee shop. It was a beautiful autumn day in Washington DC, the air was crisp and the leaves had started to turn red and gold. We eased ourselves into empty chairs. She slowly leaned forward, searching for something on my face: "How are you, dear?" I stared down at my cup of coffee as tears welled up in my eyes. I was numb. I wanted to avoid saying anything, but Martina was too dear to me to simply ignore her. Suddenly, I was overcome by uncontrollable sobs.

Martina understood that I needed help and she suggested that I see a counsellor. She knew I had accumulated all these difficult memories that needed to be sorted out so I could start to heal. Our office had hired a psychologist to treat all the staff and she asked that I meet this woman for a chat. "Please, just give it a go." I was bewildered how Americans could organise themselves so quickly, and how much attention they paid to mental health. I could hardly believe that only a day after the terrorist attacks, the organisation I worked for had already hired a psychologist who would be flown from New York City into our Washington DC office to help us deal with the shock. I was thinking how in the past ten years of my life I had never had any counselling. No one had even suggested it, let alone organised someone to work with me.

In fact, I knew almost nothing about counselling but I had a sense about what it might involve. It sounded too clinical and distant, and I was reluctant and nervous. From his Turkish perspective, Orhan Pamuk (winner of a Nobel prize and author of *Museum of Innocence*,

2008), describes a popular view of 'psychoanalysis' as the "scientific sharing of confidences invented for Westerners unaccustomed to the curative traditions of family solidarity and shared secrets" (p. 176). Indeed, counselling was equally alien to my non-Western, communal culture. We were used to solving our problems by talking to the people we knew: our family and friends. They were our counsellors. I was not comfortable talking to someone I didn't know, someone who was paid for each minute they spent listening to me, someone who knew nothing about me. How could I ever connect with and trust this stranger? It felt unnatural and imposed on me. Terms such as 'depression', 'anxiety' and 'panic attacks' did not yet exist in my vocabulary. Still, Martina was insistent. I had enormous respect for her so I decided, albeit reluctantly, to accept her suggestion. I was too tired to argue but deep down I felt annoyed by all this fuss. In fact the attention given to people around me increasingly irritated me. After all, *we* had not been hit. I did not understand why they were making it into such a big deal. Of course, I did not dare to say aloud: *Come on. This has all happened before, to me, to other people. We had no counselling, no time to cry. Pull yourself together and move on. There is no time to dwell on this thing. I survived bombing just two years ago and nothing is wrong with me.*

I thought they were overreacting. I could not stand our morning briefings and checking up on one another. I did not know that my anger and irritation was a product of something else. I did not detect the looming signs: panic attacks, flashbacks, outbursts of anger, depression and uncontrollable crying. I felt disengaged from everyone and everything around me. I withdrew into my small dark world.

The following morning I went to the appointment with the psychologist, reluctant to share anything with her. I actually did not know what I was supposed to say or do. Tell her my life story in 30 minutes? Condense the traumas and struggles to survive that had piled up over the years of war? I couldn't possibly blurt them out all at once. Confused, I forced myself to sit in the empty wooden chair. My heart and mind were in utter disarray. The psychologist told me to relax and to tell her a little bit about my life. I didn't know where to start. I have never been able to put my finger on just one incident, on something tangible, visible. This was not about a one-off event. It was an accumulation of many that had thrown my life into chaos. I had done my best to block out emotions, to repress daunting memories, to pretend nothing had happened. And now I was being invited to pour it all out in words; in *English* words.

An ache spread through my stomach while I shifted nervously in my chair. Sweat was seeping from my armpits. I shut my eyes for a second and tried to think of a suitable story to tell her, and how to phrase it in English while my mother tongue was constantly interfering. I muttered, "Too many things have happened to me since 1992 so I can only give you a snapshot." I could hear her soft voice coming from the other side of the small table standing between us. She was saying something but I was not listening; I had drifted off. I came back to the room with a jolt as she said, "Tell me whatever you want to say. I am listening."

I started to speak and in the following ten minutes I summarised the last ten years of my life. I spoke of events I wanted to forget but couldn't. This was the first time in a decade that I had revisited the previous years, and I spoke about things I had never processed, now laid bare before me. I surprised myself by listing the many shocking occurrences I had survived. Things I thought I didn't remember any more kept emerging from my subconscious, popping out from the black holes in my brain. Flashbacks, nightmares, bombs, hunger, exile. And fear. I talked in a cold, distant voice as if speaking about someone else. When I had finished I could see that she was overwhelmed. Self-consciously I glanced down at my clenched hands and then abruptly stared out the window to avoid her gaze. I felt a strong urge to escape from this place as my chaotic thoughts jostled and clashed and ran riot through my tired mind.

She rubbed her chin, swallowed, and looked me in the eye. "Look, so many things have happened to you. You should peel these layers of trauma off, but not all at once. It is not possible. Maybe we could schedule some regular sessions over the next few months." I looked around the room as if trying to find something that would make this conversation less awkward. Nothing was there. I fumbled with the pen in my hand and then dug my fingernails into my palm. "I can see no point, but thank you." I breathed out, relaxed and felt pleased that I had the courage to say it out loud and confidently. I suddenly felt lighter as I rose to my feet and turned my back to her. As far as I was concerned, the conversation was over. This decision brought me peace; but it was short-lived. At that moment, I did not know that this was the beginning of the end: the end of running away.

This conversation had cracked open the door to my inner dark world. I was afraid to face my past. I was still waiting for the right time for it to come out. I had decided not to delve into my memories because I was afraid of what I would find. I just knew that I did not want to spend the rest of my life having counselling sessions. I did not have time for them. I had other things to do. Still, deep inside me, I felt that I was simply postponing the inevitable meltdown. But for now, I was not ready.

The next couple of years passed in a blur. But something was not right. I did not have a name for this niggling disquiet and I was too afraid to confront my uneasiness. I fought it, covered it up with fake smiles; lived my life in the fast lane, filled it with people and distractions. Too often, I forced myself to be cheerful as I dragged myself off to work or study. I did everything in my power to not have time to look back. I occupied myself with reading, work, drunken nights and hanging out with friends. I talked to no one about my private battles; I guarded my secret from everyone. I noticed that I would become depressed as soon as I had time to rest and be alone with myself. I had never learned how to relax and do nothing. Whenever I was unemployed I would become anxious. Still, I thought I was tough and could go on with my life without looking back.

I was so wrong. But in 2001 I was not ready to face any of it. My brief chat with the counsellor in Washington DC was my first and last counselling session in the USA. Instead I ran away again, this time to Costa Rica in 2004, to 'heaven on earth', or so I thought.

Facing the Past Begins

In the USA in 2001, I had briefly let my past resurface but then walked away from it all. It was the first time since 1992, the beginning of the war in my home country, that I had found myself glancing back over the past years. Before that, I was constantly on the run, trying to survive. I had no time or will to reflect on my past. In the USA, I experienced the first panic attacks, flashbacks and nightmares. The terrorist attacks and September 11, 2001 reminded me of the prior war events in BiH and triggered full-blown PTSD symptoms that I did not recognise as such at the time.

Three years later, in 2004 in Costa Rica, during my studies at the UN University for Peace (UPEACE) for a Master of Arts in Gender and Peacebuilding, I experienced a return to my wartime traumas. And I also had to face another disaster: an earthquake.

I shared accommodation with a girlfriend from Tajekistan. It was a two-bedroom house in the centre of Ciudad Colón, a small town close to the capital, San José. In November 2004, two months after my arrival, I was sleeping soundly one hot, tropical night when suddenly a terrible thundering noise and a tremendous shaking woke me. I lay frozen, staring into the darkness. Then, another roaring noise. I cried out, "We are being bombed!" The room was vibrating, the walls swinging and cracking. I felt the same tremor rumbling beneath me, shaking my body, as I had felt in 1999 when NATO attacked us in Niš. The air was heavy and sticky in my mouth just as it was back then.

At first I wasn't sure if I was dreaming or if this was really happening. Everything was tumbling down—bookcases, clothes, my laptop. I watched as my books dropped from the shelves on to the floor. Others were falling on my bed, on me. I felt a sudden pain in my lower left leg as something heavy hit me. I fell to the floor as pieces of the ceiling crashed down around me. *Yes, we are being bombed, for sure.* I tried to calmly think about who could be bombing Costa Rica, and why. *Impossible. No one would bomb this place.* I was listening for aeroplanes but could only feel the trembling of the earth beneath me. I finally realised that it was not bombing but an earthquake. I felt liberated.

I heard the barefooted steps of my girlfriend quickly approaching my room. I jumped to my feet and stood under the door frame, remembering that it was the safest place during an earthquake. Tahmina ran into my arms whispering anxiously in her language. She was a small girl with long, brown hair. She buried her face in my neck and I felt her warm tears. She was speaking quickly in Tajik and I realised she was praying. She was out of her mind, quivering with fear. I felt nothing but numbness and relief that it was *only* an earthquake. I had never experienced one before. I was worried for Tahmina though, and she was sobbing uncontrollably. I tried to comfort her and gently patted her head while holding her tightly in my arms. The dishes were falling from the kitchen cupboards a few metres away making lots of noise as they smashed and scattered. I was thinking fast, asking myself what we should do next. *Should we go out or stay inside?*

I cannot tell how much time passed during the earthquake shocks but for us it felt like for ever. At some point, I decided we should go outside. I took Tahmina by the hand and we walked away from the house, stood in the middle of our garden still holding hands, and looked up at the sky. *Lots of stars tonight.* I looked over to my friend, and managed to give her a smile and say that it was all over and we were safe now.

The next day we found out that this earthquake was one of the strongest in the history of Costa Rica, with a magnitude of 6.2 on the Richter scale. More than 100 aftershocks were registered following the main quake. Eight people had died and a great deal of property had been damaged.[25] All the phone lines and towers had been destroyed and we were cut off from rest of the world for a day. But I felt calm. After all, it had not been bombs—that was the most important point as far as I was concerned.

⌘⌘⌘⌘⌘⌘

Among that year's intake of students for the Master of Arts I was the only one from the former Yugoslavia. Soon after my arrival I realised with a jolt that my studies were going to be largely based on human rights violations committed by 'my' people: the war events in the former Yugoslavia had been chosen as one of the key case studies. I had not expected that. People assumed that, having survived the war, I would be 'the expert', and would be able to comment insightfully on the terrible acts of violence that had been committed.

What did I know about the 1995 massacre at Srebrenica? What about the rapes of Bosniak women by the Serb army? Or Serb women raped by Croat and Bosniak soldiers? What about the atrocities against Albanians in Kosovo by Serbian forces that prompted the 1999 NATO bombings of Serbia? When did I learn about them? What were my thoughts about Slobodan Milošević who was the President of Serbia from 1989 to 1997, and later was tried for crimes against humanity by the International Criminal Tribunal for the former Yugoslavia in The Hague? What about my Bosnian compatriot General Ratko Mladić who is accused of being responsible for the almost four-year-

---

[25] Costa Rica, 'Disasters and Calamities' <http://costa-rica-guide.com/travel/index.php? option=com_content&task=view&id=324&Itemid=545> (accessed 14 February 2014).

long siege of Sarajevo (1992–1996) and the Srebrenica massacre? And Bosnian Serb Radovan Karadžić who is also accused of genocide and crimes against humanity—what did I know about his deeds? The truth was—back then, I did not know much at all.

On occasions, it felt like I was the one on trial for these atrocities—when in reality, when I was living in exile in Serbia from 1992 to 1999, many of us knew very little of what was happening around us. Moreover, any news we received had already been filtered through a Serbian perspective. But most importantly, I was really not politically aware or active until I studied in Costa Rica. I feel uncomfortable about my delusion and political innocence now, but this is exactly where I was at the time. I had spent the war years struggling to survive and stay safe. Until my arrival in Costa Rica I mostly avoided reading, listening or engaging in stories about my country and the horrific crimes committed. After all, I had experienced some of it, and had no desire to spend time thinking about or studying it. Of course, I was naive. How on earth could I expect to engage with peace and conflict studies in the first decade of the twenty-first century and avoid talking about war crimes in my 'own backyard'?

For some time, I was seriously considering leaving university altogether but it was too late to run away. I was in this gorgeous country, famous for its natural beauty which attracted thousands of tourists each year. I was surrounded by people from various races and ethnicities, many of them fellow survivors of war and trauma. I had to accept that the time had come to face my past—all of it. I was no longer constantly running on adrenaline for sheer survival. I was far away from my homeland and I was in a secure and secluded place with lots of time for reflection. For the first time in a decade I had no other work than to think, write and talk about the past.

The more I read and studied, the more terrified I became. Alexandra Stiglmayer's edited collection, *Mass Rape: The War Against Women in Bosnia-Herzegovina* (1994) in which she interviewed mostly Muslim survivors of rape, was one of the first books that provided me with an in-depth perspective on rapes committed by my compatriots.[26] I could not believe that all this had happened in my country. Were these

---

[26] Alexandra Stiglmayer's 1994 book, with additional pieces by Catharine MacKinnon, Rhonda Copelon, and Susan Brownmiller, and an afterword by Cynthia Enloe, was a revelation for me.

people my neighbours? What had happened to them that they became capable of acting in such atrocious ways? I kept reading obsessively— it was as if I had to catch up on a 'lost' decade in a matter of weeks. I read Ruth Seifert, Donna Pankhurst, Lepa Mladjenovic, Nancy Hartsock, Donna Hughes and many others. I was sad, depressed, and would often burst into tears in the classroom or wherever I was. I was tired, cranky and easily irritated most of the time and, for no apparent reason, angry. All sorts of memories crowded my brain; flashbacks of various events popped up, including the recent earthquake.

I would subsequently learn that this was nothing unusual; that trauma memories can arise years later, in fact, many years later. They come when we don't expect them; when we stop running for survival and have some distance, some space to pause, and look them straight in the eye; when we start to question certain things and confront them. To this day, the memories of my troubled past invade my consciousness without prompting. Often, an image, or simply a particular smell, can trigger them. The difference now is that I am equipped to react rationally rather than emotionally when this occurs.

I discovered later that I was not the only one who started the process of questioning the past while doing her studies. Ronit Yarosky, a young Jewish woman and human rights activist who lives in Israel, described the process of discovering the truth while doing her master's thesis:

> Most of these memories from my military service only came back to me after some ten years. They were transformative events, only I did not realise it at the time. The change within me began when I started to question and think and ask, while I was doing my MA research ... This was the beginning of a total, albeit slow, metamorphosis for me, my turning point—the realisation that there is more than one story in history. There are multiple stories (2012, pp. 99–100).

Like Ronit, I felt something had cracked in me during 2004, and there was no way of turning back to avoidance and ignorance of the past. The process of dealing with the past had started right there in the classroom, and in the university library where I spent hours reading. The findings and facts washed over me like a tsunami. I was drowning in the horrors that people—*my* people—had committed. Although I was one of the most engaged students in the class, I struggled with sleepless nights, flashbacks and panic attacks. I was beset by memories of war, persistent mood swings and fluctuating irrational anger. Still, I did not know how to name these symptoms nor did I think to ask for help. I did not have a clue what was going on. I knew that something was not right but could not name it. I was deeply sad, confused and troubled, but nevertheless convinced that I was tough enough to resolve the problem myself. My mind was in denial but my body was betraying me with intense pain and symptoms I could not control. I was drowning in a darkness that saturated my heart slowly but irrevocably. I convinced myself that I could rewrite my experience with a new narrative, that I could selectively forget the bad things and remember only the good ones. I was still pretending, to some degree, that I suffered from amnesia. I deluded myself.

My mental health deteriorated to the point where I was afraid to sleep alone in my house in Ciudad Colón. I tried to believe that this was all just a bad dream which would eventually vanish. As one of the characters in Erich Maria Remarque's classic *Three Comrades* (1998) says: "Sometimes I used to think that one day I should wake up, and all that had been would be over, forgotten, sunk, drowned. Nothing was for sure—not even memory" (p. 392). I was struggling to stay afloat in the sea of my traumatic experiences but was pulled into the whirlpool of emotions and experiences.

Despite being aware that the ground was shifting beneath me, I was still functioning more or less 'normally' in the eyes of friends and colleagues. I attended all classes and completed my assignments on time, often receiving the highest grades. I never asked for an extension because, in my view, to seek one was a sign of weakness. I was used to working beyond my capacities. I continued to hide my pain, and suffer through sleepless nights. Each day I would wake up, rub my eyes, take a few deep breaths, put on my 'happy face' and get on with the day. I lived a double life: a fake life with my friends and colleagues, and a real life when I was alone. I was pretending that things were fine while everything was falling apart. I did not want to disclose to anyone how I felt: ashamed and weak for not being able to control my emotions. No one knew that I was on the edge. I never thought about taking my own life, but my emotional pain was deep. I was in a pool of sadness, and joy was sucked out of me. My view of life was grim. None of my professors noticed that I had severe problems, or at least they did not tell me so. Little by little, I was sliding into mental darkness. My body and mind were raw and vulnerable to the slightest triggers. The layers of anxiety that had been building up over the years were now so thick and heavy that it was only a matter of time before they imploded.

One sunny afternoon I came back from the university to find that my house had been burgled. My laptop, with all my assignments, personal documents, and photos from the last few years, had been stolen. This event, coupled with my already strained mental state, was the breaking point, and I could no longer stay alone in my home. One of my closest classmates invited me to move into her place. I readily agreed, as I felt I was unable to look after myself. I craved warmth and affection. She welcomed me into her home and cared for me. For a few days I just lay in bed. I refused to eat, could not sleep, and was in constant fear. With my friend's gentle insistence I finally rose to my feet one morning to drink the cup of black coffee she had prepared for me. My spirits lifted briefly and I felt a sudden urge to check my emails for any news from my family or friends. It was hot and humid. I was wearing my bright yellow dressing gown, and slowly drinking my coffee while flicking through emails. I opened one that was sent by my close friend from Sarajevo, Selma. I read it, and instantly felt a horrific jagged pain stabbing every part of my body. I could barely breathe. Selma wrote that our friend Mojca had died in a car accident near Sarajevo. She was with some work colleagues when the car slipped on the icy road. She died the same day in hospital from severe injuries. She was only 31 years old. The news hit me like a powerful physical blow. I flinched. I was falling into darkness. I screamed and collapsed. I blacked out.

The next thing I remember was seeing two men in white gowns bending over me, and whispering something to each other and to my friend, in hospital. I was shaking and tears were streaming down my face. I lifted my eyes towards the doctors and heard one of them say slowly: "She has PTSD." I felt a lump in my throat. Through the blur of tears, I could see the doctors and hear what they were saying, but their voices sounded infinitely distant. The room was still. I blacked out again.

Of course I had heard about PTSD but thought it could only affect ex-combatants. It did not occur to me that civilians might suffer from such a disorder. I would only understand later that my flashbacks, nightmares, panic attacks, uncontrollable crying, irrational and misdirected anger, loss of emotional engagement and distancing myself from the people I love, were in fact symptoms of distress. I learned about it only in 2004—12 years after the war had started—the first time I experienced a nervous breakdown. It took me time to understand that a breakdown was a natural emotional reaction to abnormal and deeply traumatic events, and that it sometimes can be chronic.

I stayed in a psychiatric ward in San José Hospital for a week. I caught glimpses of people passing by my room but I could not distinguish between patients and visitors. I refused food and drink and did not want to talk to anyone. I rapidly lost weight and became too weak to walk. I could not make trips to the bathroom without assistance. I was covered in plastic tubes attached to machines which kept nutrients and water flowing through my veins. I was reduced to sobbing and despair and was at times completely numb. I tried to force my body to move, but it felt like it was cemented to the hospital bed. My mouth was sealed shut. Words could not find their way out. I could move only my eyes. From the corner of my eye, I would see the nurses measuring my blood pressure, and leaving a tray of food that would remain untouched. Each day nurses would come to bathe me. They would sit me on a chair and take off my clothes. They would lean my body against a chilly bathroom wall and I could feel the warm water droplets falling down on my face and further down on my dead limbs. My bare feet would be cold. I was indifferent to everything around me. I waited for it all to finish. My mind was blank.

I had daily visits from a psychiatrist who was trying to make me talk. He was tall with a round face and blue eyes. I guessed that he was in his late fifties. He had dark hair and his voice was soft but determined. He was a local, but spoke to me in impeccable English. I grew fond of him and although my lips were still sealed, I began looking forward to seeing him. He was the only connection I had with the outside world; someone who was trying to help me. Still, I pretended I was deaf. I had no will or energy to say anything. I was overwhelmed by helplessness: emotional 'numbing' indifference. I was so weak that I could not protest when the doctors decided to make a final check on whether something was physically wrong with me or whether the root of my problems was in my head. I was in a state of 'stupor' as they called it, in a state of inertia and lethargy. On the third day, a team of doctors wheeled me into a room to perform a CT scan of my brain. I was terrified of the long tube, but could not find words to protest. I wondered if anyone would see how upset I was and would stop. Everyone was too busy with setting up the scan machine and moving my limp body from the hospital trolley to the sliding table that would be pushed inside the CT tube. I saw the block of light coming from the tube and I held my breath. I needed to calm down but I couldn't. I squeezed the side of my right leg to check if I was alive. I felt nothing. So it did not matter what they did to me. After what seemed an eternity, they pulled my head from the tube. They rolled my body back on to the trolley and returned me to my room. I felt like a sack of potatoes that could be moved around at will. The doctors could not find anything wrong with my brain. It was 'officially' declared that it was my mental, emotional being that was in tatters. I was not sure whether that was good or bad news. All I knew was that I felt as if the end of the world was approaching fast and I was ready to vanish with it.

After about a week, the doctors decided to discharge me from the hospital. I was still very weak but well enough to stand and to start communicating with the two dear female colleagues who had been visiting me on almost a daily basis. The psychiatrist decided that I needed ongoing medication and therapy. I had been taking antidepressants for a couple of days and would continue to take them for the following few months. We agreed that because my return to BiH was imminent, starting counselling in Costa Rica would not make much sense. Instead, I was advised to seek out a psychologist trained to work with people who suffered from PTSD once I was home. I was told I needed someone with expertise in cognitive behavioural therapy (CBT)[27] who would work with me on a regular basis and for the long term. Since I had lost so much weight and was taking sedatives on a daily basis, I had to tell my parents about my medical condition. I wanted to prepare them for my new 'skinny look', but I struggled to explain that I was suffering from PTSD without them thinking that I was 'crazy'.

---

[27] CBT is considered to be one of the best therapies for people who suffer from PTSD as it helps to address and confront the root causes of a problem. It teaches the individual how to manage symptoms, to learn to accept and live with them.

Back in the former Yugoslavia there was a lot of stigma about any form of mental disorder and I was worried how my parents would react to my condition. They had always considered me a strong and capable child, the one they would proudly show off to their friends and relatives. They ignored all my weaknesses and shortcomings and always strived to present me in the best light. I had good reason to believe that they would not accept that something was 'wrong' with their little girl. Denial was a much easier option. Aung San Suu Kyi, a well-known Burmese politician and winner of the Nobel Peace Prize, has observed that there are people "who simply cannot face the truth, not just about themselves, but even about those who are near and dear to them ... There are people who always think that their children are lovely and have no faults" (2008, p. 201).

My state of mind was the result of external forces, forces beyond my control. My response to such forces was a normal human reaction to terror and trauma but still my parents struggled to understand it. They could not accept that PTSD had 'struck' their daughter and might be a lifelong response to what we all went through in the war. When I told my mother over the phone from Costa Rica that I was diagnosed with PTSD she did not hide her disbelief: "How come? They [doctors] are overreacting. You will be fine." I did not expect complete understanding from my mother but 'you will be fine' felt like an insult. It made me sound like I was a little girl who was talking nonsense. I said that I needed to take sedatives and go to therapy over the next few months, or even years, but she brushed it off. My parents were convinced that it was something like influenza or a stomach ache: you take pills and, after some weeks, feel better and move on with your life. They were also convinced that PTSD was an ailment suffered only by combatants, not by civilians; and, after all, I had not been in combat. My parents did not want to acknowledge that these were emotional scars that could last a lifetime. Nothing would be the same again.

In his powerful memoir, *Exit Wounds* (2012), Australian Major General John Cantwell, writes:

> I think of my mental scars in the same way I think of the entry and exit wounds I saw in the bodies of some of my soldiers. The entry wound is often very small; sometimes it goes unnoticed. But the projectile does its

work inside the body, tearing and destroying ... Often, the deformed and somersaulting bullet or piece of shrapnel will exit the body with great force, tearing a large exit wound in the back of the victim's body. I believe the same process applies to the mind: a traumatic memory pierces the consciousness and then tumbles through, causing an ugly, gaping wound. It's sometimes hard to determine why certain experiences breach the mind's natural defences, but their destructive wake is obvious (p. 5).

I can relate to this statement. I did not try to convince my parents that trauma had affected my life and turned it upside down. I will probably never tell them that there are scars under my skin that won't ever fade away.

And so we never talked about my state of mind again. My parents were worried that our neighbours might find out or, even worse, our relatives; that I might be perceived as 'damaged goods' and possibly unmarriageable, and need lifelong material and health support. They did not want to understand the devastating impact of war on their daughter, and they could not bear to think about the possible consequences. I could not blame them—I too needed a long time to accept the fact that trauma is not something that will vanish after a few counselling sessions but will hold my hand for the rest of my life. It will just change its appearance; sometimes it will be manageable and sometimes not. I spent many hours with my counsellor working on dealing with the pain. I did not tell anyone about my condition for a long time. I was ashamed and felt that people around me would not understand. I was angry with myself that I could not handle my reaction to trauma on my own. I considered myself weak and lacking control of my life. How could someone who seems so normal and healthy on the outside have such chaos on the inside?

From the outside, no one could tell that I was carrying scars. I was constantly afraid of people's prejudices and assumptions; afraid of losing my new job, my new partner, and my new career, if I told anyone. The idea of people looking at me as a 'sick person' horrified me. I knew how much stigma there was about people with mental health issues. But, after some time, I accepted it, as did Chris, an Iraqi ex-combatant who noted: "You're never going to be the same. You've just got to learn to live with how you are and let it not interfere with your life. I still am very vigilant, but I keep it under control" (Gonzales, 2012, p. 82).

This is exactly what I have been working on for years: to keep things under control, to accept them as they are but learn how to function on a daily basis without allowing them to mess up my life. And this is a fact of life for people struggling with past trauma. There is no cure for memory and the traumas etched within it. What one has to learn is how to manage the symptoms so they do not constantly intrude on one's life.

As if this episode and collapse had not been enough, just before I left Costa Rica, another misfortune had occurred. I was still on medication and very weak, recovering after my stay in hospital. I was on my way back from the movies with my friend Deb from the USA. It was not late, but it was dark, and we were waiting for the bus. Suddenly, a young, thin man wearing a 'hoody' over his head, and holding a knife in his right hand, ran towards me and grabbed my purse. Deb started to scream and I found myself on the ground. He dragged my weak body along the pavement. I clung to my purse, holding it as if my whole life depended on it. I saw the knife in his hand but still did not want to let go of my purse. All of my documents and my wallet were in there. The whole scene seemed to last for an eternity but it was probably no more than minute or two. I finally had to let go of it and he jumped into the car that was waiting for him. My body was bruised. The following morning we went to the police station. The police officer could read on my face that I had no hope of them ever finding my belongings. He asked me where I was from.

"Bosnia and Herzegovina," I muttered. My eyes were heavy, locked in a dull stare. I just wanted to finish this useless procedure and leave. I did not hide my emotions.

"You mean 'Botswana'."

I frowned. "No."

He pushed his chair back from his desk and laughed as if he just discovered something hilarious. "We have no such country in our system." His eyes were locked on the computer in front of him and an antiquated database that had obviously not been updated in the past ten years. "Is that a new country? What was it called before?" he asked, flustered.

I looked at him. "It is not really new. It was established in 1992 and we are now in 2005. Before it was known as 'Yugoslavia'."

"Why didn't you say so!" he exclaimed. "Here! We have Yugoslavia!"

I looked over his shoulder and, indeed, on the screen in front of me, written in big capital letters, was the name of my homeland: Y U G O S L A V I A. For a moment I was so excited that my eyes were sparkling and I could not stop smiling. My beloved and deceased country still 'existed' somewhere on this earth! Costa Rica must have been the last nation in the world which continued to use that name. Very soon after this brief encounter with the police, I left the country for good. As I had suspected, the Costa Rican police never did find my bag, or the thief.

The whole Costa Rica period became one of the most profound experiences in my life, one that will mark and change my life for ever. I reached bottom, I crashed, I melted down. I came to the point where I lost the will to live. I have never felt like that before nor since. I obviously wanted, and found, the strength to move on. I decided I wanted to live. I was still struggling and thinking I could do it on my own, but deep down I knew I needed help to pull myself out of the darkness. I clung to denial, but a door had cracked open. I was torn by grief, yearning for the life that was gone. I needed to deal with everything that happened to me regardless of the risk and the price I might have to pay; regardless that it might take the rest of my life. Once back home I continued the writing on war atrocities that I had begun in Costa Rica. It was, and still is, an important part of dealing with my past, and contributes to my ongoing survival.

I also found a counsellor with years of experience in working with ex-combatants. This was the beginning of a painful but necessary journey. For six months I travelled twice a week from Belgrade to Novi Sad to my counselling sessions. It was scary at the beginning. I cried, I was desperate, but slowly I started to recover. The therapy helped me to confront the root causes of the problem: my traumatic war experiences that I had never dealt with. I changed my view about my past. I learnt how to embrace and accept it without fear. I pushed my body and my mind to the limit. After six months I was able to stop using antidepressants and visited my counsellor only occasionally. I was not cured but I was mended. I took my life in my own hands and felt that I could take full responsibility for it again. I knew that if I needed help, it would always be there for me. That was very reassuring.

CHAPTER SIX

Between Remembering and Forgetting

> There is something incredibly lonely about grieving. It's like living in a country where no one speaks the same language as you. When you come across someone who does, you feel as though you could talk for hours.
>
> —Claire Bidwell Smith, *The Rules of Inheritance* (2012, p. 234)

My life, as is the case for many survivors, is divided into two parts: before the war, and after the war. References to my life are captured in this timeline as I am trapped and torn between the present and the past. I try to make sense of war experiences that had an impact not only on my everyday life, but on the lives of loved ones around me. I often think that I coexist as two distinct persons: one who lived before the 1990s and another whose life was marked by the beginning of the war. These two individuals look at each other in the mirror every day; they breathe together and although they have one mind and one body, they have separate existences. Daily, I walk the fine line between remembering the past and not thinking about it at all.

Psychologists such as Jens Brockmeier argue that, in fact, remembering and forgetting are two parts of "one constructive process" in which parts of the past are "deemed to be obscured, repressed or forgotten" while "selected fragments of memory" keep getting organised and reorganised into "meaningful schemata" (2002, p. 22). Selected fragments of my memory are indeed continuously organised and reorganised and have a significant presence in my mind. Flashbacks can occur at any time, often in response to triggers such as television scenes about bombing, violence or killings in any country. Certain smells and sounds can bring on particularly vivid flashbacks.

Unexpected loud noises terrify me. I am wary of fireworks and the sound of low-flying aeroplanes. I become anxious in crowded situations. In 2001, while still recovering from my recent experience of September 11 in the United States, I attempted to spend New Year's Eve on the streets of Zagreb in Croatia. I was excited until I came very close to the city centre, and was suddenly surrounded by masses of people with fireworks everywhere around me. In an instant, my good mood turned to despair; my mind was crowded with fear and I found myself squatting on the ground, shielding myself from imaginary bombs. I panicked and felt tears rolling down my cheeks. My heart was racing and I struggled to breathe. I was a wreck, terrified and ashamed. I didn't know what to say to my friend Marcel from Holland who could not understand my behaviour and was genuinely worried. I got to my feet, shook my head and looked up at him. "Sorry, I have to go back to my hotel room. I don't feel well." Disturbing thoughts raced through my mind, but I managed to sound lucid and reasonable. I tried to ignore, and fight against, the wave of images and flashbacks, reminders of the 1999 NATO bombing. All in vain.

The thump of falling shells filled my ears as I was transported back to Niš, where I had lived at the time. Memories flooded my mind: the fear of the next shell landing on top of me; the horror in the eyes of my friend who had survived a cluster bombing of the marketplace; bodies, limbs and torsos of people blown to pieces by explosives. I recalled my friend who had been operating on a man when a bomb fell in front of the hospital and the windows of the operating theatre had crashed to pieces behind her back. I could not stop thinking about this as all the other events of those years rolled over me. Puzzled, Marcel asked: "Why? What is wrong?" I did not know what to say. "I don't know. I just need to leave this place, that's all." I felt a lump in my throat while I was fighting back tears.

I was utterly unwilling to explain that fireworks reminded me of the 78 nights of bombing by NATO. I was afraid that, no matter how hard I tried to explain, the story would sound incoherent. I had not yet made sense of it to myself, so how could I expect it to make sense to someone else? It was New Year's Eve and I felt I should let Marcel go and enjoy it. I paused, looked back at him and walked away.

I also feared that my dear friend Marcel might try to legitimise the 1999 bombing. My stomach tightens with anxiety whenever I hear someone justifying NATO's 'humanitarian intervention' which I, like many others in the peace movement, consider a euphemism for 'bombing'. I react to these justifications with emotions that I cannot contain. I will never accept violence as a solution to violence, and become easily agitated when I see bombing on television.

In 2006, after I had just arrived in Australia to start my doctorate, I attended a lecture given by a colleague whose doctoral research attempted to legitimise these 'humanitarian interventions' in countries around the world. I was so upset while listening to the arguments she put forward that I could feel my heart pounding, my cheeks burning and my hands sweating. I put my hand up and with a trembling voice made a comment that violence cannot be resolved with violence. "Of course," she replied, but added that "on some occasions violence is necessary."

I disagree, but can't articulate it; emotionally I begin spiralling back to 1999. The imagery of my past slowly creeps into the here and now and takes over my mind and body. I am in the lecture theatre trying to compose myself and distract myself with other thoughts. But, I can't. Instead I am overwhelmed by electrifying fear. I am thrown back to the days and nights of bombing. I can see myself shaking under the blanket in my garage, with my hands over my ears, my eyes half shut, trying not to hear or see the flashes of bombs falling around my house. I am in a room on the first floor of the two-storey house. I want to close my eyes to avoid looking, but can't, so I concentrate on sounds. There is the hateful whistle of a powerful bomb heading towards the ground; the noise rolls into every corner of the room. The whooshing roar of a launched rocket drives me insane. That noise will stay with me for ever.

It is past 2 am. NATO's 'invisible pilots' often bomb us at this time: a time when we should be sound asleep, and not expecting a threat to our lives. In the beginning, NATO soldiers only bombed at night, and during the day we could at least breathe. But it wasn't long before daytime bombing began as well. It is chilly outside, but I am sweating. My whole body is tense and alert. My skin is covered in goosebumps. Every muscle on my face is tight. I try to contract and release them, but in vain. My feet are cold, and I can feel my blood pressure dropping. I keep the bed covers pulled around me. Fear has swallowed me.

I don't look around my room but I feel the warmth of a human body on my right side. My friend Milka is in bed next to me, holding me tight while my whole body shakes uncontrollably. I stare at the wall in front of me and the big lightning ball expanding on it. I fix my eyes on this wall. My whole world ends there. I can only imagine what lies beyond it. The ball is reflecting a silhouette of a bomb that is growing before my eyes. I can discern its direction because of the way the light falls on the wall. At the beginning, it is small and barely visible in the twilight but the closer the bomb is to the ground, the bigger its hulking shape grows. Its red and gold flashes spill over the darkness, hitting the power stations, railroad stations, bridges, military command and control centres on the ground. *Will the next one fall down right on top of us?* I sink deeper into my bed. I want the earth to open up and swallow me. The room is spinning. I feel the shock waves in my bones. The house rocks and rattles on its foundations with each tremor. This is not the first time I have been bombed, but every time feels like the first. I push myself closer to the warm body next to me. I hold my breath, transfixed on the light in front of me.

I can hear Milka's breathing. In the flashes of light I look up at her wide open eyes. She whispers, "Everything is going to be fine. This will pass very quickly. You know it will." I want so badly to trust her. I snuggle my head into her neck. The bomb finally hits the ground with a flash of detonation. The relentless brutality of bombing continues for half an hour. We lie and wait in the darkness, wondering whether the next shell will be our last. Finally, the sound of bombing echoes and fades. I stare into the darkness, listening for the return of aeroplanes. Silence. They won't come back for the next few hours at least. We know the drill because we have survived these blasts before. I sigh; the knot in my stomach slowly untightens. My head is buzzing from explosions, but I push myself from the bed and crawl to the window. Relief washes over us. I squeeze my arm to check I'm still here. It hurts. Good. I've survived another night.

I leave the lecture theatre shaking, and desperately trying not to cry. I can't crumble now. I search for something that will settle my mind, but I can't move on from the scenes of bombing in my mind. Helen, a lecturer who knows where I am from and heard my comment, comes and sits down beside me, leaning forward to take my hand. This spontaneous act of kindness eases the tension in my whole body and I start to cry. Tears stream down my cheeks. I am ashamed because I cannot control them. I take a deep breath. I can hardly move my lips and it takes all my willpower to look up at her and say, "I am sorry but I just can't accept that bombing is fine. These people did not experience it. If they did, they would never argue for it. Bombing cannot bring good to anyone." Helen looks at me with her kind blue eyes. I can feel her fingers wrapped around mine. "I know. I agree. It is good that you said so." Her smile is genuine. I lean against her and feel a bit better.

During my first months in Australia I often had such outbursts of crying, but with the passage of time they have gradually abated. Eight years later, I still consider how much energy and strength I have spent on trying to contain my experiences and feelings since the war.

Almost a decade after the NATO bombing, while teaching a course in international peacekeeping at the University of Queensland in 2008, I met an older man named Paul who told me he had been a military pilot in the Australian air force. Since we were both interested in military politics, we started discussing current affairs and the various 'humanitarian interventions' that were often led by the USA. He mentioned that he had served during the Gulf War (also known as 'Operation Desert Storm'), as Australia was a member of the international coalition.

Paul told me that while he had not been personally involved in the bombing of Serbia, *he knew people who had been involved*. He said it in a low voice and without any implied judgement. My mind was racing. I looked at him in disbelief: had he just said that he knows *the people who bombed me*? What was I supposed to do with this information? What was I supposed to say? What were the odds that the two of us would ever meet like this? His quick confession struck me as if he had told me something very confidential. I was intrigued and afraid at the same time. The pilots that bombed us for 78 days and nights suddenly became very real in my mind. I could imagine that *these people* now lived ordinary lives.

For a few moments, both of us were preoccupied with our own thoughts as we continued to walk down the hall towards the elevators that would soon separate us. I panicked at the thought of losing this unique opportunity. I wanted him to tell *the people he knew* what I thought of them.

So I told him that I had been living in Serbia at the time. His look expressed a mixture of astonishment and bewilderment. He fixed his eyes on me and said nothing for a moment or two. It was probably strange for him to meet and look into the eyes of someone who had survived such an ordeal. He said that his former colleague, a pilot from Italy, was involved in 'Operation Merciful Angel', as the NATO bombing campaign was euphemistically called. I found this name particularly disturbing and humiliating and I did not hold back in expressing what I thought of the bombings. It was so far from anything one could call 'merciful'. We talked about the 'banality' of the pilot's 'work' which entailed launching a few bombs from the Aviano airbase in Italy on to villages, towns, bridges and other infrastructure deemed by NATO to be military targets. In just 'doing their work' this pilot and his colleagues had probably never heard of, or cared about, the places they hit with their mortars. Paul told me how, for the pilots, all of this horror boiled down to 'the job' they were qualified for and were expected to do as military men. But the Italian pilot had told him how it did feel 'awkward'. Once he had launched the bombs, he would go home to his wife and children, have dinner and watch television. So he had apparently questioned his 'work' and felt somewhat uncomfortable about it.

I recall how the story about the unknown pilot struck me. I had never thought about the people, mostly men, who dropped the bombs from their invisible planes, or who launched missiles from who knows where onto Serbia. I certainly had never thought about these people as ordinary humans who would wake up each morning, drink their coffee and go to work to launch destructive weaponry on people just like them. Now, after this brief exchange with a former pilot, I wondered whether they ever had nightmares. *Had they ever considered that they might have killed a child, a woman or a man on that particular sunny day?* I was curious to find out how they made sense of their work.

I found some answers while reading John Cantwell's *Exit Wounds* (2012). A retired former Australian Major General, Cantwell was at the front line in 1991 in the first Iraq war (the 'Gulf War') when Coalition forces murdered innocent Iraqis. His book provides a humble and honest account of one man's involvement in what was dubbed 'The War on Terror'. It is a portrayal of life on a modern battlefield, where war ruins everything and leaves irreparable emotional scars. In this raw and personal exposition, Cantwell writes without shame about his struggles with post-traumatic stress disorder as a result of his deployment in Iraq and Afghanistan. It is a compelling story of the impact of war on military personnel, a tale that professional soldiers are not meant to tell. They are expected to be physically and psychologically tough and aggressive. Cantwell's account exposes the myth that we can stay unaffected by the destruction of life around us. His descriptions of how professional soldiers felt while watching the carpet bombing of Iraqi cities in 1991 is gut-wrenching:

> [O]ther men have gathered, like us, to watch *the show* [my emphasis] from behind their armoured personnel carriers. There is an occasional yell and I see a raised fist applauding the deadly work. The excitement is infectious ... For a time there is silence before I speak. 'Can you imagine what it must have been like to be under that?' Pete, his eyes wide and his voice almost reverent, responds: 'Who could live through something like that?' No one answers. The truth is I am not really thinking about the people beneath all this (pp. 10–11).

There is nothing surprising in this account, but I am disturbed by Cantwell's honesty and how he normalises the bombings as a 'show'. The excitement and exuberance on seeing bombs falling on other humans is perceived by military men as natural and logical. Military training provides a rationale for the satisfaction of having power over the lives and deaths of others (see Barry, 2010, for insight into military training). Distance from the target and psychological disengagement discourage soldiers from thinking about actual humans beneath the bombing. Indeed, to do so would make the deadly work difficult; perhaps even impossible. Soldiers need to dehumanise enemies in order to be able to kill them. There is no place for empathy and the value of human life. As Kathleen Barry points out, they need to "override their humanity" and "kill without remorse, to act without a conscience" (2010, p. 32). We should be afraid of such inhumanity encouraged by the military system. As Ivo Andrić once famously stated: "One shouldn't be afraid of humans ... but what is inhuman in them" (1978, p. 54).

In her memoir, *Ordinary Courage* (2010), Donna Mulhearn, an Australian human rights activist, writes about her experience of volunteering as a 'human shield' during the bombing of Baghdad in Iraq in 2003 by the 'Coalition of the Willing'. Donna joined hundreds of people from around the world to protect Iraqis with their own bodies, forming small teams to protect major infrastructure sites, such as water treatment plants, power stations and communication centres. She writes about Iraqis who were indeed 'beneath' the bombing; about mutilated bodies shredded by flying glass; about shrapnel lodged deep in flesh and bone; about buildings that "shake and tremble as if an earthquake has struck"; about people taking "refuge in their homes, which happen to be in the vicinity of a target" (p. 191).

I assume that from a soldier's perspective there is no difference between civilians and soldiers. There can't be in aerial bombing. I can't stop thinking, however, that in the eyes of the soldiers who bombed Serbia, Iraq and Afghanistan, innocent civilians were deemed worthless. All of them would be considered 'collateral damage', a new term invented to further dehumanise people (Caldicott, 2007, p. 16). They would remain unknown to the soldiers who launched the rockets. NATO pilots will never know which of them bears responsibility for killing three-year-old Milica Rakić who was in the bathroom of her family unit in Belgrade (Serbia) when it was bombed on 17 April 1999. Since the bombing had started, Milica had been afraid to go alone to the bathroom. But on this occasion, for the first time, when her mother Dušica offered to go with her, Milica replied, "No, I will go by myself." She wanted to prove that she was 'a big girl' now. Milica was sitting on her potty when shrapnel smashed through the walls and windows and into her tiny body. She immediately bled to death. One of the pieces of shrapnel hit the house across the road and ended up in the leg of her 21-year-old neighbour, Dražen Janković. Milica, Dražen and thousands of other children, women and men are invisible to soldiers. They will never know the names and faces of the people they injured or killed.

In *Frames of War* (2009) Judith Butler explores violence and the ways in which the West wages modern warfare. In these wars, people on the ground are easy targets who are already doomed, rather than living populations whose lives are precious and precarious. She argues that their lives are "ungrievable" (p. 38) and goes on to ask: "Why is it that we are not given the names of all the war dead, including those the US has killed, of whom we will never have the image, the name, the story, never a testimonial shard of their life, something to see, to touch, to know?" (p. 39). American soldiers lost in battle are hallowed in public obituaries which are perceived as acts of nation-building. These lives are "grievable," claims Judith Butler (2004, p. xiv). Meanwhile, Butler observes, there is a state of national melancholia that comes from the erasure from public representations of the names, images, and narratives of those people killed by the US (p. xiv). These invisible women, men and children are killed from a distance; bombed from thousands of metres away. *We* could never see their planes. *They* could never see our human faces. This fact makes their 'work' more palatable. Modern wars provide this distance of not knowing whether you just killed a human or not. It makes it much easier to kill without remorse.

Minefields

For a long time after the war ended in 1999, I had no patience for, or interest in, the frivolous and dull concerns of ordinary life. The banal conversations of some of my friends and colleagues—about shopping centres, clothing, bargain sales, reality shows, and the latest movies— would drive me to distraction. I thought it was all so pointless. I had nothing to say. I would think of people dying from violence and poverty. I would think about friends with no jobs, no security and facing a bleak future back in Bosnia and Herzegovina (BiH). But most of the time I didn't share any of these thoughts for fear of causing offence. I was aware that the emotions I had were disproportionate, but the war had altered my priorities. I had become obsessively interested in wars and the violence being unleashed around the world. Not surprisingly, I felt incredibly lonely. There was always a piece of me that felt apart from everyone else as my mind often unexpectedly drifted away.

Even now, when I step onto a soccer field or take a walk through a forest, I have flashbacks. They bring back the memory of one sunny afternoon in 2000 that I spent in eastern BiH with my friend and colleague, Saša, and our client, Savo. Saša and I were working with an international agency on a 'minority return assistance' project and our job was to meet with people who wanted to return to their pre-war houses. We worked in teams, and had a number of clients whom we visited to evaluate their needs and the suitability of their houses for a successful return. Savo was one of them. He came to our office in Banja Luka to ask for help with the rebuilding of his house. His sons had been killed in the war and his wife had recently died. He was in his early 70s and determined to return to the place he had lived all his life. He was thin and unshaven, with a sallow complexion, sparse grey hair and a deep furrow between his eyebrows. We knew how important it was for Savo and other survivors to return to their homes.

A few days later, the three of us set out to visit his home. Although we knew that his pre-war dwelling was in a small village in eastern BiH, we did not know that the whole area was now one large minefield. We left the city of Banja Luka behind and ventured deeper into the Bosnian wilderness, with its narrow roads and broad green fields. After two hours of driving we came to an area surrounded by big yellow signs with large, bold, black letters warning, *Pažnja: Mine* [Caution: Minefield]. Saša continued to drive along the narrow road passing more and more of these signs. Savo told him to stop the car and pointed his long finger towards the hills stretching out below the clear blue sky: "My home is just behind these hills. We have to go through this wood to get there."

Saša and I looked at each other, puzzled. He pulled over to the side of the road and turned off the engine. Without saying a word, we all unclipped our seat belts and got out of the four-wheel drive. I gazed up and down the dirty, dusty road. There was no one around. In front of us was one of the minefield signs. Again, Saša and I looked at each other, wondering what to do. Guessing what was on our minds, Savo said pointedly, "Just walk in my footsteps kids, and you will be fine. I know this wood as well as I know my own pocket. Just make sure you do not step anywhere else but in my footsteps." Saša stared at me. I raised my eyebrows, but said nothing.

Saša and I nodded, exchanging a quick nervous smile. Neither of us knew anything about mines, other than that BiH was full of them. But we had made a decision: we would follow Savo. We were afraid, but were not able to say no. We knew we could not possibly achieve anything with this venture. Still, something inspired us, something deeper than fear. The risk we were taking was not really about saving Savo's house. Even if the house might be repairable, no one would pay to restore a house that could only be accessed by crossing a minefield. We followed Savo because we knew how important it was for him to see his old house again.

Savo was already walking towards the wood, his face illuminated with expectation and absorbed by the nature surrounding him. I did not feel as if I would die that afternoon so I decided to trust the old man and help him in his quest. A gut-wrenching jolt of fear ran through me but I did not show it. I cast a suspicious glance at the ground beneath me and with a deep breath I walked carefully towards the woods.

It is late morning, the leaves are changing colour and are swishing and falling in the breeze. We are cautiously entering the minefield. Savo goes first, Saša second, and then me. The sun is breaking through the branches but my eyes are glued to the ground making sure my foot lands exactly in Saša's footstep. I keep my head low and don't look around. My heart is thumping so I stretch out my arms in the light breeze, thinking that they might help me to keep my balance. My legs feel heavy as I move; I hold my breath and, after each step, sigh with relief. I want to believe that we are nearly there. But the fact is we don't know how far we have to walk. We do not ask Savo.

I cannot escape the thought that, despite the beauty of nature around us, death might be waiting around the next corner. Moving my foot a few centimetres to the left or right could be the difference between life and death. One wrong step and we are *all* gone. But for Savo, the return to the house that he built with his own hands is critical to his grieving for all the losses war has brought to him and his family. I will never forget the look on his beaming face at the sight of a small ruined house in tatters, but still standing.

⌘ ⌘ ⌘ ⌘ ⌘ ⌘

A year later, in 2001, when I started work with Human Rights Watch in Washington DC, I saw for the first time a map of the minefields in BiH on the wall of our office. The map was covered in red dots marking uncleared minefield areas, including the one where I had walked that day with Saša and Savo. I was bewildered to see that my homeland, six years after the war had ended, was still full of minefields.

Later, I discovered that many minefields in BiH were not properly marked. Although the majority of them lay along the former border lines between the Serb army and the Bosniak-Croat army, people could not safely wander through any unfamiliar areas of forest in BiH because they might still contain mines. A 2011 study reported that out of almost 4 million inhabitants of BiH, approximately 920,000 were directly endangered by minefields. Almost 3% of BiH territory was not clear of mines. Still, this was an improvement from 1998 when around 8% was not clear.[28] In 2012, 3 people were killed in mine-related accidents and 9 were seriously injured.[29] In January 2014, a further 3 people were killed when they knowingly entered minefields in a desperate attempt to access the only available food crops growing near their old houses.[30] Between 1996 and 2011, out of 1,671 people who were injured by mines, 583 subsequently died.[31]

As much of the Bosnian land is still littered with mines due to their indiscriminate use during the war, this has become one of the greatest obstacles to the return of refugees to BiH. In a short documentary, *Spotlights on a Massacre* (1997), about the continuing devastating impact of mines in peacetime, young boys and girls talk about those life-changing seconds: the moment they stepped on a mine and the consequences they have to live with for the rest of their lives. As one boy, not more than seven years old, with both legs permanently disabled, says on camera: "I didn't check to see if there were any mines. We were running towards a strawberry field and I tripped on a wire connected to the mine. It exploded, I fell, and my friend was knocked down." The young people in the documentary refer to those who deposited mines in Bosnia as 'war criminals' and want them to be made accountable for the injuries and deaths their actions have caused. Unfortunately, those responsible will never be prosecuted because it is not possible to identify who planted the mines. After all, at that time landmines were lawful[32] men's 'toys'. They were—and still are in

---

[28] BH Mine Action Center (2013)

[29] Landmine and Cluster Munition Monitor (1 September 2013)

[30] BH Mine Action Center (15 January 2014)

[31] BH Mine Action Center (2013)

[32] At the time of the Bosnian war (1992–1995), the use of landmines was regulated by both customary international humanitarian law and by the 1980 Convention on Certain Conventional Weapons. In December 1997, 127 governments signed the Anti-Personnel Landmine Convention in Ottawa, Canada. BiH was amongst the signatories.

many countries—used in wars to disable 'the enemy', both soldiers and civilians, as well as the crops and livestock they depended on.

The feeling that my life had been endangered that afternoon in BiH became even stronger after I had reviewed this information. I realised just how close we had come to potential death, which made the minefield walk more prominent in my memory.

I saw Saša many years later in our home town. We were both invited to lunch at a mutual friend's place and he came to my parents' unit to pick me up. We hadn't seen each other for some time and were eager to catch up with the latest news about our lives. At one point Saša turned his head towards me and said: "Do you remember that day?" I did not have to ask which day. I nodded with a wry smile, "Of course, how can I ever forget it." We shook our heads in disbelief thinking about the foolish decision we had made. At the time we had thought that we were brave, but now we could see we had been young and stupid. I turned on the radio and 'Merlin', one of the most popular Bosnian groups, was playing one of my favourite tunes. I pumped up the volume and we both started to sing the song we knew too well: 'I cover up my fear with a smile'.

Saša has recently emigrated to Sweden. I won't see him again for a long time.

Conflicting War Memories

Each year on 4 August I privately mark the anniversary of the Croatian military operation 'Storm' which, in 1995, drove 250,000 Serbs from their homes in the region that was known as Kninska Krajina in Croatia. The operation and exodus had lasted only four days. It was the largest military operation and land offensive in Europe since the Second World War, conducted by the Croatian army and openly encouraged and supported by the USA. In Serbia, each year this date is commemorated as a national day of tragedy. Survivors come together to mourn their loved ones and to pay tribute to those who lost their lives in the course of this brutal 'ethnic cleansing'. In Croatia, however, 4 August is recognised as a day of national pride. Government officials, public figures and citizens come together to mark and celebrate this date as the most significant one in the creation of Croatian statehood. These conflicting war memories have become part of a collective remembrance cemented in school textbooks in both countries which tell the two opposing stories about the same event.[33]

On 4 August 1995 I was in Banja Luka, visiting my parents, while my brother remained on the war front. I witnessed floods of people, mainly peasants, who were fleeing from their villages and towns ahead of the advancing Croatian army. These civilians had been abandoned by the Serb army which was itself quickly overpowered by Croatian forces. Some were escaping on trucks; others were on foot, herded into groups, shuffling in the direction of my home town on their way to Serbia. But some people could not flee, among them the elderly and the sick; around 8,000 were left behind to the mercy of Croatian soldiers who looted and burned down their houses and villages.

The fleeing refugees were also fired upon by Croatian soldiers. Many of them lost their lives on their way to safety. In just two days, Banja Luka hosted tens of thousands of people and the livestock they brought with them. I was watching from my parents' verandah as women, men and children were trying to find a patch of land to camp on before continuing their trip. They arrived at the city in cars, trucks and carts with one or two plastic bags containing all their worldly possessions: some clothes, documents and a few photographs. The onslaught had come out of the blue. Yet, this was just the beginning of their story of desperation, confusion and loss.

The large majority of these people eventually settled in Serbia, though some remained in Banja Luka, and others later resettled in parts of Europe, the USA and Australia. We watched as hungry and thirsty cows, sheep and dogs wandered around the city with their owners. People were sleeping on pavements and in schoolyards; anywhere they could find some space. The city officials quickly created makeshift accommodation, turning sporting halls and other public properties into refugee housing. My family discussed what we could do to help and decided to pack our old clothes, toys and some food in big plastic bags and take them to a hall called 'Borik'. Many of the people I met there seemed tired of living, exhausted by the effort to understand what had just happened and how to deal with this inhumane mass violence. Their eyes were empty, and surrounded by

---

[33] For more on memory and identity see Sabrina Ramet, 'Memory and identity in the Yugoslav successor states' (8 June 2013, p. 871).

dark circles, a sign of many sleepless nights. I wanted to pull my hair out and scream. Instead, I talked to a few women and their children about what had happened to them.

The city was overcrowded with people, livestock and pets. It was impossible to accommodate 250,000 refugees in our small town as this was equivalent to the number of actual residents. People were hanging around, not knowing what to do. We were all sinking into a sense of hopelessness and fear. The traffic was chaotic and most of the roads were blocked by large groups of people with nowhere to go. In the meantime, the Croatian army was advancing and there were rumours that soldiers would arrive in Banja Luka in just a matter of days. My parents panicked and wanted to send me back to Serbia as soon as possible. My brother arrived unexpectedly on our doorstep and told us that we should pack one bag with the main necessities and be prepared to leave at short notice. He was supposed to withdraw with the Serb army and advised us not to wait for him, but to go our separate ways and eventually meet him somewhere in Serbia. My parents did not want to go anywhere. They did not want to be rescued. "We have nowhere to go. We can't leave our unit. This is all we have." I knew that there was nothing I could do to change their minds. Despite ongoing deaths, some people were still in denial that their next door neighbour might be capable of killing them if they didn't flee. They believed and hoped that something like that wouldn't happen to them. Unfortunately, such wishful thinking cost many of them their lives.

Although they decided to stay, my parents wanted to see me out of the city as soon as possible. They worked in the post office and decided to put me on one of the mail trucks that went to Serbia daily. We estimated that the journey would take around 24 hours and would require a great deal of patience because everyone was travelling in the same direction. There was no semblance of order on the clogged roads, with vehicles sharing the road with horse-drawn carts, livestock and tractors.

I shed a lot of tears during that trip, seeing masses of exhausted, tired, dirty and hungry people. I can still see two young women changing their babies' nappies on the back of the cart in front of us. Their bodies are swinging from side to side as we drive on a rutted, narrow road through a village near the border with Serbia. Bumping over the gouged earth, I look at one of the women. Her sad, small face is framed by a thin sky-blue scarf and long black hair. Her cheeks are contorted in an expression of acute suffering. Her face is grey with grief. I see sweat dripping from her forehead. She seems oblivious to the people and noise around her, fully absorbed in the baby lying on a piece of brightly patched cloth. The boy is no more than one year old. I can see his thick dark hair; his small fists are up in the air as if trying to reach for his mother. With one hand she hooks a long piece of hair behind her ear. With the other she gently strokes his head. She catches my eye. We look at each other for a brief moment. In the midst of this pain we manage to exchange humanity. She smiles and the lines around her eyes crinkle. I smile back and wave my hand. This image will haunt me, searing itself into the deep recesses of my soul. We continue to move slowly along the narrow dusty road that will take us all to safety. Our truck is only metres away from the cart that is taking these women and their children to an uncertain freedom. We are all heading in the same direction, but our lives will part very soon.

It is hot, and most people do not have access to basic hygiene. The sweat runs down my back, under my armpits. I sob as I watch men, women and children catching bread and water that is being thrown to them by local villagers. I turn around and realise I am not the only one. Lots of us are crying, sweating. A stinking cloud of engine exhaust fumes mixed with the smell of people who have not bathed for days, washes over me. As we near the border with Serbia, we encounter people who come out of their homes and from the side of the road with bread, fruit and bottles of fresh, cold water for us. As they throw the food to us, it is scattered by the wind, but eventually caught by exhausted people. A ripple of excitement surges through me. For a brief moment I am happy to see humanity in action: simultaneously painful and beautiful. Time has become elastic; what feels like minutes must be hours. Sunset comes and goes and darkness envelopes us. In normal, pre-war times this trip would take five hours, but it takes us almost 24 hours to reach Belgrade, the capital of Serbia. I am dizzy and exhausted when we reach the city. It has been the longest day of my life. But I almost wish it wouldn't finish. There is no one to welcome me at the end of the road.

Tens of thousands of people arrived in Serbia and were accommodated in abandoned child-care centres and other institutions turned into refugee camps. Some of them live in these decrepit places to this day.[34] They crossed the bridge which stretched from hell to security—not to paradise. Their whole lives before 4 August 1995 were erased and become a distant memory. No more daily routine for these people: going to work, drinking coffee with their next-door neighbours on a hot summer night, having parties to celebrate birthdays. All gone in 24 hours. The war had barrelled into their lives, wiping out the known and secure, leaving them in a chaos of wild uncertainties.

But these lives did not matter much to the international community. The exodus of 250,000 people took place virtually unnoticed by the world community, and without humanitarian intervention. To this day, no one has been held accountable for the 'ethnic cleansing' in Croatia's Krajina region.[35] In *Madness Visible: A Memoir of War* (2004) journalist Janine di Giovanni acknowledges the lack of interest by the international media in these Serb refugees. She describes what the so-called temporary accommodations for people who fled the military operation 'Storm', looked like:

> I found my friend Zoran, a Serb from Sarajevo, living in a filthy refugee camp outside of the city. The place was full of Krajina refugees, old women in head scarves and old men playing cards. There was the usual smell of refugees, of misery, of a communal toilet for hundreds and a communal kitchen where one pot cooked everyone's food. *The only difference was that these were Serbian refugees; there were no television crews or reporters writing about their plight* [my emphasis] (p. 68).

---

[34] According to a 2014 report by the United Nations High Commissioner for Refugees (UNHCR), by mid-2013 there were still 57,076 refugees and 227,585 internally displaced persons (IDPs) residing in Serbia. It is the country of first resort in the region for forced displacements (UNHCR 2014; see also Vlada Republike Srbije, 'Izbjeglice u Srbiji' <http://www.srbija.gov.rs/pages/article.php?id=45>).

[35] In 2011, two Croatian generals, Ante Gotovina and Mladen Markač, were sentenced to 24 years and 18 years respectively in relation to the killing of ethnic Serbs in an offensive to retake Croatia's Krajina region. Judges at the time ruled that they were part of a criminal conspiracy led by the late Croatian President Franjo Tudjman to "permanently and forcibly remove" the Serb civilian population from Krajina. However, a year later, on 16 November 2012, the United Nations International Criminal Tribunal for the Former Yugoslavia (ICTY) overturned the convictions and acquitted both generals. This decision was welcomed in Croatia and condemned in Serbia (*BBC News Europe*, 17 November 2012).

Many of these refugees would not return to their pre-war settlements. Some vowed they would never go back. There was nothing to return to for many of them: their houses had been destroyed, and families and friends had been killed or had fled. For others, only their houses remained. These people had become strangers in their own city, displaced from their pre-war residencies which were now occupied by unknown persons. This is a common story for all who were displaced—we found ourselves in places we did not want to occupy and had to learn how to live in them.

I was 22 at the time, and this was but one incident in a chain of events that would permanently mark my life. Life before the war seemed like a dream: unreal and too good to be true. I spent the trip back to Serbia absorbing the misery around me and sobbing. I kept wondering why we had allowed this to happen to us. As British author Rebecca West wrote in 1941 in her novel *Black Lamb and Grey Falcon*: "Why did the Yugoslavs choose to perish? It must be reiterated that it was their choice, made out of full knowledge. On none of them did their fates steal unawares" (1941/2007, p. 1,144).

About the wars in Yugoslavia in the 1990s, Laura Silber and Allan Little write that Yugoslavia "did not die a natural death" but was "rather deliberately and systematically killed off by men who had nothing to gain and everything to lose from a peaceful transition from state socialism and one-party rule to free-market economy" (1997, p. 25). I agree that we Yugoslavs are in part responsible for its death, but it was also due to a failure of the international community. I believe the wars could have been prevented.[36] But the USA and Western Europe were unwilling to recognise that, after Tito's death in 1980, Yugoslavia was disintegrating, and that those in authority were not interested in regulating this process peacefully (Glenny, 1996, p. 235). After all, the Balkans had always been portrayed as a violent and destructive region. While travelling through Yugoslavia for the first time at the brink of the Second World War, Rebecca West had

---

[36] On 16 December 1991, the European Union (EU) recognised Slovenia's and Croatia's independence. Germany had been the first to recognise these two independent states and was pressuring its allies to follow suit. This was later criticised as a premature, erroneous and misguided move and was even seen as one of the causes of the war that led to the dissolution of Yugoslavia. For more details see Blitz (2006, p. 57); von Bogdandy, Wolfrum and Philipp (2005, p. 183); Ramet and Coffin (2001, pp. 48–64).

stated: "Violence was indeed all I knew of the Balkans: all I knew of the South Slavs" (1941/2007, p. 21).

In the long history of Balkan violence and conflict that goes back centuries, the so-called Third Balkan War from 1992 to 1995, the war I survived, stands out. It was my first war. For my parents it was the second; and for my grandparents, the third.[37] It was a civil war fought between former friends and neighbours; between teachers and their students. Elvir Kulin was my brother's age, in his early twenties, when the hostilities began. While my brother was drafted into the Bosnian Serb army, Elvir was drafted into the Bosnian Muslim army, and soon found himself on the front line. In his memoir, *In a Bosnian Trench: A Wartime Memoir of a Muslim Bosnian Soldier* (2005), he recalls how he was given an assignment to look after a group of prisoners, Bosnian Serbs, some of whom had been mobilised as older disabled soldiers, and others who were Bosnian Serb civilians who had refused to join the Bosnian army. Kulin writes about the absurdity of the Bosnian war, and about the young men who were forcibly recruited as soldiers and struggled to make sense of it all. He describes how, during this assignment, he found himself eye to eye with a man who had been his teacher several years earlier.

> Ten men escorted by a Bosnian soldier arrived. I handed shovels to them. They didn't speak. All were around my age except a man who was in his fifties. I recognized him. His name was Krsto, and he was my former elementary school teacher ... As Krsto looked at me now, I felt embarrassed and ashamed. I wanted to say something to him but didn't know what ... I offered him a cigarette (p. 93).

Krsto was a senior man of authority whom Kulin respected. But now Kulin was expected to treat him as an enemy. He felt "embarrassed and ashamed," feelings that one should not experience in relation to an *enemy*.

This is just one example of the myriad of complexities associated with the Bosnian war that go beyond what are often described as 'ancient hatreds' between the three ethnic groups who live in BiH (Bosnian Muslims, Orthodox Christian Serbs, Catholic Croats). The

---

[37] My grandparents survived the First World War (1914–1918) and the Second World War (1939–1945). My parents survived the Second World War and the recent Bosnian War (1992–1995).

confusion about the roles soldiers were meant to play in the war— about being in a position to decide on a person's life or death; being forced to torture and kill former neighbours, lovers and friends—is something that will leave psychological scars for decades. Yet despite the madness of war, humanity can be preserved. Even if it is just in the form of a cigarette.

My friend Eldin recently told me a similar story. Eldin was only 19 when the Bosnian war started. He lived in my home town and as a Bosniak he faced the real danger of being forcibly conscripted into the Serb army. Through some personal connections, he managed to make a fake identification card with a Serb name on it, and decided to try his luck, cross the border between BiH and Croatia, and flee to safety. In the autumn of 1992, he took one of the local buses to Zagreb. He was afraid, but felt he had nothing to lose. After an hour he arrived at the Serb checkpoint. All passengers were required to show their IDs to an inspector. When it was his turn, he froze with fear. Here in front of him was his lifelong childhood Serb friend, Milan. Eldin stood before him and handed over his fake ID. They looked each other in the eye. They were both stunned and too afraid to speak. If they gave any sign that they knew each other it could be fatal. Still, they spoke with their eyes, transfixed on memories of their shared past which blurred into this life-or-death moment. Eldin knew that his life depended on his former friend, the Serb inspector, who could reveal his fake identity and imprison him. That moment of waiting lasted less than a minute but seemed like an eternity. Finally, Milan said: "Thanks. You can go now." These two childhood friends have never met again.

Some people who survived the war, such as my friend Eldin, feel an urge to "bear witness for those who can't speak" (Hunt, 2004, p. 15) about past events that marked their lives. But even these people often need a long time to open up and speak about their traumatic past. Others, such as one of my close friends who came to Australia during the BiH war as a refugee, are still afraid of confronting their past even now, almost two decades after the war (pers. comm., March 2013):

> I could not afford the time to work on myself. I was a single mother with a teenage daughter at the time my panic attacks were most severe. When

I had a panic attack I would often end up in a hospital, but would go out as soon as I felt a bit better. My daughter could not be left alone. She was 12. She did not understand what I was going through and she was sick of my mental collapses. One day she told me, 'Mom, you better pull yourself together or kill yourself'. I then decided to cement all those memories deep inside me. I am aware, of course, that this is not a solution at all, that putting a lid on bad memories won't solve the problems, but may even exacerbate them and rupture through other illnesses of psychosomatic character. Still, the time has passed and I have no energy and will to go through it all now.

My friend had to put aside her healing for the time being, or possibly for good. Many civilians suffer from war in silence with their sadness hidden behind fake smiles. As Primo Levi argues, they have chosen to keep their "burdensome memories" at bay through the creation of a defensive "*cordon sanitaire*" (1988, pp. 17–18). They avoid facing and dealing with the past, hoping that one day its ghosts will stop haunting them once and for all. People have chosen 'amnesia' since some level of forgetting may be desirable as a way of preventing a constant intrusion of the past upon the present, blocking the experience of the here and now. However, to expect that the past can be simply forgotten is naïve and unrealistic since the experiences of trauma and war do not belong to past time (Shepherdson, 2008, p. 107).

For a long time, I felt too embarrassed to talk about my trauma because I thought (as do many other survivors) that the horrors I had survived were infinitesimally small compared to others; for instance, those of my friend Elma who had lived for four years under siege in Sarajevo, or Nenad, my next-door neighbour who lost his 22-year-old brother Predrag only a month before the Dayton Peace Agreement was signed in November 1995. For a long time I tried to bury my emotions and to deal with them on my own. But gradually I realised that my own experiences, and how I internalised them, *did* matter. It might not be the worst trauma to someone else, but it was the worst for me.

During and after the war people were divided, cultures erased, lifelong friends became enemies. How do we (re)imagine life together after such mayhem that is imprinted on each part of our bodies and minds? American author, Joan Nestle, moved by Lara Fergus' novel, *My Sister Chaos*, about war, displacements and sisterhood, writes in her review of the book: "How do we find a way back into the belief that any kind of hope is possible, that even when all the boundaries have shifted and no amount of exerted control will bring back what has been lost, how do we find the contours of possibilities?" (forthcoming 2014).

Eldin's story of his childhood friend's humanity, and many other accounts of reaching 'the other side', tell us that it is possible to 'shift the boundaries' once more: to see former 'enemies' reconciling and learning to live together again. My neighbour Avdo returned to the unit from which he had been expelled during the war. He now mixes again with pre-war neighbours. It will never be the same as before, but it is possible to live, if not together, at least side by side. People in BiH have no choice but to share space and land.

It will take decades for BiH to recover, but its people have to find strength to move on with their daily lives and struggles. They have to find the courage to live between remembering and forgetting; between two parallel worlds of sorrow and reality. Between their memories of their homeland as it was before the war, and the new lives they now lead across the world in Europe, America, Australia— or still in their fractured homeland.

Epilogue

Troubled Homeland

I don't miss home, *mati*. I'm there all the time. In the past. In fiction.

—Ismet Prcic, *Shards* (2011, p. 41)

"Hamzo, look how mama dives!"

A woman in her late thirties, with long brown hair piled on top of her head and a girl sitting on her shoulders, is looking over at little Hamzo. Pinching her nostrils firmly closed while standing up to her belly in the water, she starts to count slowly: "One ... Two ..." On "Three!" she disappears into the sky-blue Adriatic Sea.

I glance over at Hamzo, just four years old and shaking in his father's big arms. He is naked except for a pair of flippers that look gigantic on his small body. Hamzo doesn't look impressed by his mother and does not seem eager to follow her into the water.

It was a sunny June afternoon in Mali Drvenik, a small, tucked-away town in Croatia. I was standing up to my knees in the chilly Adriatic sea, trying to make up my mind whether I wanted to dive in or not. Like Hamzo, I was cold. After a long, wet winter, the water was not yet warm enough for those who had escaped to the coast before the season was in full swing.

While watching Hamzo and his family, images from my own childhood holidays came back to me. I could see myself as a skinny little girl, with my parents and my older brother, on the Adriatic coast, camping somewhere along the Makarska Riviera. Today, just like back then (in the 1980s), I could see and hear people from different parts of Bosnia and Herzegovina (BiH), as they were sunbaking on the beach. Their voices and faces blurred. It could easily be 1988, but it was now the summer of 2013, and long years of violence, destruction and poverty had passed since then. Yet, children were as eager as ever to learn to swim, and were shouting, splashing and laughing. Their mothers were encouraging them, while making sandwiches out of bread, tomato and *pašteta* [pâté],[38] still the favourite snack food of all generations growing up in ex-Yugoslavia.

Still standing in the water, I thought again how much it felt and looked like the pre-war years, with Bosniaks, Croats and Serbs from BiH sharing a vast blue sea and beach with mostly Slovakian and Czech people. Before the war, when Czechoslovakia was one country, our beaches were swamped by its citizens who loved our coast. Now, after their peaceful split, Czechs and Slovaks still find the Croatian coast attractive and relatively cheap. I could hear different accents and variations of my language mixed up with Slovak and Czech. I felt happy for a moment—*it feels so good to be back home*, I thought.

I realised that I was part of a multi-ethnic group. Such groupings are rare in 2013 in my 'ethnically cleansed' homeland. It felt like being in an old movie from my childhood, except that the 100,000 people who had died in the Bosnian wars and the 8,000 still missing[39] were deprived of enjoying today's holiday. Along with many current Bosnian citizens facing poverty, they will not be able to stand in the sea up to their waists and think about when we all lived in one state called Yugoslavia: a state that has been erased; a state whose borders have changed too many times.

Not everyone is as nostalgic about the 'good old days' as I am. During my time in Mali Drvenik, I met a young couple who were selling souvenirs and swimming gear to tourists. I bought a small blue boat decorated with yellow and red fishes for my son. We started to chat about the Croatian beaches—rocky, not sandy—for which

---

[38] *Pašteta* is a thinly pureed pâté usually made from chicken or, less commonly, tuna or salmon.

[39] As of mid-August 2013, the fate and whereabouts of 7,800 people who vanished during the conflict in BiH remains unknown. In the 22 years since the Balkan conflict started, almost 35,000 people have been reported missing to the International Committee of the Red Cross (ICRC, 22 August, 2013).

you need a pair of *šlapas* (light, colourful sandals) to ease your often painful entrance into the sea. I told them, half-jokingly, how Australia has beaches with beautiful white sand, but that the ocean has sharks and deadly 'stingers' (jellyfish)—dangers that we don't have to worry about here. Most people from the Balkans are terrified of sharks. I am always on guard when swimming in the ocean. Despite the assertions by my Australian friends that shark attacks are 'extremely rare', and that surfers are their 'targets' rather than swimmers, I can never fully relax in the Pacific Ocean. I love the Adriatic Sea where you can swim as far as you wish with no fear at all.

The three of us laughed together and as a way of saying goodbye I concluded (as a good old nostalgic ex-Yugoslav) that there is 'no sea like *naše* [ours]'. In pronouncing *naše* I realised I was making a mistake, but it was too late. Their faces suddenly froze and they said nothing. An uncomfortable silence enveloped us all as I had made a lapsus linguae. The reality is that the sea is not *naše* any more, but *njihovo* [theirs]: Croatian.

Children in Drevenik do not care about the ethnicity of their playmates; unlike adults, who now *do* care—a lot. My ten-year-old cousin Stefan lives in an 'ethnically cleansed' town comprised of almost 95% Serbs. He has never heard certain Bosniak words and names and different Bosnian accents. This is not surprising given that children, and many adults, seldom cross the ethnic borders unless absolutely necessary. Yet, at the Adriatic Sea in Mali Drvenik, my cousin befriended: Nezira from Zenica; Albert from Slovakia; Denis from Travnik; and Rian from Sarajevo. Faced with different slang and accents, at one point Stefan asked me: "What does *ba* mean?" It is an expression used mostly by people living in the central Bosnia and Sarajevo region. *Ba* is a saying that has no particular meaning; it is similar to 'hey' in English. Bosnians use it a lot, although they find it difficult to explain what it means. I couldn't explain it either.

My cousin's questions and curiosity about Bosniak names, and a dialect that was all too familiar to me but foreign to him, was a reminder that there is a new generation of young people growing up in ex-Yugoslavia who know nothing about 'the good old days' and for whom 'the 1990s civil war' is an abstract term, just as 'the Second World War' had been for me. For him, and for his peers, the name of his birthplace, 'Bosnia', is a foreign and disliked term. Serbia is his motherland.

On our way back home, while driving through the countryside along the border with Croatia, Stefan's mother, Jelena, suddenly turned her head to him and said with urgency in her voice, "When we travelled along this way during the war we could not turn the car lights on at night." He took his eyes off his cell phone, paused for a brief moment, and asked: "Why not?" She pointed towards the river and explained: "Because Croatians were shooting at us across the Sava River." His face was blank and he returned to his electronic game. Like his peers, he lives in the world of computer games and has no interest in the matters his mother is eager to teach him.

I, on the other hand, was stunned by Jelena's remarks and felt intense discomfort. We had just enjoyed a nice relaxing holiday but it was obvious that we cannot ever escape reminders of the war imprinted everywhere around us. It seems that every piece of this beautiful land has been part of killing fields that had drowned in blood. I curled into my seat at the back and gazed towards the calm bluish river that hides stories of anguish, torture and death; of bodies floating and finally sinking deep down into it. I thought it was no coincidence that Jelena made her comment at this particular place.

The Sava River has a very special meaning for Serbs. During the Second World War, the corpses from the extermination camps of Jasenovac and Stara Grdiška floated down this river.[40] The river was a mass grave and this is how I will always remember Sava. Like other children in ex-Yugoslavia, I grew up learning this history from our school textbooks.

I sank more deeply into my car seat and wondered: *What will become of us? What will become of Stefan and his peers? Will this cycle of dark memories ever stop following us? Does each new generation of the former Yugoslavia need to experience war and trauma?*

My dark thoughts were interrupted by Jelena's chatter coming from the front of the car. I looked into the rear-view mirror and our eyes met. She was in a good mood. Jelena was chatting with Stefan

---

[40] From August 1941 to April 1945, hundreds of thousands of Serbs, Jews and Romas, as well as anti-fascists of many nationalities, were murdered at the death camp known as Jasenovac. Jasenovac has a similar significance for Serbs as Auschwitz has for Jewish people. It was the largest concentration and extermination camp in Croatia. Estimates of the total numbers of men, women and children killed in this camp range from 300,000 to 700,000. And yet, despite the scale of the crimes committed there, most of the world has never heard of Jasenovac. See Lampe (2000), p. 211; Singleton (1985), p. 177; and Mojzes (2011), p. 56.

about their recent visit to Greece. She told me that while holidaying in Greece, a local man had asked her: "Where are you from?" "From Serbia!" she had responded. "I did not want to explain to him where we are really from," she told me with an apologetic half-smile. I was confused but said nothing. I was wondering what there was to explain. It is an easy question, and should have been an even easier answer. But, the reality is that our identities have become complex, and confused: part of a continuous search for meaning. Jelena and many other Serbs who live in Republika Srpska do not recognise BiH as their homeland. They have chosen Serbia instead.

Every year when I visit my homeland I am told that the past year has been 'the most difficult year since the war ended'. I have heard this sentence so many times I am not sure whether to believe it any more. It seems impossible to survive without jobs, salaries, and pensions in a country which, as my colleague Hariz Halilovich puts it, is in "a no-war, no-peace situation. Bodies are still being exhumed, some war criminals are under arrest, some are still at large. But the most disappointing thing is that the politics of that brutal time are still so much alive" (in Charter, 9 April 2012).

When I was visiting BiH in 2013, the latest shocking revelation preoccupying my friends was that a child can actually die while waiting for an identification number simply because Bosnian politicians seem unable to pass a law that would provide such a number. In June 2013, demonstrations were held in Sarajevo after a six-week-old baby girl, Berina Hamidović, died. She did not have a passport to cross the border from Bosnia to get to a hospital in Serbia. Due to a political row, Bosnian authorities were not issuing identification numbers, so her treatment was delayed for several days. This is *2013* Sarajevo, not *1993*! I thought we had moved on from violence and recklessness, towards a more peaceful existence in which we strive to preserve human life rather than discard it. In disbelief and bewilderment, I watched television reports showing demonstrators calling on lawmakers to put public interest before the political divisions that have rendered some of Bosnia's institutions dysfunctional.

This was the first news I received after an absence of a year and a half from the region. It was the tragedy that greeted me, that reminded me that I was indeed back in my still dysfunctional country, my homeland. Sabrina Ramet, an expert on Yugoslavian history and politics, has recently described BiH as a political anomaly, with two largely autonomous 'entities' operating within the framework of the state, [with] a flag designed by an international administrator, a wordless national anthem, and a constitution written in English, for which there is still no official Bosnian translation (2013, p. 12).

The people of BiH, women in particular, are impacted by these 'anomalies' on a daily basis. Many female war victims still struggle to exercise their legal and socio-economic rights.

After I returned from my holiday in Mali Drvenik I met with two women, Milica and Spasenija. Both are survivors of rape. Milica and her three young children were detained in the Bosniak-Croat rape camp in the municipalities of Bosanski Brod and Odžak in 1992.[41] Her youngest daughter, Ljiljana, was only nine months old. Milica was repeatedly gang-raped in front of her children. Ever since that dreadful time her son (who was five years old) has had a permanent speech impediment caused by shock.

Both women wanted to share their stories and I promised to talk and write about their ordeals. I knew how important it was for them to speak, and for me to listen. As Elisabeth Porter argues, "without such listening, stories remain untold or fall on deaf ears, the truth is not incorporated into history, and pleas for understanding and justice go unheeded" (2007, p. 22). Showing compassion and respect for these women is also important. So far, few people have cared to listen to their stories, let alone do something to assist them in their fight for justice.

While Milica, Spasenija and many other women were able to return to their pre-war houses, large numbers of survivors of rape left BiH altogether and resettled in other countries. Teta [Aunty] Mira, who now regularly babysits my son in Brisbane, is one of them. She came one Thursday morning, as she usually does. I was about to leave home for work when we started to talk about women who have been victims of wartime rape. Out of the blue, Teta Mira told me that she had been in a rape camp in 1992 with her two sons. I did not ask for such a 'confession'—she felt the need to tell me her story. She

---

[41] Anuradha Kumar has written about Serb women being raped in these municipalities in *Human Rights: Global Perspectives* (2002, p. 111). See also Human Rights Watch, *Global Report on Women's Human Rights (1990–1995)* (August 1995), pp. 21–25.

was clearly distressed; her hands were trembling, and her whole body was shaking with pain as she began to describe the scenes from the camp. I poured her a glass of water and we sat together at the table. With clinical precision Teta Mira recalled dates, times, and the names of the female victims and the male perpetrators, while describing the horrors that happened to her and her family more than 20 years ago.

I pretended to be calm but was speechless. I could not believe that Teta Mira, a good-natured woman in her mid-50s who had cared for my son for more than a year, had survived such atrocities. The possibility had never even crossed my mind. She did not actually say that she had been raped but that she witnessed many women and young girls being taken away to be gang-raped. Once she had finished speaking, I could see that she felt better. I was reluctant to leave her but I had to go to work. We hugged and I rushed through the door which slammed behind me. I stood for a moment on the verandah, struggling with emotions that overwhelmed me. So many untold stories ... so much violence to remember ... I then slowly walked to my car, took a deep breath and started the engine. Another day of my life was before me.

⌘⌘⌘⌘⌘⌘

When in Australia, I dream of returning to live in BiH. I become romantic and nostalgic, but once back, I need no more than a few days to miss my exile and to admit that I do not want to live in BiH again. I am always confronted by the harsh reality that people can die just because no one cares. In BiH, we have been used to seeing lots of beggars for several years, many of them Roma children, but the face of extreme poverty has changed. While I was drinking a coffee in a local cake shop, a young girl (no more than five years old) suddenly appeared next to me. Puzzled, I thought she must be from one of the nearby tables, sharing cake with her parents. But I was wrong. She smiled at me and stretched out her small arm: "Do you have some *marka* (local currency)?" She bent down for a moment to pick up a coin that someone had lost.

Other people have also asked me for *marka*. They were mostly young women or older men who did not look like 'typical' beggars. They looked 'normal', and wore clean, everyday clothing, except for one woman who was completely covered from head to toe. I couldn't see any part of her body, not even her eyes since she looked constantly at her feet. It was rumoured that she was a young woman from the city who disguised herself so no one could recognise her. She must be ashamed, my friends told me. I replied that she had no reason to be ashamed of poverty. It is the people, the men, who lead this country, who should be ashamed.

The situation is not much different in neighbouring Serbia. While I was doing fieldwork in Belgrade in 2013, the nanny for my nine-month-old son was Milena, a 38-year-old woman originally from Croatia, who had left home with her family in 1991 when the war started there. Milena was born of a 'mixed marriage', with her father Croat and her mother Serb. Her family moved to Serbia out of fear that they would be killed or abused because of her mother's ethnicity. They fled in a hurry, leaving their home and a holiday house on the Adriatic coast behind. For the past 20 years Milena's parents and brother have been living in a small unit, paying rent with the meagre income Milena's mother earns. To date, all attempts to have their properties returned have been unsuccessful.

Milena's mother also works as a nanny, for ten hours a day, Monday to Friday, for 300 euros. From her tiny salary, she pays her health insurance and pension fund. Being a nanny in Serbia entails cooking, cleaning, ironing, shopping, helping with homework, washing dishes and baking. Child care has become a form of modern-day slavery. A friend who works for an anti-trafficking organisation in Serbia says that many people walk a fine line between slavery and employment. This distinction has become more subtle and complex since there is an army of unemployed people of all ages who wander about, desperate to do anything. And if nothing comes of it, they try to emigrate. People like Milena's mother have no one to complain to. The answer to any complaint is: "If you don't like it, leave. There is always someone else in the queue waiting to do your work." And unfortunately that is true.

Milena is a construction engineer who managed to finish her studies in 2002 while caring for two babies. She worked hard to graduate, hoping to work on infrastructure projects such as streets, tunnels and highways. Eleven years later she is a housewife whose daily life has been reduced to shopping at the local market and disciplining her two teenage sons. She knows all the local peasants and often goes to the market with her younger son who proudly told me that he occasionally gets free paprika, or an apple or potato. "I got two apples and one tomato today for free," he boasted to me, as Milena glowed with happiness. I did not know what to say. Had we come to the point that we have to be happy about receiving a free potato at the market?

Milena had never been a nanny before, but she was more than happy to help me out. I felt bad about giving her instructions for my son's care since she is highly qualified in her field. She is sad, but has not lost hope that she will eventually find a job in Serbia as an engineer. She keeps responding to local newspaper ads for positions in her profession although she knows that what she really needs is a 'connection'. It is nearly impossible to secure any reasonable job without enlisting nepotism or bribery; or being prepared to endure (sexual) harassment. Milena told me that she had recently met one of her former professors in the neighbourhood. After telling him that she still does not have work as an engineer (or any work whatsoever), he winked at her and said with a wry smile, "You know you are attractive. You should use that asset to get yourself a job." Milena was quite incensed by his remark but she said nothing. She felt powerless. She was afraid to insult him since he may well be one of the 'connections' she will need to help her get a job.

Although Milena would love to expand her search, going abroad is out of question. I look at her and see thousands of young women and men in Serbia and BiH, experts in their fields, who sit at home while, as many of them have told me, life passes them by.

Sometimes employment can be achieved by using capital to start a business. In this case, even those with no schooling can become employers if they have sufficient funds. They employ people like Milena who are desperate to do any kind of work. In Bijeljina, a city near the border with Serbia, Ana, who has a high school diploma, owns a boutique. When one of her staff members went on holiday, she employed a woman who had graduated with a degree from the University of Technology three years earlier. Ana told me that the woman was so happy to be offered temporary work as a salesperson that she said: "Thanks so much for thinking of me. It is good that I can leave my house for a while. I am so bored!"

Most of the young women I meet seem desperate, but some are also bitter and committed to maintaining the traditional ways of life. In a Belgrade beauty parlour I was having a discussion with young women about giving birth. All of them were appalled at the idea of having their partner next to them during this time. One of them, a mother of a nine-month-old boy, commented angrily: "It is disgusting. I mean to give birth in general. I don't want my husband to be disgusted by me and never be attracted to me again." When I told them that, in Australia, it is the norm rather than the exception to have a partner next to you while giving birth, and that this is considered a very precious time, they were surprised, and said that wouldn't happen in Serbia for "thousands of years." They did not welcome the prospect and couldn't understand why women would support such an idea.

Mira, a hairdresser in her early thirties who had been displaced by war and then settled in Bijeljina in BiH, told me that she can "only dream of going to the coast" for a holiday with her family since her husband has no job. He was a mechanic, but the business that employed him had closed down. They tried unsuccessfully to emigrate to Austria. Mira mentioned that her salary covers only "fuel to get me to work, and nappies." Although her husband has been unemployed for more than a year, it is 'culturally unacceptable' for him to care for their two baby girls. Instead, Mira must drive them to her mother's home on the other side of the city, on her way to work. She has no money to pay for child care which would cost $100 per month. Mira told me: "Life is just passing us by," and they will spend it in poverty. Her brother-in-law and his wife, who now live in Austria, took Mira and her husband to the coast on two consecutive years and paid for their holiday. But she did not feel comfortable about the arrangement since they had no money to contribute, not even for daily expenses. She said:

> I would lie on the beach starving to death but I had no money to even buy a sandwich. So, I would wait till one of them got hungry so they would invite us to eat too. It is humiliating. What sort of vacation is that? It is better to go nowhere than to wait for food like a dog (pers. comm., June 2013).

Many of my friends have family abroad, and it is the diaspora who often feed the families 'back home'. We spend lots of money on our families and friends. The expenditure does not end with buying aeroplane tickets, gifts and souvenirs, or wiring money on a regular basis; the real spending spree hits us once we arrive back home. There is a common belief that we are *puni k'o brod* [full of money] and it is an unwritten rule that we will always pay for everything for everyone. Many people don't want to go back home because they have had enough of giving away money to relatives, friends and charities. They are tired of listening to the same old stories about poverty and the 'economic crisis' each year. They listen to long desperate monologues and feel guilty that they have 'made it' while their families and friends can barely survive. A friend of mine spoke bitterly about an expatriate now living in Holland: "She is *puna k'o brod*, she can get herself a taxi; I don't need to drive her around." I was surprised as they had been close friends. I wondered whether she thought the same about me.

To compensate for the guilt of having 'made it', we ensure we always have $20, $50 and $100 notes to give away to cousins and children, or to buy food or drinks, and to pay for general bills, doctors' fees, and medicines for our parents. We hire cars and drive our aged relatives to cemeteries since that is often the only opportunity they have to visit the graves of loved ones. I smiled wryly when a friend told me: "Yesterday I drove my parents to Tuzla to visit the cemetery. That is what we do lately … We drive to graveyards when we get here. Bizarre."

I don't blame those who no longer return home, but instead send money from time to time, call their family on the phone, or 'have coffee over Skype'. Like other Australians, they would rather go to Thailand to sunbake, or to New Zealand to ski. They pay off their mortgages and spend time with their adopted community. I can't. I have an enormous urge to go home. I simply must go or I feel that I will die. That is how strong the urge is.

Many people I encounter in my homeland, even some with whom I meet to talk about business matters, want to know how they can emigrate to Australia. Those of us who have made the transition are used to being asked how we managed it, and whether we have any advice. It often feels like being a therapist: listening to story after story of desperation, wanting to help, but not wanting to give false hope and raise expectations. People talk about their desperate living conditions and we feel uncomfortable, if not guilty, about the fortunate lives we lead. One young man, an actor in a grassroots theatre, and a refugee and father of two, insisted that we meet and talk about my research. As soon as we met, I realised that he wanted to vent his rage and bitterness to someone—anyone—about the country in which he lives. He had not received a salary for the past two years. "If only I had a monthly salary ..." he said wistfully. "Poverty is boring. I am sick of not having money for coffee. This is a tainted environment that cannot stand smart and enterprising people. If you are intelligent, you are gone, finished."

People are so desperate that even without a salary, they think they have to 'keep their job'. One woman who hasn't been paid for eighteen months told me: "It is hard but we have to work." In such terrible living conditions, countless people have either left or plan to leave. An acquaintance from my home town summed up the situation in today's BiH (pers. comm., June 2013):

> Bosnia is a champion in 'brain drain' in the region. In the last few years 150,000 people have left and migration is a good business here. There are agencies that have specialised in certain fields: law, engineering, medicine. My son and his wife, who both have relatively good jobs here, want to go to Norway. They study Norwegian and have an agency helping them to find jobs there. Poor kids, they are killing themselves day and night with that strange language! So, even people who have relatively good jobs, who are not jobless, are desperate. They say they can't live in this contaminated environment any more. They can't work with conservative and backward people. They don't have anyone to go with to the coast or have fun with because people around them, their close friends, have nothing. The emotion which now prevails in Bosnia is despair. I thought that we reached the bottom five years ago but I can see now that it can be worse.

There is a joke in BiH that goes: "You know you are Bosnian when you have at least three passports, and have lived in four countries in the last twelve years." I have two passports, and have lived in four countries over the past twelve years. I live between two worlds: one that is left behind me, BiH; and another, before me, Australia. I could not find two countries further apart. Life in these two countries is a contrast of black and white. But this contrast helps me to see the beauty and ugliness in both. Going back and forth provides insight and the chance to reflect on things I would never notice if I had not emigrated. There is sadness, but also excitement about my discoveries each year when I return to the place where I was born. The place that provides me with comfort, but also triggers anxiety. The place I love and hate at the same time.

Postscript: 'Bosnian Spring'

In February 2014, BiH experienced riots escalating to a level of violence not seen since the end of the civil war in the 1990s. The citizens of BiH—many of them making up the massive pool of unemployed labour—were rising up against their corrupt government demanding bread, work and social justice for all. Tens of thousands of workers, students and other citizens took to the streets across BiH to call for the resignations of local, municipal and federal government officials. The protests were sparked by decades of endemic corruption, increasing poverty, economic stagnation and social inequality.

I followed the news intently for a few days. For a moment I felt that there was hope: the protests transcended ethnic, nationalist and religious lines. They unified the BiH people who despair about a small but powerful and toxic cleptocracy that rules their lives. I held my breath when I saw a photo of four young men holding three flags (Serbian, Croatian and Bosnian) which they had tied to one another. Their eyes were glowing and faces shining. I looked at that photo over and over again. I was proud and happy. For a moment, I was hopeful that another future is possible.

APPENDIX

Timeline of Yugoslavia's Disintegration

YEAR	MONTH	EVENT
1980	May	President of the Socialist Federative Republic of Yugoslavia (SFRY), Josip Broz Tito, dies. He was President from 1953 to 1980.
1989	May	Slobodan Milošević becomes President of Serbia.
1990	January	The Communist Party of Yugoslavia is dissolved.
	July	The Parliament of Slovenia votes in favour of independence from Yugoslavia.
	July/ September	The Parliament of Bosnia and Herzegovina (BiH) changes its constitution in July to officially become the home of Bosniaks, Serbs and Croats, and in September votes to stay within the SFRY.
	November	First multi-party election in BiH. Alija Izetbegović, a Bosniak politician, becomes the first President of BiH. He served until 1996.
	December	Slovenia votes for independence from Yugoslavia in a referendum with 95% voter support and 93% voter turnout.
1991	March	The war in Croatia begins.
	May	Croatia votes for independence in a referendum, with 94% voter support and 86% voter turnout.
	June	Slovenia declares independence on 27 June, triggering the Ten-Day War (which lasted until 6 July) between the Slovenian Territorial Defence and the Yugoslav People's Army (JNA).
	September	Macedonia votes for independence with 95% voter support and 75% voter turnout. At the end of September, a referendum in Kosovo also results in a vote in favour of independence.

YEAR	MONTH	EVENT
	October	Croatia declares independence from Yugoslavia.
	November	Bosnian Serbs living in BiH vote in favour of a referendum to remain in Yugoslavia, with 98% voter support and 85% voter turnout. The Bosnian government declares the referendum unconstitutional.
1992	January	Republika Srpska (RS) is established by the Bosnian Serbs but is not recognised internationally or by the Bosnian government.
	February	A referendum on independence is held in BiH. A majority of Bosniaks and Croats vote in favour, but most Serbs boycott the vote. Voter turnout is only 63% with votes in favour of independence 99%.
	April	BiH declares independence which results in the start of the Bosnian War and the siege of Sarajevo. (The siege of Sarajevo lasts from 5 April 1992 to 29 February 1996.)
1993	May	The International Criminal Tribunal for the former Yugoslavia (ICTY) is set up by Resolution 827 of the United Nations Security Council.
1995	April	The first trial of the ICTY to include sexual violence as an indictable crime by an international court (*Duško Tadić case*). Sentencing judgment handed down in January 2000.
	July	The Srebrenica genocide occurs, in which approximately 8,000 Muslim men and boys are killed by the Army of Republika Srpska (VRS) under the command of General Ratko Mladić. (Srebrenica is a town in eastern Bosnia.)
	August	Military operation 'Storm' begins, the biggest military operation run by the Croatian armed forces which sees the forcible expulsion of approximately 250,000 Serbs from Croatia. It is the largest single act of 'ethnic cleansing' committed in the war.
	November	The War in Croatia ends.
	December	The Dayton Peace Agreement formally ends the Bosnian war. It is brokered by the USA and involves the President of the Federative Republic of Yugoslavia (now known as Serbia), Slobodan Milošević; the President of Croatia, Franjo Tudman; and the President of BiH, Alija Izetbegović. (Milošević represents the Bosnian Serb interests due to the absence of Radovan Karadžić.)
1996	February	The siege of Sarajevo ends.
1997	March	The Kosovo Liberation Army, an ethnic-Albanian paramilitary organisation, increases its activity fighting against Serbian military and security forces.

YEAR	MONTH	EVENT
1998	February	Kosovo begins full-scale armed conflict with Serbia.
	November	The first conviction of an accused person for rape as torture by the ICTY occurs (*Čelebići Case*).
1999	March	After peace talks fail, the North Atlantic Treaty Organization (NATO) launches air strikes in Kosovo and Serbia. This is despite failing to gain the approval of the United Nations Security Council for such an operation.
	June	The Kosovo War with Serbia ends. NATO air strikes cease and Serbian military forces withdraw from Kosovo.
2000	July	The first case is heard by the ICTY which concentrates entirely on charges of sexual violence (*Prosecutor vs Furundžija*).
	October	In the face of trade sanctions and a crumbling economy, support for Slobodan Milošević crumbles and he steps down.
2001	February	The ICTY rules that the act of rape is recognised as a crime against humanity (*Foča Rape Case*).
	April	Slobodan Milošević is arrested. His trial begins in 2002.
2006	March	Slobodan Milošević, the former Yugoslav President, dies in his prison cell before the completion of his trial. He was charged with war crimes, including genocide and crimes against humanity. The trial had lasted for five years at the time of his death.
	June	Montenegro declares independence.
2008	February	Kosovo declares independence from Serbia.
	July	Radovan Karadžić, the first President of RS, is arrested, after 12 years as a fugitive, having been indicted for war crimes by the ICTY.
2011	May	General Ratko Mladić is captured in Serbia and extradited, accused of committing war crimes, crimes against humanity and genocide.
2012	November	Ante Gotovina and Mladen Markač, who both served in the Croatian army, are acquitted on appeal after being found guilty at trial by the ICTY. They were both charged with war crimes and crimes against humanity committed during the military operation 'Storm'.
2014	February	Unrest that has not been seen since the end of the war breaks out in BiH. A series of often violent riots and demonstrations spreads throughout the country due to poverty, corruption and the high unemployment rate.

GLOSSARY

Banja Luka
(also Banjaluka)

The political and administrative capital of Republika Srpska.

Bosnia and
Herzegovina (BiH)
(also Bosnia, Bosnia-
Herzegovina)

The modern-day state that declared its independence and received international recognition on 6 April 1992. This recognition was followed by three years of civil war.

Bosniak
(also Bosnian
Muslim)

Bosniaks (Muslims) are one of the three constitutive peoples of Bosnia and Herzegovina, along with Serbs and Croats.

Bosnian language

The language spoken by Bosniaks. One of the three official languages of Bosnia and Herzegovina, along with Serbian and Croatian.

Bosnians

Describes all people who live in Bosnia and Herzegovina regardless of their ethnic, religious or regional identities.

Brčko District

The Brčko District was the subject of disputes and international arbitration and was attached neither to the Federation of Bosnia and Herzegovina nor to the Republika Srpska. In 2000, the International Arbitrary Commission placed Brčko under the administration of Bosnia and Herzegovina, as a separate self-governing district. Thus, Bosnia and Herzegovina comprises two entities plus the Brčko District.

Croat
(also Bosnian Croat)

Croats (Catholic Christians) are one of the three constitutive peoples of Bosnia and Herzegovina, along with Bosniaks and Serbs.

Croatian language   The language spoken by Croats in Bosnia and Herzegovina. One of the three official languages of Bosnia and Herzegovina, along with Serbian and Bosnian.

Dayton Peace Agreement   The 1995 Dayton Peace Agreement ended the war in Bosnia and Herzegovina and established the state of Bosnia and Herzegovina as a sovereign country with two separate entities: a Bosniak-Croat Federation of Bosnia and Herzegovina (51% of the territory); and the Bosnian Serb Republic, or Republika Srpska (49% of the territory); each with its own president, government, parliament, police and other bodies.

Federation of Bosnia and Herzegovina   Also referred to as 'Bosniak-Croat Federation', 'Muslim-Croat Federation' or 'Federation of BiH'. One of two entities within the country of Bosnia and Herzegovina (the other being Republika Srpska). It is inhabited primarily by Bosniaks and Bosnian Croats. The Federation of BiH consists of ten cantons (which, in administrative terms, are further split into 80 municipalities).

marka   The *konvertibilna marka* (KM) is the official Bosnian postwar currency that was established by the Dayton Peace Agreement and introduced as the currency in 1998. It replaced the Bosnia and Herzegovina dinar, the Croatian kuna and the Republika Srpska dinar.

Republika Srpska (RS)   Also referred to as the 'Bosnian Serb Republic'. One of two entities within the country of Bosnia and Herzegovina (the other being the Federation of Bosnia and Herzegovina). It is inhabited primarily by Serbs.

Sarajevo (*see also*: 'Siege of Sarajevo')   The capital of Bosnia and Herzegovina and the political and administrative capital of the Federation of Bosnia and Herzegovina.

Serbian language   The language spoken by Serbs in Bosnia and Herzegovina. One of the three official languages of Bosnia and Herzegovina, along with Croatian and Bosnian.

Serbo-Croatian language   Commonly referred to as *naš jezik* [our language]. It was the shared language of Bosnians prior to the war in the 1990s.

Serbs (also Bosnian Serbs)   Serbs (Orthodox Christians) are one of the three constitutive peoples of Bosnia and Herzegovina, along with Bosniaks and Croats.

Glossary

Siege of Sarajevo
(*see also*: 'Sarajevo')

Between April 1992 and February 1996, Sarajevo was besieged by the troops of the Army of Republika Srpska (VRS). This was the longest siege of a capital city in the history of modern warfare.

šljivovica
(also *slivovitz*)

Plum brandy. Produced in Eastern and Central Europe (commercial and home-made varieties).

Socialist Federative Republic of Yugoslavia (SFRY)
[Socijalistićka Federativna Republika Jugoslavija (SFRJ)]

Today referred to as 'the Former Yugoslavia', 'ex-Yugoslavia' or 'ex-YU'. Existing from 1945 to 1992, it was a socialist state and a federation made up of six socialist republics: Bosnia and Herzegovina, Croatia, Macedonia, Montenegro, Serbia, and Slovenia. Serbia, in addition, included two autonomous provinces: Vojvodina and Kosovo.

BIBLIOGRAPHY

Abarbanel, Avigail (ed.) (2012) *Beyond Tribal Loyalties: Personal Stories of Jewish Peace Activists*. Cambridge Scholars Publishing, Newcastle upon Tyne.

Adler, Patricia A. and Peter Adler (1987) *Membership Roles in Field Research*. Sage Publications Inc., Thousand Oaks, California.

Alvesson, Mats (2002) *Postmodernism and Social Research*. Open University Press, Buckingham.

Andrić, Ivo (1960) 'Razaranja' [Destruction] in *Lica, zbirka pripovedaka*. Mladost, Zagreb, p. 131.

Andrić, Ivo (1978) *Znakovi pored puta*. Svjetlost, Sarajevo.

Arendt, Hannah (1977) *Eichmann in Jerusalem: A Report on the Banality of Evil*. Penguin Books, New York.

Arendt, Hannah (2009) *Responsibility and Judgment*. Random House, New York.

Asselin, Marilyn E. (2003) 'Insider research: Issues to consider when doing qualitative research in your own setting' *Journal for Nurses in Professional Development* 19 (2), pp. 99–103.

Atkinson, Judy (2002) *Trauma Trails, Recreating Song Lines: The Transgenerational Effects of Trauma in Indigenous Australia*. Spinifex Press, North Melbourne.

Aung San Suu Kyi (2008) *The Voice of Hope: Conversations with Alan Clements*. Seven Stories Press, New York.

Australian Bureau of Statistics (2011) 'Migration Australia 2009–10' cat. no. 3412.0 <http://www.ausstats.abs.gov.au/Ausstats/subscriber.nsf/0/CAC6E05106F66A1 3CA2578B000119F19/$File/34120_2009-10.pdf> (accessed 17 October 2012).

Bakić-Hayden, Milica and Robert M. Hayden (1992) 'Orientalist variations on the theme "Balkans": Symbolic geography in recent Yugoslav cultural politics' *Slavic Review* 51 (1), pp. 1–15.

Barclay, Paul (15 October 2012) 'John Cantwell' [audio interview] *Big Ideas* <http://www.abc.net.au/radionational/programs/bigideas/2012-10-15/4309418> (accessed 17 October 2012).

Barry, Kathleen (2010) *Unmaking War, Remaking Men: How Empathy Can Reshape Our Politics, Our Soldiers and Ourselves*. Spinifex Press, North Melbourne.

Bartsch, Karl and Evelyn Bartsch (1995) *Stress and Trauma Healing: A Manual for Caregivers*. Mennonite Central Committee, Vuleak Trust and Diakonia Council of Churches, Durban.

Bašić, Aida (2004) *Trauma-Market*. Omnibus, Sarajevo.

BBC News (15 April 1999) 'NATO pilot bombed refugees' <http://news.bbc.co.uk/2/hi/europe/319943.stm> (accessed 15 January 2013).

BBC News (7 May 1999) 'NATO bombs hit hospital <http://news.bbc.co.uk/2/hi/europe/337989.stm> (accessed 22 February 2013).

BBC News (31 May 1999) 'Civilian deaths "necessary price"', <http://news.bbc. co.uk/2/hi/europe/357355.stm> (accessed 13 February 2013).

BBC News (9 June 2005) 'Timeline: Siege of Srebrenica' <http://news.bbc.co.uk/2/ hi/675945.stm> (accessed 12 January 2014).

BBC News Europe (17 November 2012) 'Hague war court acquits Croatian Generals Gotovina and Markač' <http://www.bbc.co.uk/news/world-europe-20352187> (accessed 31 January 2014).

BH Mine Action Center (2013) 'Izvještaj o protivminskom djelovanju u Bosni i Hercegovini za period januar-juni 2013' Sarajevo <http://www.bhmac.org/ba/ stream.daenet?kat=45> (accessed 28 February 2014).

BH Mine Action Center (15 January 2014) 'Upozorenje-Mine tihe ubice!!!' <http:// www.bhmac.org/ba/stream.daenet?kat=2> (accessed 30 January 2014).

Bidwell Smith, Claire (2012) *The Rules of Inheritance: A Memoir.* Hudson Street Press (Penguin Group), New York.

Blitz, Brad K. (2006) *War and Change in the Balkans: Nationalism, Conflict and Cooperation.* Cambridge University Press, Cambridge.

Bobis, Merlinda (2011) *Fish-Hair Woman.* Spinifex Press, North Melbourne.

Bottomley, Gillian (1992) *From Another Place: Migration and the Politics of Culture.* Cambridge University Press, Cambridge.

Brannick, Teresa and David Coghlan (2007) 'In defense of being "native": The case for insider academic research' *Organizational Research Methods* 10 (1), pp. 59–74.

Brecht, Bertolt (1941/1972) *Mother Courage and Her Children* [play] trans. Ralph Manheim. Random House/Pantheon Books, New York.

Brecht, Bertolt (1975) 'When leaders speak of peace' in *Selected Poems*, trans. H.R. Hays. Harcourt Brace, New York.

Bringa, Tone (1995) *Being Muslim the Bosnian Way: Identity and Community in a Central Bosnian Village.* Princeton University Press, Princeton.

Brockmeier, Jens (2002) 'Remembering and forgetting: Narrative as cultural memory' *Culture Psychology* 8 (1), pp. 15–43.

Broz, Svetlana (2005) *Good People in an Evil Time: Portraits of Complicity and Resistance in the Bosnian War.* Other Press, New York.

Bulgakov, Mikhail (1996) *The Master and Margarita.* Vintage Books, New York.

Butler, Judith (2004) *Precarious Life: The Powers of Mourning and Violence.* Verso, London.

Butler, Judith (2005) *Giving an Account of Oneself.* Fordham University Press, New York.

Butler, Judith (2009) *Frames of War: When Is Life Grievable?* Verso, London.

Buttry, Daniel L. (2011) *Blessed Are the Peacemakers.* David Crumm Media, LLC, Canton, Michigan.

Caldicott, Helen (2007) *War in Heaven: The Arms Race in Outer Space.* The New Press, New York.

Campbell, David (1998) *National Deconstruction: Violence, Identity, and Justice in Bosnia.* University of Minnesota Press, Minneapolis.

Cantwell, John (2012) *Exit Wounds: One Australian's War on Terror.* Melbourne University Press, Melbourne.

Centar za uklanjanje mina (2011) 'Izvještaj o protivminskom djelovanju za 2011. godinu' [Report about anti-mining action in Bosnia and Herzegovina in 2011] <http://www.bhmac.org/ba/stream.daenet?kat=80> (6 May 2012).

Charter, David (9 April 2012) 'Bosnia, the broken country' *The Australian* <http:// www.theaustralian.com.au/news/world/bosnia-the-broken-country/story-fnb64oi6-1226321616546#> (accessed 15 February 2014).

Bibliography

Clancy, Tim (2007) *Bosnia and Herzegovina: The Bradt Travel Guide.* The Globe Pequot Press, Guilford, Connecticut.

Cockburn, Cynthia (2001) 'The gendered dynamics of armed conflict and political violence' in Caroline N. O. Moser and Fiona Clark (eds) *Victims, Perpetrators or Actors? Gender, Armed Conflict and Political Violence.* Zed Books, London.

Cockburn, Cynthia and Dubravka Žarkov (eds) (2002) *The Postwar Moment: Militaries, Masculinities and International Peacekeeping, Bosnia and the Netherlands.* Lawrence and Wishart, London.

Connolly, Kate (16 September 2012) 'Bernhard Schlink: Being German is a huge burden', *The Guardian* <http://www.theguardian.com/world/2012/sep/16/bernhard-schlink-germany-burden-euro-crisis> (accessed 29 November 2013).

Cook, Judith A. and Mary Margaret Fonow (1986) 'Knowledge and women's interests: Issues of epistemology and methodology in feminist sociological research' *Sociological Enquiry* 56 (1), pp. 2–29.

Copelan, Rhonda (1994) 'Surfacing gender: Reconceptualizing crimes against women in times of war' in Alexandra Stiglmayer (ed.) *Mass Rape: The War Against Women in Bosnia-Herzegovina.* University of Nebraska Press, Lincoln, pp. 197–218.

Corbin Dwyer, Sonya and Jennifer L. Buckle (2009) 'The space between: On being an insider-outsider in qualitative research' *International Journal of Qualitative Methods* 8 (1), pp. 54–63.

Des Forges, Alison (1999) *Leave None to Tell the Story: Genocide in Rwanda.* Human Rights Watch, New York.

di Giovanni, Janine (2004) *Madness Visible: A Memoir of War.* Bloomsbury Publishing, London.

Donais, Timothy and Andreas Pickel (1 June 2003) 'The international engineering of a multiethnic state in Bosnia: Bound to fail, yet likely to persist' (Presented at the CPSA Annual Conference, Halifax, Nova Scotia) <http://www.cpsa-acsp.ca/paper-2003/pickel.pdf> (accessed 30 April 2012).

Drakulić, Slavenka (1992) *How We Survived Communism and Even Laughed.* W.W. Norton and Company, New York.

Drakulić, Slavenka (17 February 2012) 'Can Hollywood tell the truth about the war in Bosnia?' *The Guardian* <http://www.theguardian.com/commentisfree/2012/feb/17/bosnia-in-the-land-of-blood-and-honey> (accessed 29 November 2013).

Drakulić, Slavenka (14 January 2014) 'The dogs of Sarajevo' *Eurozine* <http://www.eurozine.com/articles/2014-01-21-drakulic-en.html> (accessed 28 January 2014).

Duggan, Dave (2008) *AH 6905* [stage play] in *Plays in a Peace Process.* Guildhall Press, Derry.

Dzidic, Denis (6 April 2012) 'Bosnia still living with consequences of war' *Balkan Transitional Justice* <http://www.balkaninsight.com/en/article/bosnia-still-living-with-consequences-of-war> (accessed 29 November 2013).

Dzidic, Denis (4 April 2013) 'Karadzic "sacrificed himself for Serbs", says Dodik' *Balkan Transitional Justice* <http://www.balkaninsight.com/en/article/karadzic-s-request-to-subpoena-oric-denied-again> (accessed 29 November 2013).

Edwards, Rob (6 March 2013) 'Iraq's depleted uranium clean-up to cost $30m as contamination spreads' *The Guardian* <http://www.theguardian.com/environment/2013/mar/06/iraq-depleted-uranium-clean-up-contamination-spreads> (accessed December 2013).

Eisikovits, Nir (2009) *Sympathizing With the Enemy: Reconciliation, Transitional Justice, Negotiation.* Republic of Letters, Martinus Nijhoff Publishers, Boston.

Ensler, Eve (2008) *Insecure at Last: A Political Memoir*. Villard Books, New York.

Fergus, Lara (2010) *My Sister Chaos*. Spinifex Press, North Melbourne.

Filipović, Zlata (2006) *Zlata's Diary: A Child's Life in Wartime Sarajevo*. Penguin Books, New York.

Fischer, Martina (ed.) (2006) *Peacebuilding and Civil Society in Bosnia-Herzegovina: Ten Years After Dayton*. Lit Verlag, Berlin.

Forča, Ksenija and Majda Puača (2007) 'Nationalism entails discrimination' in Helena Rill, Tamara Šmidling and Ana Bitoljanu (eds) *20 Pieces of Encouragement for Awakening and Change: Peacebuilding in the Region of the Former Yugoslavia*. Centre for Nonviolent Action, Sarajevo.

Foss, Karen A. and Sonja K. Foss (1994) 'Personal experience as evidence in feminist scholarship' *Western Journal of Communication* 58 (1), pp. 39–43.

Funder, Anna (2011) *All That I Am*. Penguin Australia, Camberwell.

Galtung, Johan, Carl G. Jacobsen and Kai Frithjof Brand-Jacobsen (2002) *Searching for Peace: The Road to TRANSCEND*. Pluto Press, London.

Glenny, Misha (1996) *The Fall of Yugoslavia: The Third Balkan War*. Penguin Books, New York.

Goldstein, Joshua S. (2011) *Winning the War on War: The Decline of Armed Conflict Worldwide*. Penguin Books, New York.

Gonzales, Laurence (2012) *Surviving Survival: The Art and Science of Resilience*. W.W. Norton & Company, New York.

Govier, Trudy (2002) *Forgiveness and Revenge*. Routledge, London.

Greenberg, Robert D. (2008) *Language and Identity in the Balkans: Serbo-Croatian and Its Disintegration*. Oxford University Press, Oxford.

Guillaumin, Colette (1995) *Racism, Sexism, Power and Ideology*. Routledge, London and New York.

Hartsock, Nancy (1989) 'Masculinity, heroism and the making of war' in Adrienne Harris and Ynestra King (eds) *Rocking the Ship of State: Toward a Feminist Peace Politics*. Westview Press, Boulder, pp. 133–152.

Hawthorne, Susan (2002) *Wild Politics: Feminism, Globalisation and Bio/diversity*. Spinifex Press, North Melbourne.

Hawthorne, Susan (2011) *Valence: Considering War Through Poetry and Theory*. Spinifex Press, North Melbourne.

Helms, Elissa (2013) *Innocence and Victimhood: Gender, Nation, and Women's Activism in Postwar Bosnia-Herzegovina*. University of Wisconsin Press, Madison.

Hemon, Aleksandar (15 January 2012) 'National subjects' *Guernica*, <http://www.guernicamag.com/features/hemon_1_15_12/> (accessed 6 December 2013).

Herman, Judith (1992) *Trauma and Recovery*. Harper Collins, London.

Hronešová, Jessie (2012) *Everyday Ethno-National Identities of Young People in Bosnia and Herzegovina*. Peter Lang, Frankfurt.

Humanitarian Law Center (11 January 2008) 'Court files from trials of members of the "Scorpions" paramilitary unit for crimes against civilians in Srebrenica' <http://www.hlc-rdc.org/?p=13477&lang=de.> (accessed January 2014).

Human Rights Watch (August 1995) 'Assault by Bosnian Croats, Bosnian Government and Muslim forces', *Global Report on Women's Human Rights (1990–1995)*. Human Rights Watch, New York and London <http://www.hrw.org/sites/default/files/reports/general958.pdf> (accessed 17 February 2014).

Hunt, Swanee (2004) *This Was Not Our War: Bosnian Women Reclaiming the Peace*. Duke University Press, Durham, North Carolina.

Hunt, Swanee (2011) *Worlds Apart: Bosnian Lessons for Global Security*. Duke University Press, Durham, North Carolina.

Bibliography

Husanovic, Jasmina (2009) 'The politics of gender, witnessing, postcoloniality and trauma: Bosnian feminist trajectories' *Feminist Theory* 10 (1), pp. 99–119.

International Committee of the Red Cross Resource Centre (ICRC) (22 August 2013) 'Western Balkans: Authorities must support families of missing persons' <http://www.icrc.org/eng/resources/documents/interview/2013/08-28-disappeared-missing-western-balkans-milner.htm> (accessed 1 February 2014).

Johnson, Sonia (1987) *Going Out of Our Minds: The Metaphysics of Liberation*. The Crossing Press, Freedom, California.

Jokanović, Žarko (2013) *Jovanka Broz: Moj Život Moja Istina*. Blic, Beograd.

Jurisevic, Craig (2010) *Blood on My Hands: A Surgeon at War*. Wild Dingo Press, Melbourne.

Kanuha, Valli Kalei (2000) '"Being" native versus "going native": Conducting social work research as an insider' *Social Work* 45 (5), pp. 439–447.

Karlaš, Radmila (2009) *Four Leaf Clover*. Grafid, Banja Luka.

Karlaš, Radmila (2010) *The Silence of Mestizos*. Grafid, Banja Luka.

Kašić, Biljana (1993/2007) 'Crossing the Lines' [poem], Women's Lobby, Zagreb, Croatia; also in Women in Black (ed.) *Women's Side of War*. Art Grafik, Belgrade.

Kaufmann, Chaim (1996) 'Possible and impossible solutions to ethnic civil wars' *International Security* 20 (4), pp. 136–175.

Kulin, Elvir with Maury Hirschkorn (2005) *In a Bosnian Trench: A Wartime Memoir of a Muslim Bosnian Soldier*. Trafford Publishing, Victoria, British Columbia.

Kumar, Anuradha (2002) *Human Rights: Global Perspectives*. Sarap and Sons, Delhi.

Lampe, John R. (2000) *Yugoslavia as History: Twice There Was a Country*. Cambridge University Press, Cambridge.

Landmine and Cluster Munition Monitor (1 September 2013) Bosnia and Herzegovina 'Casualties and victims assistance' <http://www.the-monitor.org/index.php/cp/display/region_profiles/theme/2466> (accessed 30 January 2014).

Lennon, John and Malcolm Foley (2000) *Dark Tourism: The Attraction of Death and Disaster*. Thomson Learning, London.

Levi, Primo (1988) *The Drowned and the Saved*. Michael Joseph, London.

Levine, Peter A. (1997) *Waking the Tiger: Healing Trauma*. North Atlantic Books, Berkeley, California.

Leydesdorff, Selma (2011) *Surviving the Bosnian Genocide: The Women of Srebrenica Speak*. Indiana University Press, Bloomington.

Lloyd, Betty-Ann, Frances Ennis and Tannis Atkinson (1994) *The Power of Woman-positive Literacy Work: Program-based Action Research*. Fernwood Publishing, Halifax, Nova Scotia.

Lugones, Maria C. and Elizabeth V. Spelman (1990) 'Have we got a theory for you! Feminist theory, cultural imperialism and the demand for "The woman's voice"' in Azizah Y. al-Hibri and Margaret A. Simons (eds) *Hypatia Reborn: Essays in Feminist Philosophy*. Indiana University Press, Bloomington, pp. 18–33.

Lupis, Ivan, Vlatka Mihelić and Ivana Nizich (1994) 'War crimes in Bosnia-Herzegovina: U.N. cease-fire won't help Banjaluka' *Human Rights Watch* 6 (8) <http://www.hrw.org/legacy/reports/1994/bosnia2/> (accessed 6 December 2013).

Mandelstam, Nadezhda (1970) *Vospominaniya*. Chekhov, New York.

Mandelstam, Nadezhda (2002) *Hope Against Hope*. Random House, New York.

Marcuse, Herbert (1964) *One-Dimensional Man: Studies in the Ideology of Advanced Industrial Society*. Beacon Press, Boston.

Mardešić, Petar and Zvonimir Dugački (1961) *Geografski atlas Jugoslavije*. Znanje, Zagreb.

Massey, Garth, Randy Hodson and Duško Sekulić (2006) 'Ethnic intolerance and ethnic conflict in the dissolution of Yugoslavia' *Ethnic and Racial Studies* 29 (5), pp. 797–827.

Meier, Iren (2008) [no title, comment on rape of girls and women in war] in Lina Vušković and Zorica Trifunović (eds) *Women's Side of War* [original title: *Ženska strana rata* (2007)]. Women in Black, Belgrade.

Milojević, Ivana (2013) *Breathing: Violence In, Peace Out.* University of Queensland Press, St Lucia.

Milojević, Ivana and Slobodanka Markov (2008) 'Gender, militarism and the view of the future: Students' views on the introduction of the civilian service in Serbia' *Journal of Peace Education* 5 (2), pp. 175–191.

Milošević, Dijana (2011) 'Theatre as a way of creating sense: Performance and peacebuilding in the region of the former Yugoslavia' in Cynthia E. Cohen, Roberto Gutiérrez Varea and Polly O. Walker (eds) *Acting Together: Performance and the Creative Transformation of Conflict.* New Village Press, New York.

Mirjana (2005) motion picture, 'Vizantija' Udruženja filmskih radnika, Pale.

Mladjenović, Lepa (2003) 'Feminist politics in the anti-war movement in Belgrade: *To shoot or not to shoot?*' in Wenona Giles, Malathi de Alwis, Edith Klein, Neluka Silva (eds) *Feminists Under Fire: Exchanges Across War Zones.* Between the Lines, Toronto, pp. 157–166.

Mladjenović, Lepa and Donna M. Hughes (2001) 'Feminist resistance to war and violence in Serbia' in Marguerite R. Waller and Jennifer Rycenga (eds) *Frontline Feminisms: Women, War, and Resistance.* Routledge, New York, pp. 241–271.

Mladjenović, Lepa and Divna Matijasevic (1996) 'SOS Belgrade July 1993–1995: Dirty streets' in Chris Corrin (ed.) *Women in a Violent World: Feminist Analyses and Resistance Across 'Europe'.* Edinburgh University Press, Edinburgh, pp. 119–132.

Mohanty, Chandra Talpade (1992) 'Feminist encounters: Locating the politics of experience' in Michèle Barrett and Anne Phillips (eds) *Destabilizing Theory: Contemporary Feminist Debates.* Stanford University Press, Stanford.

Mojzes, Paul (2011) *Balkan Genocides: Holocaust and Ethnic Cleansing in the Twentieth Century.* Rowman and Littlefield Publishers, Washington.

Mulhearn, Donna (2010) *Ordinary Courage: My Journey to Baghdad as a Human Shield.* Murdoch Books, Sydney.

Nestle, Joan (forthcoming 2014) '"All maps are lies": A Review of *My Sister Chaos* by Lara Fergus' in *Sinister Wisdom* 94 (Special issue on lesbians and exile, Yasmin Tambiah and Joan Nestle eds).

Nikolić-Ristanović, Vesna and Nataša Hanak (2006) 'Truth, reconciliation, and the Serbian Victimology Society' *Peace Review: A Journal of Social Justice* 18 (3), pp. 379–387.

Nizich, Ivana (1994) 'Violations of the rules of war by Bosnian Croat and Muslim forces in Bosnia-Herzegovina' *Hastings Women's Law Journal* 5 (1), pp. 25–52.

Norton-Taylor, Richard (24 April 1999) 'Serb TV station was legitimate target, says Blair' *The Guardian* <http://www.theguardian.com/world/1999/apr/24/balkans3>.

Pamuk, Orhan (2008) *Museum of Innocence.* Random House, New York.

Pankhurst, Donna (2000) 'Women, Gender and Peacebuilding', Working Paper No 5, Center for Conflict Resolution, Department of Peace Studies, University of Bradford, England.

Porter, Elisabeth (2007) 'Women's truth narratives: The power of compassionate listening' in *Critical Half: Bi-Annual Journal of Women for Women International* 5 (2), pp. 20–25.

Prcic, Ismet (2011) *Shards.* Grove Press, New York.

PressTV (16 April 2012) 'For every US troop killed, 25 veterans commit suicide' <http://www.presstv.ir/detail/236543.html> (accessed 6 December 2013).

Puljek-Shank, Amela (2007) 'Trauma and reconciliation' in Helena Rill, Tamara Šmidling and Ana Bitoljanu (eds) *20 Pieces of Encouragement for Awakening and Change: Peacebuilding in the Region of the Former Yugoslavia.* Centre for Nonviolent Action, Sarajevo.

Ramet, Sabrina P. (2013) 'Bosnia-Herzegovina since Dayton—An introduction' in Ola Listhaug and Sabrina P. Ramet (eds) *Bosnia-Herzegovina Since Dayton: Civic and Uncivic Values.* Logo Editore, Ravenna.

Ramet, Sabrina P. (8 June 2013) 'Memory and identity in the Yugoslav successor states' *Nationalities Papers: The Journal of Nationalism and Ethnicity* 41 (6), pp. 871–881 <http://www.tandfonline.com/doi/abs/10.1080/00905992.2013.801419?journ alCode=cnap20#.Uvc-j42W-bJ> (accessed 31 January 2014).

Ramet, Sabrina P. and Letty Coffin (January–February 2001) 'German Foreign Policy vis-à-vis the Yugoslav Successor States, 1991–99' *Problems of Post-Communism* 48 (1), pp. 48–64.

Raymond, Janice G. (1986/2001) *A Passion for Friends: Toward a Philosophy of Female Affection.* Beacon Press, Boston; Spinifex Press, North Melbourne.

Remarque, Erich Maria (1966) *All Quiet on the Western Front*, trans. A.W. Wheen. Folio Society, London.

Remarque, Erich Maria (1998) *Three Comrades*, trans. A.W. Wheen. Random House, New York.

Ricoeur, Paul (2004) *Memory, History, Forgetting.* University of Chicago Press, Chicago.

Sandić-Hadžihasanović, Gordana (19 May 2013) 'Twenty years on: The unfinished lives of Bosnia's Romeo and Juliet', Radio Free Europe/Radio Liberty <http://www.rferl.org/content/bosnia-love-story-sarajevo-war/24990732.html> (accessed December 2013).

Šantić, Aleksa (1896/2006) 'Ostajte ovdje' [Stay here], poem, *Spirit of Bosnia* 1 (4) <http://www.spiritofbosnia.org/volume-1-no-4-2006-october/stay-here/> (accessed December 2013).

Scarry, Elaine (1985) *The Body in Pain: The Making and Unmaking of the World.* Oxford University Press, Oxford.

Schlink, Bernhard (2010) *Guilt About the Past.* House of Anansi Press, Toronto.

Schöpflin, George (2000) *Nations, Identity, Power: The New Politics of Europe.* C. Hurst & Co. Publishers, London.

Scott, Kim (2013) 'A Fantasy of Sand and Sea' in Rosie Scott and Tom Keneally (eds) *A Country Too Far: Writings on Asylum Seekers.* Penguin Books, Melbourne.

Seifert, Ruth (1996) 'The second front: The logic of sexual violence in wars' *Women's Studies International Forum* 19, pp. 35–43.

Selimović, Meša (1975) *Sabrana Dela: Pisci, Mišljenja i Razgovori.* Sloboda, Beograd.

Selimović, Meša (1996) *Death and the Dervish.* Northwestern University Press, Evanston, Illinois.

Shepherdson, Charles (2008) *Lacan and the Limits of Language.* Fordham University Press, New York.

Silber, Laura and Allan Little (1997) *Yugoslavia: Death of a Nation.* Penguin Books, New York.

Simić, Olivera (2005a) 'Gender, conflict, and reconciliation: Where are the *Men*, what about *Women*?' *Journal for Political Theory and Research on Globalisation, Development and Gender Issues*, pp. 1–13. Also at <http://www.globalizacija.com/doc_en/e0065sim.htm>.

Simić, Olivera (2005b) 'Sexual abuse of women and exploitation of children by peacekeepers: Case of Bosnia and Herzegovina and Democratic Republic of Congo' *Journal for Political Theory and Research on Globalisation, Development and Gender Issues* 10, pp. 1–14.

Simić, Olivera (2008) 'A tour to a site of genocide: Mothers, borders and bones' *Journal of International Women's Studies* 9 (3), pp. 304–314.

Simić, Olivera (2009a) 'Remembering, visiting and placing the dead: Law, authority and genocide in Srebrenica' *Law Text Culture* 13, pp. 273–311.

Simić, Olivera (2009b) 'Rethinking "sexual exploitation" in UN peacekeeping operations' *Women's Studies International Forum* 32 (4), pp. 288–295.

Simić, Olivera (2009c) 'What remains of Srebrenica? Motherhood, transitional justice and yearning for the truth' *Journal of International Women's Studies* 10 (4), pp. 220–236.

Simić, Olivera (2009d) 'Who should be a peacekeeper?' *Peace Review: A Journal of Social Justice* 21 (3), pp. 395–402.

Simić, Olivera (2009e) 'Activism for peace in Bosnia and Herzegovina: A gender perspective' *Global Media Journal* (American Edition) 8 (15) <http://www98.griffith.edu.au/dspace/bitstream/handle/10072/37902/66703_1.pdf.jsessionid=AECDDDFB22C1E84AAC644FC59A889CEF?sequence=1>.

Simić, Olivera (2010a) 'Breathing sense into women's lives shattered by war: DAH Theatre Belgrade' *Law Text Culture* 14, pp. 117–133.

Simić, Olivera (2010b) '"Boys will be boys": Human trafficking and UN peacekeeping in Bosnia and Kosovo' in Leslie Holmes (ed.) *Trafficking and Human Rights: European and Asia-Pacific Perspectives*. Edward Elgar, Cheltenham, pp. 79–95.

Simić, Olivera (2010c) 'Does the presence of women really matter? Towards combating male sexual violence in peacekeeping operations' *International Peacekeeping* 17 (2), pp. 188–199.

Simić, Olivera (2011) 'Bringing "justice" home: Bosnians, war criminals and the interaction between the cosmopolitan and the local' *German Law Journal* 12, pp. 1,388–1,407.

Simić, Olivera and Kathleen Daly (2011) '"One pair of shoes, one life": Steps towards accountability for genocide in Srebrenica' *International Journal of Transitional Justice* 5 (3), pp. 477–491.

Simić, Olivera (2012a) 'After the war in Bosnia: Radmila's life under handbrake' *German Law Journal* 13 (6) pp. 659–678 <http://www.germanlawjournal.com/index.php?pageID=11&artID=1442>.

Simić, Olivera (2012b) 'Challenging Bosnian women's identity as rape victims, as unending victims: The "other" sex in times of war' *Journal of International Women's Studies* 13 (4), pp. 129–142.

Simić, Olivera (2012c) *Regulation of Sexual Conduct in UN Peacekeeping Operations.* Springer, Berlin <http://www.springer.com/law/international/book/978-3-642-28483-0> PDF file.

Simić, Olivera (2012d) 'Surviving peace' *Griffith Review* 35: *Surviving* <http://griffithreview.com/edition-35-surviving/surviving-peace>.

Simić, Olivera, Elma Softic-Kaunitz and Maria Tumarkin (2012) 'Letters from Sarajevo: Three ways of remembering' in Julianne Schultz (ed.) *Griffith REVIEW 37: Small World*. Griffith University, Brisbane / Text Publishing, Melbourne <http://griffithreview.com/edition-37-small-world/>.

Bibliography

Simić, Olivera, Zala Volčič and Catherine R. Philpot (2012) 'Peace psychology in the Balkans: In times past, present and future' in Olivera Simić, Zala Volčič and Catherine R. Philpot (eds) *Peace Psychology in the Balkans: Dealing With a Violent Past While Building Peace*. Springer, New York, pp. 1–14.

Simić, Olivera, Zala Volčič and Catherine R. Philpot (eds) (2012) *Peace Psychology in the Balkans: Dealing With a Violent Past While Building Peace*. Springer, New York <http://www.springer.com/psychology/personality+26+social+psychology/book/978-1-4614-1947-1> PDF file.

Simić, Olivera (2013a) '"The day after": Ex-combatants live in Belgrade Theatre Performance *Tanatos*', *History of Communism in Europe* 4.

Simić, Olivera (2013b) 'Memorial culture in the former Yugoslavia: Mothers of Srebrenica and the destruction of artefacts by the ICTY' in Olivera Simić and Peter D. Rush (eds) *The Arts of Transitional Justice: Culture, Activism and Memory After Atrocity*. Springer, New York, pp. 155–172.

Simić, Olivera (2013c) '"Pillar of shame": Civil society, the UN responsibility and genocide in Srebrenica' in Olivera Simić and Zala Volčič (eds) *Transitional Justice and Civil Society in the Balkans*. Springer, New York, 181–200.

Simić, Olivera and Dijana Milošević (2013) 'Enacting justice: The role of Dah Theatre Company in transitional justice processes in Serbia and beyond' in Olivera Simić and Peter D. Rush (eds) *The Arts of Transitional Justice: Culture, Activism and Memory After Atrocity*. Springer, New York, pp. 99–113.

Simić, Olivera and Zala Volčič (2013) 'Localizing transitional justice: Civil society practices and initiatives in the Balkans' in Olivera Simić and Zala Volčič (eds) *Transitional Justice and Civil Society in the Balkans*. Springer, New York, pp. 1–16.

Simić, Olivera and Zala Volčič (eds) (2013) *Transitional Justice and Civil Society in the Balkans*. Springer, New York <http://www.springer.com/psychology/personality+%26+social+psychology/book/978-1-4614-5421-2> PDF file.

Simić, Olivera and Peter D. Rush (eds) (2014) *The Arts of Transitional Justice: Culture, Activism, and Memory After Atrocity*. Springer, New York <http://www.springer.com/psychology/community+psychology/book/978-1-4614-8384-7> PDF file.

Simić, Olivera with Ivana Milojević (31 March 2014) 'Dialogues between excombatants and youth in Serbia: A constructive use of war experience' *Peacebuilding* 2 (1) <http://www.tandfonline.com/doi/abs/10.1080/21647259.2014.899134#.U0xzmaLZV8E>.

Simić, Olivera (forthcoming 2014a) 'European Union and the Western Balkans: Time to move away from retributive justice?' in Soeren Keil and Zeynep Arkan (eds) *The EU and Member State Building: European Foreign Policy and Intervention in the Western Balkans*. Routledge.

Simić, Olivera (forthcoming 2014b) 'Increasing women's presence in peacekeeping operations: The rationales and realities of 'gender balance' in Gina Heathcote and Dianne Otto (eds) *Rethinking Peacekeeping, Gender Equality and Collective Security*. Palgrave-Macmillan.

Simić, Olivera (forthcoming 2014c) 'One step forward, two steps back: Gender (in)equality in Bosnia and Herzegovina' in Sabrina P. Ramet *Gender Equality and Gender Politics in Southeastern Europe: A Question of Justice*. Palgrave-Macmillan.

Singleton, Fred (1985) *A Short History of the Yugoslav People*. Cambridge University Press, Cambridge.

Softić-Kaunitz, Elma (1996) *Sarajevo Days, Sarajevo Nights*, trans. Nada Conić. Hungry Mind Press, St Paul, Minnesota.

Soh, C. Sarah (2008) *The Comfort Women: Sexual Violence and Postcolonial Memory in Korea and Japan*. The University of Chicago Press, Chicago.

Sontag, Susan (2004) *Regarding the Pain of Others*. Picador, New York.

Spender, Dale (1982) *Women of Ideas (and What Men Have Done to Them)*. Routledge & Kegan Paul, London.

Špirić, Željko (ed.) (2008) *Ratna Psihotrauma Srpskih Veterana* [Serbian]. *Čigoja štampa*, Beograd.

Spotlights on a Massacre (1997) documentary, Handicap International and Little Bear <http://www.youtube.com/watch?v=djVs4YTIxOg>.

Stiglmayer, Alexandra (ed.) (1994) *Mass Rape: The War Against Women in Bosnia-Herzegovina*. University of Nebraska Press, Lincoln.

Tanesini, Alessandra (1999) *An Introduction to Feminist Epistemologies*. Blackwell Publishers, Malden, Massachusetts.

Tedeschi, Richard G. and Lawrence G. Calhoun (1996) 'The posttraumatic growth inventory: Measuring the positive legacy of trauma' *Journal of Traumatic Stress* 9 (3), pp. 455–471.

Todorova, Maria N. (1997) *Imagining the Balkans*. Oxford University Press, Oxford.

Tumarkin, Maria M. (2005) *Traumascapes*. Melbourne University Press, Melbourne.

Tumarkin, Maria M. (2007) *Courage*. Melbourne University Press, Melbourne.

Tumarkin, Maria M. (2010) *Otherland: A Journey With My Daughter*. Random House, North Sydney.

Tumarkin, Maria M. (2011) 'Beyond truth and justice' *Griffith REVIEW* 33 <http://griffithreview.com/edition-33-such-is-life/beyond-truth-and-justice/all-pages> (accessed 6 December 2013).

Ugrešić, Dubravka (2003) 'Because we're just boys' in Ammu Joseph and Kalpana Sharma (eds) *Terror, Counter Terror: Women Speak Out*. Kali for Women, New Delhi.

Ugrešić, Dubravka (2008) *The Ministry of Pain*. Telegram Books, London.

United Human Rights Council (n.d.) 'Genocide in Rwanda', <http://www.united humanrights.org/genocide/genocide_in_rwanda.htm> (accessed 29 January 2014).

United Nations (27 May 1994) 'Final Report of the United Nations Commission of Experts', S/1994/674/Add.2 (Vol. 4). See <http://www.icty.org/x/file/About/OTP/un_commission_of_experts_report1994_en.pdf.> and <http://www.ess.uwe.ac.uk/comexpert/ANX/VIII-01.htm#II.C.1> (accessed 29 January 2014).

United Nations High Commissioner for Refugees (2014) Regional operations profile – South-Eastern Europe – Serbia <http://www.unhcr.org/pages/49e48d9f6.html> (accessed 30 January 2014).

United Nations International Criminal Tribunal for the Former Yugoslavia (ICTY) (14 July 1997) *Prosecutor v. Dusko Tadic*, Case No. IT-94-1-T, Sentencing Judgement <http://www.icty.org/x/cases/tadic/tjug/en/tad-sj970714e.pdf> (accessed 29 January 2014).

United Nations International Criminal Tribunal for the Former Yugoslavia (ICTY) (13 June 2000) Final Report to the Prosecutor by the Committee Established to Review the NATO Bombing Campaign Against the Federal Republic of Yugoslavia <http://www.icty.org/sid/10052#IVB4> (accessed 15 January 2013).

University of Texas Libraries (n.d.) 'Bosnia maps', Perry-Castañeda Library Map Collections <http://www.lib.utexas.edu/maps/bosnia.html> (accessed 12 February 2014).

Uzzell, David (1989) 'The hot interpretation of war and conflict' in David Uzzell (ed.) *Heritage Interpretation Vol. 1: The Natural and Built Environment*. Belhaven Press, London, pp. 33–46.

Vlaisavljević, Ugo (2010) 'Tri nacije kao tri ratne naracije' *Up&Underground* 17–18, pp. 26–39.

von Bogdandy, Armin, Rüdiger Wolfrum and Christiane E. Philipp (2005) *Max*

Bibliography

Planck Yearbook of United Nations Law. Martinus Nijhoff Publishers, Leiden, The Netherlands.

Vulliamy, Ed (2012) *The War is Dead, Long Live the War. Bosnia: The Reckoning*. The Bodley Head, London.

Walker, Martin (4 May 1999) '"Soft bomb" knocks out power plants' *The Guardian* <http://www.theguardian.com/world/1999/may/04/martinwalker1> (accessed December 2013).

West, Rebecca (1941/2007) *Black Lamb and Grey Falcon*. The Viking Press / Penguin Books, New York.

Women in Black (31 October 2005) 'Serbia and Montenegro: Women, peace, security' Conference Report [quoting from the contribution of Sonja Biserko of the Helsinki Committee for Human Rights in Serbia] <http://www.wluml.org/node/2637> (accessed 5 May 2012).

Women in Black (ed.) (2007) *Women's Side of War*. Art Grafik, Belgrade.

Woolf, Virginia (1938/2006) *Three Guineas*. Houghton Mifflin Harcourt, Boston.

Yarosky, Ronit (2012) 'The whole truth' in Avigail Abarbanel (ed.) *Beyond Tribal Loyalties: Personal Stories of Jewish Peace Activists*. Cambridge Scholars Publishing, Newcastle upon Tyne.

Yuval-Davis, Nira (2010) 'Theorizing identity: Beyond the 'us' and 'them' dichotomy' *Patterns of Prejudice* 44 (3), pp. 261–280.

INDEX

Index

mugging, in Costa Rica, 126–7
Mulhearn, Donna, 136
multiculturalism, 82

nationalism, 33–4
NATO bombings, 32, 62–72, 111, 130–4, 167
nervous breakdown, 122–3
Nestle, Joan, 149–50
Niš, 21, 62, 64, 66

ostracism, 50, 51–2
Otto, Dianne, 72
'outsider' perspective, 2

Pamuk, Orhan, 112–13
peace building, 72–7
Politkovskaya, Anna, 52
Porter, Elisabeth, 156
post-traumatic stress disorder (PTSD), 111–12, 113, 115–16, 120–6, 135
Prijedor, 46
privacy, 11
protests, against NATO bombing, 66
Puljek-Shank, Amela, 76

Rakić, Milica, 136
Ramet, Sabrina, 155
rape, 16, 16n4, 17, 99n22, 101, 118, 157
rape camps, 17, 17n6, 156–7, 156n41
reconciliation, 75–6, 102
refugee camps, 67–70, 70–2, 145
refugees and displaced persons, bombing of Albanian refugees, 64; from civil war, 4; in Serbia, 141, 142–6, 145n34
Remarque, Erich, 41, 120
Republika Srpska (RS), administrative capital, 10; attack on Sarajevo, 30; establishment, 2n1, 166; map, xii
Roma people, 14, 71, 84, 154n40
Rwandan genocide, 99n22

Sanski, 58
Šantić, Aleksa, 61
Sarajevo, aftermath of war, 87; beggars, 83, 84; siege of, 30, 55–6, 78, 87–8, 97–8, 166; street animals, 83–4, 85, 85n20
Sava River, 154
Scarry, Elaine, 41
Schlink, Bernhard, 37
'Scorpions', 32, 32n9
Second World War, extermination camps, 14, 154, 154n40; inter-ethnic violence, 14
Selimović, Meša, 1, 4, 10
September 11 terrorist attacks, 109–10, 112

Serb army (Vojska Republike Srpske), drafting of soldiers, 20
Serb ethnic identity, 21–2, 155
Serbia, 'ethnic cleansing', 141–2; NATO bombings, 32, 62–72, 111, 130–4; poverty, 158; refugees, 141, 142–6, 145n34
Serbian language, 23–4
Serbo-Croatian language, 22–3, 24
Shea, Jamie, 64
Silber, Laura, 146
slavery, 158
Smajlović, Vedran, 87–8
Šmidling, Tamara, 76
smuggling, 67–70
Sofia, black market, 67, 68
Softić-Kaunitz, Elma, 87, 88, 89–92; letter to Maria Tumarkin, 92–4; Sarajevo Days, Sarajevo Nights, 90, 91, 94–5, 97–8
Sontag, Susan, 15, 59
Soviet Union, repression under Stalin, 95–6
Špirić, Željko, 43
Srebrenica massacre, 28, 31–2, 32n9, 54, 58, 74, 74n18, 102, 118
Stara Grdiška extermination camp, 154
Stiglmayer, Alexandra, 118
student in exile in Serbia, 21, 62, 118; experience of NATO bombings, 62–3, 66, 130–4; in refugee camp, 67–70, 72–3; in residential accommodation, 62, 70, 73; trips home to Banja Luka, 20–1, 65–6, 142–4
suicide, 43
surviving war, personal impact of, 73–7

'target' brooches and T-shirts, 66, 66n17
Tedeschi, Richard, 44
Ten-Day War, 165
Third Balkan War, 147
Tito, Josip Broz, death of, 12–13, 165
trauma memories, 111–12, 113, 115–16, 119–26
trust, 75, 76
Tudjman, Franjo, 145n35
Tumarkin, Maria, 19, 53, 76, 89; letter from Olivera, 83–92; letter to Elma Softić-Kaunitz, 89–91; letter to Olivera and Elma, 94–7

Ugrešić, Dubravka, 23
ultra-right nationalism, 33–4
United Nations Children's Fund (UNICEF), minority return assistance project, 70–1, 103, 138–9

'victim of war' role, 100–4
Vrbas River, 10–11
Vukić, Radislav, 18–19
Vukovar, 15
Vulliamy, Ed, 100

war, masculinity of, 39–44
war crimes, in Banja Luka, 16; difficulties of
    discussing, 55–9; writing about atrocities
    committed by 'own people', 6, 6n3,
    27–9, 31–3, 35–9, 45–9, 47–9, 56–7,
    58–9, 75
war experiences, 'amnesia' about, 39, 120,
    149; examples of humanity, 34, 35,
    147–8, 150; facing the past, 115, 117–27;
    making sense of, 129–31; sharing stories
    about, 61–2; soldier's perspective, 134–6
war industry, 99–100
'war survivor' identity, 74
'War on Terror', 135
war-torn social fabric, 33
West, Rebecca, 146
women, against war, 40–41, 47; and peace,
    104; poverty, 16, 157, 159–160; victims
    of violence, 16, 73, 101, 112, 118, 156;
    see also feminism; girls; rape; rape camps
Women in Black, 74
Woolf, Virginia, 41
'wounded healers', 7
writing, power of, 94–7; process of, 38–9

Yarosky, Ronit, 119
Yugoslavia, map, xi; reasons for disintegration,
    146, 146n36; timeline of disintegration,
    165–7; under Tito, 12–13, 14–15, 22
Yugoslavian identity, 9–10, 22, 79
'Yuval', 92

Živanović, Miodrag, 25.

OTHER BOOKS FROM SPINIFEX PRESS

Unmaking War Remaking Men: How Empathy Can Reshape Our Politics, Our Soldiers and Ourselves
Kathleen Barry

In *Unmaking War Remaking Men*, Kathleen Barry explores soldiers' experiences through a politics of empathy. By revealing how men's lives are made expendable for combat, she shows how military training drives them to kill without thinking and without remorse, only to suffer both trauma and loss of their own souls. With the politics of empathy, she sheds new light on the experiences of those who are invaded and occupied and shows how resistance rises among them.

In an era of perpetual war, Kathleen Barry asks the important questions: How do we learn and teach violence, and what does killing do both to us and our society? A provocative, impassioned and necessary exploration of a topic too often cloaked by euphemisms and evasions.

—Jeff Sparrow, *Overland*

Rights: AU & NZ
ISBN: 1876756861
eBook: available

Valence: Considering War through Poetry and Theory

Susan Hawthorne

In this remarkable annotated poem, Susan Hawthorne commits to words the horrors of war that have been left unspoken. She shatters the conspiracy of silence and dares to draw links between militarism, fundamentalism and the sex industry. She rails against the violence of war and contemplates the link between place and the history of war that is infused into the earth. With a fresh examination of her surroundings, she considers the endless cycle of war that survives on the persistence of hope—hope of an end to war, hope of an end to suffering. This is a hope that Susan Hawthorne does not ultimately share, but her courage in telling the truth about war through her poetry is a gift for readers.

Valence is a powerful book on a number of levels. It contains a powerful anti-war poem, rich in imagery and history, full of passion and measured anger. It also operates on a more direct level, directly confronting the culture, language and history of war. In the end it doesn't fit well in Auden's poetic valley—it is a work that demands to be widely read. Perhaps it should be compulsory reading in the period leading up to the 100th anniversary of the Gallipoli landings.

—Mark Roberts, *Rochford Street Review*

Rights: World
ISBN: 1876756985
eBook: available

Last Walk in Naryshkin Park
Rose Zwi

Naryshkin Park is a place where lovers once walked. On 2 October 1941, it became the site of a mass grave. Rose Zwi deftly weaves together clues from survivors' accounts, old photographs, official documents and archival research to form a many-layered account of the proud history and tragic destruction of the Jews of Lithuania.

The lightness of her touch and her transparent desire to heal rifts between people, make her a powerful advocate.

—Miriam Cosic, *Australian Review of Books*

Rights: World
ISBN: 9781875559725
eBook: available

September 11, 2001: Feminist Perspectives

Bronwyn Winter, Susan Hawthorne (eds)

After September 11, feminists around the world spoke out, wrote for newspapers, for email lists and for the Internet. But in the male-dominated mass media, it was hard to find feminist perspectives. This collection brings together women who discuss the connections between war, terrorism, fundamentalism, racism, global capitalism and male violence. From the USA to Afghanistan, from Pakistan to Palestine, from Australia to Europe they have deconstructed this story and retold it from a feminist perspective in a powerful indictment of current global politics.

September 11, 2001: Feminist Perspectives *is an inspiring monument to the many voices of reason, compassion and wisdom that have cried out in dissent of this ongoing madness. It is an invaluable intervention from those who hold up more than half the sky, and is essential reading for all men and women to better inform themselves of the meanings and ramifications of '9/11', the current Terror War, and mass violence in general.*

—Arnaud Gallois, *Melbourne Journal of Politics*

Rights: World
ISBN: 9781876756277
eBook: available

Fish-Hair Woman
Merlinda Bobis

1987. The Philippine government fights a total war against insurgency. The village of Iraya is militarised. The days are violent and the nights heavy with fireflies in the river where the dead are dumped. With her twelve-metre hair, Estrella, the Fish-Hair Woman, trawls corpses from the water that tastes of lemon grass. She falls in love with the Australian Tony McIntyre who disappears in the conflict. Ten years later, his son travels to Manila to find his father.

To read Fish-Hair Woman *is to enter a kind of entrancement, at once strange, haunting, beautiful and terrifying. This is an extraordinary novel of compelling originality in which we learn that testimony is solidarity and that the loss and retrieval of any story of historical suffering implicates us all.*

—Gail Jones, author of *Five Bells*

Rights: World X Philippines
ISBN: 9781876756970
eBook: available

If you would like to know more about *Spinifex Press*
write for a free catalogue or visit our website.

SPINIFEX PRESS

PO Box 212 North Melbourne
Victoria 3051 Australia
www.spinifexpress.com.au